# PUBLIC BUILDINGS

## Volume One

# PUBLIC BUILDINGS

## ARCHITECTURE UNDER THE PUBLIC WORKS ADMINISTRATION 1933-39

### VOLUME I

Projects Constructed by Federal and Other Governmental Bodies
Between the Years 1933 and 1939
With the Assistance of the Public Works Administration

by
C. W. SHORT - Public Works Administration
R. STANLEY-BROWN - Public Buildings Administration

New Introduction by RICHARD GUY WILSON

A DA CAPO PAPERBACK

Library of Congress Cataloging in Publication Data

Short C. W. (Charles Wilkins), 1884–1954.
  Public buildings.

  (A Da Capo paperback)
  Reprint. Originally published as 1 v. work: Washington: U.S. G.P.O.,
1939.
  "Projects constructed by federal and other governmental bodies between
the years 1933 and 1939 with the assistance of the Public Works Administra-
tion."
  Includes index.
  1. United States—Public buildings. 2. Architecture and state—United
States. I. Stanley-Brown, R. (Rudolph), 1889–1944. II. United States.
Public Works Administration. III. Title.
NA4208.S46   1986                720′.973                85-32560
ISBN 0-306-80265-1 (pbk.)

This Da Capo Press paperback edition of *Public Buildings: Architecture
under the Public Works Administration 1933–39* is an unabridged republication of
the first half (through page 343) of the book entitled *Public Buildings: A
Survey of Architecture of Projects Constructed by Federal and Other Governmental
Bodies Between the Years 1933 and 1939 with the Assistance of the Public Works
Administration.* Originally published in Washington, D.C. in 1939, this
book is here supplemented with a new introduction
by Richard Guy Wilson.

New introduction © 1986 by Richard Guy Wilson

Published by Da Capo Press, Inc.
A Subsidiary of Plenum Publishing Corporation
233 Spring Street, New York, N.Y. 10013

# TABLE OF CONTENTS

# PREFACE

The information in this book is based on a report made for the President in May 1939 by the "Committee on Architectural Surveys." The report was called "Survey of the Architecture of Completed Projects of the Public Works Administration." The Committee consisted of the two authors of this book, who were appointed by the then Administrator of the Federal Emergency Administration of Public Works and by the then Director of Procurement of the Treasury Department. Since the report was compiled, the Public Works Administration and the Public Buildings Branch of the Procurement Division were transferred to the Federal Works Agency, on July 1, 1939, together with the Works Progress Administration, the Public Roads Administration, and the United States Housing Authority, in accordanec with the reorganization plan of President Franklin D. Roosevelt.

In order to obtain the best and most representative selection of projects for that Survey, a Selection Committee was formed consisting of four architects, three being in the Government and one who was brought in from private practice for this purpose. The exact information about each Nonfederal project was obtained from the records by representatives brought in from each of the Regional Offices of the P. W. A. The information about Federal projects was obtained by direct contact with the departments, bureaus, and agencies of the Federal Government.

The opinions expressed in this volume are those of the authors only.

# INTRODUCTION TO THE
# DA CAPO EDITION

*Public Buildings* provides a unique survey of American architecture and public works between the years 1933 and 1939. Illustrated are the extremes of architectural taste, from conservative colonial through the moderne and radical modernism, along with work in housing, highways, dams, waterworks, sewage plants, and even shipbuilding, airplanes, and streamlined locomotives. In one sense the book is a chronicle of the increasing modernization of the United States, the growing impact of the government at all levels, and the overwhelming presence of the machine—from the automobile to electricity—in all areas of American life. The book is also a political document with a specific purpose: to persuade and silence critics of Franklin Delano Roosevelt's New Deal. Only through a political perspective can some of the unique features of *Public Buildings* be understood.

*        *        *

The Public Works Administration, or the PWA, was one of the many "alphabet agencies" spawned in 1933 with Roosevelt's ascension to the White House.[1] The second part of the National Industrial Recovery Act of June 1933, title II, "Public Works and Construction Projects" created the PWA. The act's intentions were "to increase the consumption of agricultural products by increasing purchasing power, to reduce and relieve unemployment, to improve standards of labor, and otherwise rehabilitate industry and to conserve natural resources."[2] Roosevelt's executive order 6174 created the Federal Emergency Administration of Public Works, or PWA, and appointed as its head Harold L. Ickes, the Secretary of the Interior. Ickes' positions were entirely separate, and he remained as head of the PWA until July, 1939— when, as explained in the original introduction, the PWA was combined with similar programs into the Federal Works Agency. Ickes summarized the PWA's task in 1933: "Our business is to put men to work, to do it quickly, and to do it intelligently."[3] To this end the PWA and the Procurement Division of the Treasury Department—responsible for Federal Buildings—had by 1939 allotted funds through grants and loans to over 34,500 projects and helped to bring into the economy nearly 7 billion dollars in new construction costs. Chapters I—VIII of the book explain in some detail the policies and working of the PWA and a few of its accomplishments. Not so apparent is the political purpose of the book.

Already in 1939 Roosevelt and his advisors were thinking about the 1940 election and his unprecedented run for a third term. The administration was under constant attack for creating haphazard "make work" and "boondoggling" programs, such as the out-of-work artists and writers employed by the Works Progress (later Projects) Administration (WPA), the youths hired by the Civilian Conservation Corps, and others. In contrast to the hard-to-quantify and -qualify accomplishments of such programs, the PWA had real buildings, dams, and roads to its credit.

The PWA did put people back to work through its loans and grants, but behind this stated purpose a more subtle agenda existed: to provide decent housing for the poor, to bring better public buildings of all types to Americans, to modernize America through roads, water systems, and electricity, and to wrest from private interests the right to operate public utilities. By 1938 Ickes became very definite on the PWA's role: "For a hundred years the municipalities of America have been fighting for the right to build and operate their own public utilities . . . [for] municipalities to manufacture and distribute electric energy at a minimum cost to their citizens." The facts of governmental policy and success were there and needed to be told to the public.[4]

For the bureaucrats at PWA and the Treasury Department's Procurement Division, an internal political reason existed for telling their story: the competition from other agencies, especially the WPA. Created in 1935, the WPA threatened the funds and the purposes of the PWA, directly employing architects to design buildings as well as allocating funds to construct them. In the end, the WPA's involvement in architecture was minor in comparison to the PWA, though the WPA did carry out some decorations. Here also conflict and confusion exist. All of the major art schemes in Federal Buildings during the period, including the murals and sculpture shown in *Public Buildings* (pages 648-649), came not from the WPA but from the Treasury Department's Section of Painting and Sculpture, later known as the Section of Fine Arts. Both at the time and also later, especially among scholars, tremendous confusion, not to say inaccuracies have existed over the terms, and most of the architecture popularly known as WPA is really PWA. Similarly, WPA art does exist, but it is not the murals in Federal post offices and court houses, which came from the Treasury Department's Fine Art Section.[5]

[1]"Alphabets and Architects," *The American Architect,* 148 (January 1936), p. 18. Much of the PWA archives was sold for scrap paper during World War II. Still, a considerable amount survives and is at the National Archives, Record Group 135.
[2]*Principal Acts and Executive Orders Pertaining to Public Works Administration* (Washington, D.C.: Government Printing Office, July, 1938).
[3]Harold L. Ickes, "Public Works in the New Deal," *The Architectural Forum,* 59 (September, 1933), 151; see also pages 152-161.

[4]Harold L. Ickes, "Our Right to Power," *Collier's,* 102 (November 12, 1938), 18. See also *The Congressional Digest,* June-July, 1938, pp. 175-177.
[5]The best study of the Treasury Fine Art Section is: Marlene Park and Gerald E. Markowitz, *Democratic Vistas: Post Offices and Public Art in the New Deal* (Philadelphia: Temple University Press, 1984). See also William F. McDonald, *Federal Relief Administration and the Arts* (Columbus: Ohio State University Press, 1969).

The immediate background to *Public Buildings* was a report of eight large photographic albums (weighing about 150 lbs.) titled, *Photographic Report to the President, "Survey of the Architecture of Completed Projects of the PWA 1939,"* and is referred to in the original introduction. This contained some 1,700 PWA projects in a format very similar to *Public Buildings,* generally one page with a photograph, plan, and small text. An interesting feature of volumes 7 and 8 was a poor-design section: "The following illustrations show examples of buildings where the exterior design is not as of as high a standard as most of the others illustrated in this report."[6] From this report, 650 projects were selected for the permanent published record.

Complementary with *Public Buildings,* the PWA also issued a smaller book, *America Builds, The Record of PWA,* which spelled out in detail the legal and historical background of PWA and summarized its accomplishments in areas such as schools, electric power, health, sewage, water, and public housing. In addition to proclaiming the triumphs of PWA building activity, *America Builds* detailed the economic stimulation of such projects as the Alameda County Courthouse in Oakland, California (on p. 62-63 in *Public Buildings;* architects, W. G. Corlett and J. W. Plachek), which included building materials from 18 different states—temperature control units from Wisconsin, cast iron pipe from Alabama, and glass from Oklahoma.[7] A series of case histories outlined PWA successes: the Triborough Bridge, the Florida Keys highway, and others.

*Public Buildings* accomplished many of its political purposes. Widely reviewed by the professional architectural press, the book was also picked up by *Life* magazine, which ran a seven-page feature of photographs drawn from the book. *Life* enthused: "Franklin D. Roosevelt has made Cheops, Pericles, Augustus, Chin Shih Huang Ti, the Medicis, and Peter the Great look like a club of birdhouse-builders. For one Great Pyramid or Great Wall, PWA has raised up scores of tremendous dams. For one Parthenon, it has reared thousands of glistening city halls, courthouses, post offices, schoolhouses. For one 366-mile Appian Way, it has laid 50,000 miles of highway over the hills and valleys of America."[8] The *Life* magazine article noted the confusion between PWA and WPA and came down firmly on the side of the PWA.

A more subtle political message also emerges from *Public Buildings.* Conspicuously absent were the names of the architects and engineers involved on the different projects. Many of the architectural reviewers criticized this feature and the President of the American Institute of Architects wrote a letter of protest to the head of the Federal Works Agency.[9] John M. Carmody, the administrator, replied that the decision not to include architects' names came because "building contractors and manufacturers and vendors" might also request identification. C. W. Short, one of the authors of the book, also replied in a number of letters to different magazines with even more elaborate excuses; the listing of names could

be interpreted as advertising, or the credit for actual designs could not be determined. In some cases, he claimed, there had been too many people who deserved credit—110 architects for the Los Angeles Schools, for example—and the feelings of those architects whose projects were not selected for inclusion might be hurt.[10]

Masked behind these timid excuses was a far more important polemical stance: philosophically the PWA stood for communitarianism; the buildings were *public buildings,* created for the public and as expressions of public will. The success of each project and the entire PWA was not due to individual talent or genius, but the product of many individuals, from designers to bricklayers, dragline operators, and bureaucrats. To single out an architect as the creator (and the hero) would defeat the message of the book, and the purpose of the PWA and of the entire New Deal.

Unfortunately for later generations of architectural scholars, the absence of architectural credits has reduced the effective use of the book. To redress this shortcoming an index to be published with Volume II of this reprinting will include the names of the architects where they can be determined from the records.

The authors of *Public Buildings,* Charles W. Short of the PWA and Rudolph Stanley Brown of the Treasury Department's Public Buildings Division, deserve some comment. Both were architects. Short (1884-1954), was born in Cincinnati and studied architecture in England, then worked for Ralph Adams Cram. During World War I he worked in the Department of Labor's United States Housing Corporation, and then returned to private practice in Cincinnati, before being called to Washington to become an architectural advisor to the PWA.[11] Stanley-Brown (1889-1944) of Cleveland, studied architecture for two-and-a-half years at Columbia and then spent 1912-1914 at the *Ecole des Beaux-Arts.* He also had been in private practice in Cleveland before accepting a job in 1936 with the Treasury Department.[12]

Stylistically, the wide variety shown in *Public Buildings* gives rejoinder to the frequent generalization about the official, governmental, moderne style based in classicism, or what is sometimes called, "WPA Modern." A careful reading of the introductory text indicates that the authors, Short and Stanley-Brown, preferred the modern style, but deliberately chose a tremendous range of styles for the book. Undoubtedly, a political agenda dictated this decision: the book should both survey the work being done, and indicate the ecumenical nature of American architecture. The implicit message was that the Federal government was not going to demand an unpopular modern style. Some reviewers lambasted this nonpartisan stylistic stance. A critic for *Architectural Forum* claimed: "Here, on page after page, are the buildings that graced the pages of magazines twenty years ago: public libraries straight out of the golden age of Carrère and Hastings; Spanish Colonial that even the Jerry-builders now hesitate to foist upon

[6] *Photographic Report to the President, "Survey of the Architecture of Completed Projects of the PWA 1939,"* vol. 7, p. 1451, National Archives (Still Photographs Collection), Record Group 135.
[7] Public Works Division, *American Builds, The Record of PWA* (Washington, D.C.: Government Printing Office, 1939), p. 25.
[8] "PWA has Changed Face of U.S." *Life,* 8, no. 14 (April 1, 1940), p. 62.
[9] "With Record Readers," *The Architectural Record,* 87 (May 1940), p. 10.

[10] "To Read or Not to Read," *Pencil Points,* 21 (February–March, 1940) p. 28.
[11] *The New York Times,* April 17, 1954, p. 13.
[12] Stanley Brown's membership application is on file at the AIA Archives, Washington, D.C. Additionally, I am indebted to Richard Chafee of Providence, Rhode Island, and to Tony Wren, the AIA archivist for assistance and information. See also *New York Times,* February 9, 1944, p. 50.

their customers; . . . the tired ghost of early Modernistic . . ."[13]

The noted critic Fredrick A. Gutheim in an article went even further, and felt the entire PWA program "has not produced one architectural masterpiece."[14] Gutheim chose to illustrate his article with several modern buildings such as the Coolspring School, Indiana (p. 164) by John Lloyd Wright; and the Municipal Incinerator, Shreveport, Louisiana (p. 471) by Jones, Roessle, Olschner and Weiner (with Samuel Weiner as main designer). Both of these buildings were fairly well known in the architectural press at the time, and in fact the Shreveport Incinerator had been singled out for praise by Lewis Mumford in one of his *New Yorker* columns.[15] Implicitly, Gutheim suggested that these buildings offered a possible solution to what he termed the "architectural problem of our time." For Gutheim, the questions concerned the character of "modern civilization" and the way out of the "jungle" of Colonial Williamsburg reproductions and half-modern modernism. As for the solution to the dilemma of a modern American architecture, Gutheim felt that PWA not only had contributed nothing, but actually hindered its development by accepting anything that came along.[16]

Yet as Gutheim grudgingly admitted, and is apparent from the book, the PWA did not judge style; it was an operation that passed only on the worthiness of the project. The one exception was the Procurement Division of the Treasury, which did have architects on staff and designed some — not all — of the post offices and other Federal buildings.[17] To look to the PWA for a solution to stylistic matters was inaccurate and wrong. While many PWA-sponsored buildings and construction projects are missing from this book, the range of those included is overwhelming, from George Grant Elmslie's Oliver P. Morton School in Hammond, Indiana (p. 259) to Shepley, Bulfinch and Abbott's High School of Fitchburg, Massachusetts (p. 190), and from C. N. Crawford's Santa Maria, California City Hall (p. 32) to Fred Willson's Gallatin County Courthouse, Bozeman, Montana (p. 54). This diversity of styles and approaches was chosen to show the good work possible by the government. Communities which never had substantial public buildings now had their fair share. Similarly, the two pages (pp. 648-649) of the Treasury Department's Fine Art section showed some art work in Washington, D.C., but also a piece of sculpture by Edmond R. Amateis in the post office at Ilion, New York and murals by Ross Moffett, Arthur Covey, and Clay Spohn at post offices in, respectively, Holyoke, Massachusetts; Torrington, Connecticut; and Montebello, California. Across the country the government brought not only buildings but art to the people.

Some of the work shown in *Public Buildings* had a mixed parentage and indicates some of the problems in unraveling the origins of Roosevelt's New Deal. The only project to receive four pages (pp. 516-519), and one of the centerpieces of the Roosevelt administration, was Boulder Dam on the Colorado River between Arizona and Nevada. Actually the design of the dam began in the mid-1920s and was completed in 1932 under the Hoover administration. Site work had begun in 1930 and the contract for construction was awarded in March 1931 when work began immediately. By the time Roosevelt entered the White house construction was well advanced, though funds were lagging. The PWA helped supply money to the Bureau of Reclamation for its continuation. So politically-charged was the dam that the original name, "Hoover Dam," was changed to "Boulder Dam" by Secretary of the Interior Ickes. In 1947 under a Republican Congress the name was changed back to Hoover Dam. The apparent success of the Hoover/Boulder Dam project, in which an actual town was built (Boulder City, Nevada), certainly provided the impetus for the Roosevelt administration to set up the Tennessee Valley Authority, not shown in the book, as well as other dams, Fort Peck (p. 510-511), Bonneville (pp. 524-525), and for the entire Federal program for non-governmental building and construction.[18]

The involvement of the national government in non-Federal building marked a significant change from prior practice. For many years the military had constructed living quarters for its personnel; and the Architect of the Treasury had designed Federal buildings, such as courthouses and post offices. But the government, except during World War I, never had concerned itself with housing. With the PWA this changed. In the 1920s some architectural reformers such as Catherine Bauer, Edith Wilmer Wood, Clarence Stein, Henry Wright and others, inspired by the success of the Netherlands and Germany, called for the government to create decent housing.[19] The omnibus 1933 NRA legislation included a section on low-cost housing and slum clearance. A Housing Division was established under the direction of Robert Korn, an architect, then Colonel Horatio Hackett, an engineer, and finally, A. R. Clas. In 1937 the Wagner-Steagall bill created the United States Housing Authority, which took over the PWA's housing role. Embedded in the legislative and bureaucratic maze of these years were several significant changes in attitude to public housing. Initially low-cost housing was to be produced through private or local initiative, and, while funded by PWA, the emphasis was on reducing unemployment.

This approach was unsuccessful, and in 1935-36 the PWA set up the Emergency Housing Corporation, which became directly involved in acquiring and condemning land, designing and building units. One result was the *Unit Plan Book* or a set of standards — size, siting, materials, room arrangement, etc. (p. 654-655) — that architects could apply. The standards led to a predetermined low-cost character that would rule American public housing far beyond the 1930s.[20] Architecturally and socially the results were mixed and ranged from large apartment block housing projects, such as the

[13]"Books", *Architectural Forum* 72 (March, 1940), p. 22; see also "Book Reviews," *The Architectural Record* 87 (May, 1940), p. 122.

[14]Frederick A. Gutheim "Seven Years of Public Buildings" *The Magazine of Art,* 33 (July, 1940), p. 433; see also his "The Quality of Public Works," *American Magazine of Art* 27 (April, 1934), pp. 183-187.

[15]Lewis Mumford, "The Skyline: The Golden Age in the West and the South", *The New Yorker* (April 30, 1938), p. 50; "Municipal Incinerator, Shreveport, Louisiana," *The Architectural Forum* 63 (October, 1935), pp. 482-488. "Coolspring School, Coolspring Indiana," *The Architectural Forum* 71 (September, 1939), pp. 173-175.

[16]Gutheim, *op. cit.* p. 443.

[17]"Architecture and Government," *The American Architect,* 150 (January, 1937), p. 24; see also "Alphabets and Architects", *op. cit.,* p. 17-18.

[18]Harold L. Ickes, *The Secret Diaries of Harold L. Ickes* (New York: Simon & Schuster, 1953), vol. 1, pp. 37-38. See also Richard Guy Wilson, "Machine-Age Iconography in the American West: The Design of Hoover Dam," *Pacific Historical Review* Vol. LIV (Nov., 1985), pp. 463-493.

[19]Catherine Bauer, *Modern Housing* (Boston: Houghton Mifflin, 1934); Carol Aronovici, "Housing Based on Social and Economic Need Jutifies Federal Aid," *The American Architect,* 143 (November, 1933), pp. 10-14.

[20]Alfred Feilheimer, "Planning American Standards for Low-Rent Housing," *The American Architect,* 146 (February, 1935), pp. 12-18, and "Federal Housing Construction," *Architectural Record,* 77 (March, 1935), pp. 186-190.

Williamsburg Houses, New York, (pp. 662-663) to single-story duplexes in the Virgin Islands (p. 666). While in later years the large Williamsburg Houses complex has been cited as an example of all that is wrong in public housing, at the time it was highly praised.[21]

Responsibility for the failure of most public housing of the 1930s goes far beyond purely architectural considerations and should be linked to public attitudes toward slums and the city. The call for a total demolition and renewal did not begin in the 1930s, and can be traced back to the earlier turn-of-the-century City Beautiful Movement as well as Le Corbusier, but the PWA put into operation a slum-clearance system that would be continued after World War II. Perhaps urban renewal and public housing were misguided, but the attempt was a noble one, guided by the best minds of the period.

In a far more successful vein and noted in the book (pp. XV, XVIII-XXII) was the educational building activity of the PWA. The PWA brought new facilities, a high standard of construction, and safety to school buildings across the U.S. By 1936 over 70 percent of all school construction came through the PWA.[22]

[21]Talbot Faulkner Hamlin, "New York Housing," *Pencil Points,* 19 (May, 1938), pp. 281-292.
[22]"Architecture and the Government," *op. cit.,* p. 25.

*Public Buildings* concerns only a small sample of PWA projects. Not included are 34,000 others, some completed after 1939, or the work of the TVA; the towns of the Resettlement Administration such as Roosevelt, New Jersey, and Greenbelt, Maryland; and such highway projects as the George Washington Memorial Parkway in Washington, D.C. and the Blue Ridge Parkway in Virginia and North Carolina. Obviously the Federal government played a major role in shaping the land and the buildings of America, and by extension, the way of life for its people.

*Public Buildings* has to be viewed from the perspective of its period and its intentions. The book is an architectural record and a socio-political tract. It demonstrates some of the changes that were occurring. It should inspire us to look more carefully at the 1930s and to our own public buildings. For, as the authors claim at the opening, "Men build temples to the things they love."

—RICHARD GUY WILSON
University of Virginia
Charlottesville, VA
December, 1985

# NOTE TO VOLUME I

Originally published as one thick eight-pound book, *Public Buildings* appears in this reprint edition as a two-volume set. Volume I contains many of the more traditional public buildings: courthouses, libraries, city halls, and schools. Volume II contains more "public works": dams, highways, sewage plants, bridges, water works, and hospitals. Volume I shows state and local projects built with the assistance of PWA funds, while the Federal projects dominate Volume II.

The arrangement calls for some comment. The plan of the original book, never spelled out, is keyed to the PWA's seven geographical regions, which run east to west in numerical progression. Yet within each region the projects appear in neither alphabetical nor geographical order; buildings from the same state in the same category (e.g. city halls in Pawtucket, p. 1, and Cranston, Rhode Island, p. 6) are separated by buildings from other states. This suggests a deliberate design on the part of Short and Stanley-Brown, the original editors, to emphasize certain architectural styles. The Pawtucket City Hall was clearly the most moderne in its region, which may account for its prominence as the first building in the book.

Short and Stanley-Brown did not disown traditional styles in architecture (how could they?) but they seem to have included examples only if indigenous to the region and not an importation. They accepted Colonial or Georgian revival for Cranston, Rhode Island (p. 6, Benjamin Wright, architect) and Pocomoke City, Maryland (p. 12, Buckles and Fenhagen, architects). But in Santa Cruz, California (p. 34, C. J. Ryland, architect) they chose a building designed in the Spanish Ranch House style. Interspersed were examples of the moderne irrespective of place: Sioux City, South Dakota or Kansas City, Missouri. Short and Stanley-Brown note on page II that "the trend toward the 'modern' is evident throughout the country, but varies, like the Federal work, in the different states." They felt that the best modern architecture was happening in California—the state furthest from European influence, so they observed.

The almost complete absence of anything resembling the International Style underlines the conservative nature of most PWA architecture. Short and Stanley-Brown could have included several of the Los Angeles schools designed by Richard Neutra, but did not. *Public Buildings,* with its panoramic view of architecture under the New Deal, should reopen debate on the nature of American design during this period, its successes and failures and its legacy.

—R.G.W.

# CHAPTER I

# INTRODUCTION

Men build temples to the things they love. During the 10 years of post-war boom the finest buildings in this country were being constructed to serve business and commercial interests. Today, on the other hand, we are watching structures being erected everywhere to fit the needs of humanity in general. Hospitals are being built, floods are being controlled, new and humane prisons and asylums are replacing the old which were intended merely as places of confinement and not education, slums are being cleaned up, and in all building, as in town planning, sanitary and healthful conditions of life are being stressed.

For the first time the people have been building public works in unison, bettering the living conditions of all men. This change is partly due to the years of financial depression and unemployment following 1929, when it became necessary for the Federal Government to assist the States and other public bodies by providing financial aid for the construction of necessary public works and thereby affording employment in the building industry.

The greater part of work constructed during the past 6 years by public bodies, such as towns, cities, counties, and States and by the various Federal departments, was financed with the assistance of the Federal Government. As the information concerning such a vast number of public buildings has been brought together, by P. W. A., for the first time in one place, it has now become possible to review the architecture of a great number of public buildings in all parts of the country over a considerable period of time. Comparisons of design in style and planning, of the trends of design in the different sections of the country, and the varied developments which have been made in construction can all be studied. The numerous interesting architectural and engineering features and details of such structures are available on a comparative basis. As a result of this situation, this book is written to make available to the public the general information and some examples of the work that has been done during this period and to serve as a reference book for architects, engineers, students, school bodies, and others interested in architectural design.

Architecture like all art is never static but is undergoing a continual process of change. This change is due not only to the developments of new needs, new materials, and new methods of construction but also to the desire, inherent in successive generations of man, to produce something better and different from that accomplished by the preceding generations, something which will outlast the short span of a lifetime and will remain as monuments for the generations to come. This desire for change, however, is offset and balanced to a great extent by an equally human desire to preserve tradition. Today architecture in the United States is passing through a period of transition from eclectic design to something new and different, thus creating a condition which has much in common with that which existed in Italy in the fifteenth century when the architecture of the Middle Ages was changing to that of the Renaissance. Today, as then, changes in the character and style of architectural design occur slowly and constitute an evolution rather than a revolution.

In this book the term "architecture" is used in its broad sense to include not only plan and design, but proper use of materials, good construction, cost, the relationship to location, climate, site, to other structures and to a city or town plan, and includes, as well, the adaptation of a given structure to social and humanitarian needs and its success in the protection against hazards to life and health, such as fire, earthquake, and lack of sanitation. Such work may have been designed by an engineer or an architect.

In this discussion, for the purpose of comparison and not for the purpose of definition, we use the word "modern" as describing the evolving style of the present time which is based on evolutions from other styles of architecture and on the changes that have developed in needs, requirements, and construction. It does not apply to those designs which are not based on such evolutions and developments, but, on the contrary, are based chiefly on decoration or those which are an attempt to create something entirely new for present needs without regard to anything that has gone before, which for the purpose of clarification, we might call "modernistic design."

In the projects selected for this publication we have attempted to show some of the best examples of the different types of buildings and other structures which are the most interesting from architectural and engineering viewpoints. Size and cost have not been criterions in choosing these examples. The smallest sewage-disposal plant is given equal standing with the greatest power projects, and many very expensive buildings have been omitted altogether as having little or no architectural merit. Bridges, dams, and well designed landscaping are all included. Many projects contain more than one building. For example, some university projects include auditoriums, gymnasiums, libraries, dormitories, administrative buildings, and structures of other natures. Projects which were primarily for provision of electric power, gas, water, and sewage disposal, often included many small as well as large buildings. Every State in the Union is represented, thus adding to the value of comparisons.

The projects illustrated were completed or substantially completed by January 1, 1939, and do not include any of those financed from the Congressional appropriation of 1938. The 1938 program is not included herein because at the time this study began, only a few of those projects were completed. The construction of P. W. A. projects began soon after the N. I. R. Act in 1933 and has continued through the various subsequent Congressional appropriations in 1935, in 1936, in 1937, and in 1938. Some of the projects such as the large conservation dams, are still under construction at this time.

The extent to which public works were constructed during the 6 years prior to 1939 may be seen from the fact that up to January 1, 1938, allotments were made by the P. W. A. for 15,976 Federal and 10,498 Non-federal projects, a total of 26,474 projects, of which 8,259 were for building projects only. Approximately 17,300 buildings were erected, of which 2,200 were accessory to projects for sewers, gas, power, and water supply. The buildings or structures illustrated herein represent 620 selected projects. As of October 1, 1939, 7,993 additional projects, including 10,350 buildings, have been completed or are under construction under the 1938 appropriation of Congress.

The allotments were divided into two classes. One consisted of Federal projects which, with very few exceptions, had been planned and designed by architectural and engineering organizations of the various departments of the Federal Government; the other consisted of Non-federal projects which had been planned and designed by architects and engineers in private practice, employed by the owners.

The outstanding accomplishments in planning of both Federal and Non-federal buildings are the elimination of waste space, economy in cost, and proper consideration of light, ventilation, and sanitation; while in design, careful study of line, scale, and proportion, greater simplicity and an extremely sparing use of ornament, and a skillful and effective handling of materials, are noteworthy characteristics.

The architectural quality of the Federal projects is far better than that of the buildings constructed by the Federal Government during the two previous decades. Many of the post offices and courthouses and other buildings designed by the Public Buildings Branch of the Procurement Division of the Treasury Department (now the Public Buildings Administration of the Federal Works Agency) have a high degree of architectural merit. The Navy Department has erected some excellent structures, and the great dams built by the Reclamation Service and the Army engineers are among the finest examples of modern design. The small structures erected by the National Park Service in our national parks have great architectural interest and charm, and many other Federal agencies have contributed much to the advancement of architecture.

Traditional design predominates in Federal work although some trend toward the "modern" may be noted, particularly in the Middle West where the traditions of the architexture of western Europe are not so deeply rooted. Viewed as a whole the average architectural quality of design of the Federal work appears to be higher than the average of the Non-federal. However, there are a greater number of really outstanding examples of architectural design in the Non-federal buildings than can be found in the Federal work.

Traditional and "modern" design are more equally divided in Non-federal work. The trend toward the "modern" is evident throughout the country, but varies, like the Federal work, in the different States. And this variation is in quantity as well as quality, probably due to densities of population, wealth, background and tradition, local pride, culture, and the availability of competent architects and engineers.

The Non-federal projects vary greatly in architectural quality from very good to extremely bad. Many really fine examples of architecture in Non-federal work are distributed throughout the country but the greatest quantity of the best work is to be found in two areas, one of which is California and the other the Atlantic seaboard from Massachusetts to Pennsylvania, inclusive.

The greatest architectural advance has been made in the designing of utilitarian buildings, such as those connected with sewage and garbage-disposal plants and water-supply systems, which in former times were invariably ugly but which in many cases in the past 6 years have become structures of great aesthetic merit. Some of the best architecturally outstanding buildings in all types may be found in California. This is probably a result not only of good designing but also to the great advance made in the use of concrete as a finishing material and, to some extent, to the protective requirements against seismic disturbances. Also, the Triborough Bridge, tunnel approaches, and parkways in New York City; several of the New England schools; the State Prison at Atlanta; several beautiful bridges in Florida; the Exposition Building at Shreveport, Louisiana; several of the courthouses and city halls of Texas and New Mexico; some of the public buildings in Kansas City and St. Louis; the coastal bridges of Oregon, and several schools in Mississippi are all worthy of special note.

The designers of public works during the past 6 years have borrowed much from the general current that is flowing away from traditional design toward something new, but in reviewing their work from a close perspective it seems very evident that they have decidedly contributed to the movement. Where they have designed traditionally there is less copying of old buildings and details than formerly. Retaining the character of a given style, they have instilled new life into it by the use of new materials or new motifs and have thereby given it a freshness which protects it against the charge of being archaeology. Where they have used the "modern" style, the design sometimes shows the influence of the character and style evolved by various living European architects, but in general this is not the case. Most of the architects who have attempted to diverge from tradition seem to have attacked their problems from the point of view first of plan requirements, secondly of construction, and thirdly of type of materials to be used, with the result that in the more successful buildings of this character a style has emerged that may perhaps be the seed of the long sought "school of American design".

It is a fundamental principle of architecture that the best buildings are always those which are built throughout to comply with the structure best suited to the needs of the project. Excessive ornamentation is not only unnecessary, but in many cases definitely detracts from the aesthetic values of a building. As all building is designed to fulfill human needs, structural requirements may, in the last analysis, be considered to be the human ones. The best designs of public buildings that have been produced in the past 6 years indicates definite efforts to provide structures to fit our present civilization rather than to make our civilization fit into buildings that were designed for other ages.

So it is that this vast building program presents us with a great vision, that of man building primarily for love of and to fulfill the needs of his fellowmen. Perhaps future generations will classify these years as one of the epoch-making periods of advancement in the civilization not only of our own country but also of the human race.

*CHAPTER II*

# SCOPE OF STUDY AND GENERAL DATA

The structures chosen for illustration in this book were selected from over 1,700 projects which were included in the Survey prepared by the Committee on Architectural Surveys mentioned in the preface. The photographs in that Survey were selected from pictures of approximately 1,550 Federal and 5,900 Non-federal projects which had in turn been culled from the great mass of available material on more than 26,000 projects. The work for the Survey necessitated a study of plans and documents, the examination of over 10,000 photographs, and a limited amount of field inspection.

To obtain a general idea of the financial extent to which the P. W. A. assisted in the construction of the enormous number of public buildings erected during the past 6 years, it is necessary to review some items of cost at this time. Detailed statistics are given in Chapter X.

The estimated cost of construction only, of approximately 17,250 *buildings* erected during this period was:

| | | |
|---|---|---|
| On Federal projects (approx.)... | $ 321,289,000 | |
| On Non-federal projects (approx.). | 1,100,070,600 | |
| | | $1,421,359,600 |

It is to be remembered that some of the buildings have not yet been completed, so the final cost can be estimated only. On *all types of projects*, prior to the 1938 program, the total funds that will have been provided by P. W. A. and owners when all the projects are completed will be:

| | | |
|---|---|---|
| On Federal projects (approx.)....[1] | $1,703,000,000 | |
| On Non-federal projects (approx.). [2] | 2,757,500,000 | |
| | | $4,460,500,000 |

[1] Included in this are $136,667,750 for 51 housing projects.
[2] Included in this are $200,974,500 for railway loans.

When all of these projects are completed, P. W. A. will have provided in *loans and grants:*

| | | |
|---|---|---|
| On Federal projects (approx.).... | $1,703,000,000 | |
| On Non-federal projects (approx.). | 1,652,775,000 | |
| | | $3,355,775,000 |

The P. W. A. overhead costs on all projects up to 1939 was $89,144,361. It is difficult to determine what portion of this is applicable to Federal projects, but, assuming we allocate the whole sum to the cost of the Non-federal projects, it is of interest to note that this overhead was only 3.23 percent of the cost of Non-federal projects. The cost of the land, which is also included in the total cost, amounted to approximately $34,000,000 on Non-federal projects, and $25,938,000 on Federal projects.

It must be remembered that there will be no return to the Government on any funds from the Federal allotments except from the revenue-producing projects, such as Boulder Dam, the Bonneville project, Grand Coulee, and projects of the Tennessee Valley Authority. There will be a return on the loans made in Non-federal allotments and the interest accrued on those loans. The time of repayment of loans varied according to the project, the desire of the owners, and the ability of the owners to make payments up to a period of 30 years. The loans were made on a basis to yield 4 percent per annum.

Therefore, if we deduct the interest already earned and the amount of the loans, which would ultimately be repaid in full, from the total funds that will have been provided at completion of the projects by the P. W. A. (including overhead costs), we may obtain an approximate idea of the net cost to the Government of these *Non-federal projects:*

| | | |
|---|---|---|
| Funds that will have been provided............ | $1,652,774,300 | |
| P. W. A. overhead.......................... | 89,144,300 | |
| | 1,741,918,600 | |
| Interest earned.............. $ 18,278,500 | | |
| Allotted loans.............. 785,249,300 | | |
| | 803,527,800 | |
| Estimated maximum final cost to Government... | 938,390,800 | |

It will be seen that the estimated maximum final cost to the Government, which may be assumed as net cost for the purpose of this analysis, is approximately 54 percent of the funds that will have been provided by the Government for these Non-federal projects when they have all been completed. This does not take into consideration the accruing interest which will be paid up to the time of the expiration of the various loans, which will probably amount to over $2,000,000 and will thereby reduce this net cost to approximately 42 percent of the funds provided.

It is very interesting that the above estimate of the final maximum cost to the Government ($938,390,800) is only 34 percent of the total cost of construction of the Non-federal projects; and when all the interest will have been paid it will probably be less than 26.8 percent.

Until 1938, streets and highways comprised the greatest number of projects, but building projects had the largest total allotments in money. There were 10,808 projects for streets and highways and 8,259 projects for buildings. As has been stated before, there were approximately 17,250 buildings constructed on all the different kinds of projects. (In the 1938 program the projects for buildings were almost twice the number of those for streets and highways.) The amounts of allotments to the different States for all types of projects have followed generally in ratio to the population. Allotments were made to 82 Federal departments, bureaus, and agencies, which are listed in Chapter X under Statistics.

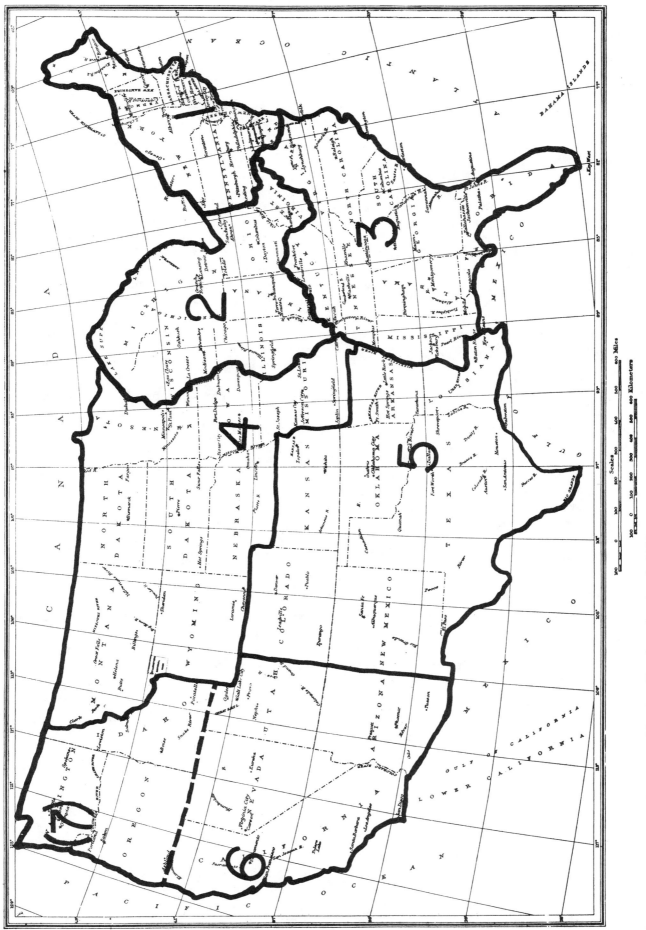

REGION No. 7 was made a part of Region No. 6 on October 1, 1939.

*CHAPTER III*

# POLICIES OF THE P. W. A.

That the lay reader may more clearly understand the operations of the P. W. A. and the extent to which it enters into the construction of a project, it is advisable to review briefly, in general outline, the functions of that organization.

The P. W. A. does not design any buildings or projects. It does not write the specifications or make any drawings. The character of architecture, the materials to be used and the type of construction are left entirely to the private architects and engineers employed by the owners on Non-federal projects and those employed by the Federal agencies on Federal projects. The P. W. A. acts somewhat in the nature of a bank or a large building and loan association.

The engineer sent to a project as an inspector is there for the purpose of seeing that the project is constructed in accordance with the owner's plans and specifications on which the P. W. A. made its grant or its loan and grant. He also ascertains that the policies of the Government, chiefly concerning fair and adequate competition in the purchase of materials and labor, are properly adhered to by the contractors and everyone concerned. He checks the expenditures of funds, because part of those funds are advanced by the Government. He reports only to the P. W. A.

When an owner makes an application for funds to the P. W. A., the application contains the proposed solution of the problem, the estimated cost, a preliminary plan and a brief description of the materials and construction to be used, together with data concerning the financial status of the owner and the legality of the proposed project. The P. W. A. does not undertake at any time to assume any responsibility for, or to make any changes in design or specifications unless it may be obvious that the plans are technically or economically unsound.

The application is examined to judge the usefulness, suitability, necessity, and desirability of the project; the adequacy in scope of the project for the purpose for which it is intended; the reasonableness of cost; and the financial ability of the owner to complete the project and, where a loan is made, if the loan is adequately secured. If the loan is secured by revenue bonds, instead of general obligation bonds, careful examination must be made to ascertain that the project should produce sufficient revenue to secure and pay off the loan within the period for which it is to be made. Also, the general technical soundness is studied to judge whether the project would be properly constructed for the purpose for which it is to be built, if carried out in accordance with the

plans and descriptions of the owner.

The working drawings and specifications, which generally are completed after the application has been approved, must be in compliance with local building codes, or with good practice where such codes do not exist. They must make adequate provision for sanitation, light, and air, and for the reduction of fire hazards to buildings and occupants.

The only requirements concerning the architects and engineers selected by the owner are that they must be in good standing, competent for the nature of the work to be constructed, and that the fees to be paid for their services are reasonable in amount.

The Government requires that an award of contract must be made to the lowest responsible bidder on all principal contracts. The bidder must be in good standing and competent. The contracts require that construction be completed within a time limit. No change orders affecting changes in cost may be executed by the owner or contractor without the approval of the P. W. A., as it is financially interested in the cost.

The Government requirements pertaining to materials are very explicit. Both the source of the material and the manufacturer must be in the United States and only by special approval may the raw or finished material be from a foreign source.

The owner may request a loan only, or a loan for any amount up to 55 percent of the total cost of the project plus a grant from the Government of 45 percent of that cost. When the allotment has been made and before contracts are awarded, the owner must deposit in a bank part of its share of the estimated cost of construction, which at completion may not be less than 55 percent of the total cost of the project when the allotment includes a grant of 45 percent.

The total cost of a project is composed of the preliminary costs and costs of land, construction, architect's or engineer's fees, legal fees, interest on loans during construction, and miscellaneous costs.

On Federal projects the allotments made by the P. W. A. are grants up to 100 percent of the estimated cost of the project. Under the N. I. R. Act a very small number of loans were made to semipublic bodies created for the benefit of the public, such as the railroads and limited dividend corporations to construct low-cost housing projects (slum clearance, etc.). This policy was soon changed in the later acts of Congress making appropriations to P. W. A., and all allotments were restricted to recognized public bodies.

# CHAPTER IV

# ACCOMPLISHMENTS

Invention follows upon invention in the world today, technical improvement upon technical improvement. Science is reaching out and is touching all walks of life and its transformations occur with almost bewildering rapidity. Humanity is striving to adjust itself to the new methods of living and its faster tempo of life and to gear its economy to the infinitely increased speed of production. These changes have affected the building industry as well as the planning and designing of the architects and engineers. Scientific improvements have been made in the fields of equipment, processes and materials and some of the best of these have been used in the construction of public works.

## Improvements in Equipment, Processes, and Materials

In practically all public buildings there has been a great improvement during the past 6 years in plumbing, ventilation, lighting and electrical equipment. Modern sanitary plumbing has been adequately provided; ventilation assured, either direct or mechanical; lighting, both direct and electrical, has been improved and much of the most modern electrical equipment, such as fire-alarm systems, police radio call systems, new locking devices, etc., have come into general use.

Air conditioning, although not yet perfected, has been installed in many schools, courthouses, and other buildings in which public gatherings are held. This treating and cooling of air is a great advance in the art of living and soon it should be more generally used, especially in the hospitals in the South where there is much unnecessary suffering brought about by the heat, when perspiration causes bandages to chafe, and even the touch of a pillow becomes intolerable to a patient; and exhausted doctors and nurses struggle to do their best under a terrific handicap.

Furniture for schools, hospitals, and courthouses has been usually well designed and of the best manufacture, and most of the furniture equipment for all types of buildings has been satisfactory with the exception of prisons where the type of beds provided for prisoners shows little improvement.

All civilizations have realized the value of large and pure water supplies, but never before has water been put to so many varied uses as it is today. Clear and pure supplies of water have been made available to the citizens of most of our urban centers through conservation and water-supply projects, and by the requirements of law. Water has also been harnessed to turn the wheels of great power plants to provide the electricity for many factories and towns. Water is carried over vast tracts of arid desert to create fertile fields out of shifting sand dunes. It seems that we could have no more fitting monuments to our civilization than the great Boulder Dam on the Colorado River between Arizona and Nevada, the Grand Coulee Dam and the Bonneville Dam in Oregon.

The outstanding feature of dam construction during the past 5 years has been the increasing interest in the importance of thorough exploration of foundations by geologists, both below and on the flanks of dams. Diamond drilling is now recognized as a necessary exploration for dams of any great size. Grouting to great depths, where fissures are found in any part of the impounded area, has become common practice.

The practice of grouting concrete to fill possible voids has greatly increased. This is carried out through grout pipes which are introduced into the concrete when it is poured. After it is thoroughly set, grout is driven in under as high a pressure as 1,000 pounds per square inch. On the Boulder Dam the chemical heat of the setting concrete was absorbed by refrigeration, provided by means of pipes run through the concrete. At a slow enough rate of deposit the concrete will cool by conduction and radiation but the Boulder Dam method of refrigeration made possible great speed of construction and saved a year or more of time.

In earth dams "core walls" are being much less used today. Careful classification of materials and greater consolidation are practiced. The spillways are generally of concrete. The use of the "sheep's foot roller" has become much more common and this machine has been greatly increased in size and efficiency. A photograph of one of these rollers at work on the Fork Peck Dam is shown on the left. The "feet"

on the drum, which are about 7 inches long and 3 inches thick, give the greatest compression that can be obtained on the layers of soil under the surface, although the top may remain disturbed. Proper grading of materials and the laying of the central part of the dam in water, using clays for this portion, has become normal construction.

The necessity of providing some means of preventing the silting up of dams is an obstacle in the way of much dam construction. Each dam is a special case and it seems probable that some projects should be delayed until soil conservation has been properly carried out over a considerable area around the dam site.

Water purification has already reached such a peak of perfection that there have been few innovations. Practically all filters are now of the mechanical type, "slow sand" having been given up. Hardness, salinity, and the presence of any elements detrimental to health must be eliminated. For example, it was discovered that much well water, particularly in the West, contains small amounts of the element fluorine which is responsible for decay of children's teeth. Where this condition existed and no other source of water supply was available, families having young children were urged to make use of filters or small distilling equipment adaptable to domestic use in order to provide distilled water. In filtration plants there have been changes in coagulants, the trend being largely toward ferric chloride. This was formerly so costly that other chemicals were generally used even if they were less effective. Many chemicals used in this manner were, however, found to be byproducts of other industries and the price of ferric chloride has therefore been greatly reduced, thereby making it a good competitor of other chemicals. Lime waste from the manufacture of acetylene gas is almost entirely bought up by filtration plants when they are in the same location and this constitutes a substantial economy.

In sewage disposal, chemical precipitation is coming back into more general use due to the progressive cheapening of chemicals. The development of the vacuum filter, which will produce a fairly dry sludge cake, has made possible the economical incineration of sewage sludge, especially as it does not require land for exterior sludge drying. This overcomes the necessity of buying expensive land in cities and eliminates objectionable odors. The installation of these new methods permits the development of the land around the plants into parks. Exterior sludge drying is still generally used where land costs are low and in the smaller plants. In plants where the ultimate in sewage treatment is required, magnetite filters have come into more general use, especially due to the greater ease of cleaning and the smaller space required, than is the case with fine sand in the final treatment of the effluent.

In refuse incinerators the only developments have been the progressively larger sizes of the units and improvements in heat economizers. Power has become, quite generally, a byproduct during most of the year.

The importance of adequate transportation facilities to all the nations is increasing. This country is further ahead in this field than any other country in the world. Our boulevards, ramps, and great scientifically planned highways amaze and attract not only foreign visitors but also us. These vast schemes of road construction are part of the modern idea of the necessity of building for the good of the general public. The medical aid, necessities and luxuries of life can be brought to the majority of the citizens of the land, and the citizens can easily transport themselves or their goods to all sections of the country.

Bridges are integral parts of highway systems. There has been great improvement in design in this field. Most of those built of steel are more beautiful in line and proportion than those constructed before 1933 with the exception of some notable examples such as the George Washington Bridge which spans the Hudson River. Even the steel framing has generally been studied to produce artistic effects in line and in texture, as can be seen in the Triborough Bridge over the East River in New York City. In many cases the bridges have been designed to fit the surrounding scenery, such as those in the public parkways.

One new development in bridge engineering is the use of open-grid flooring (subway grating). This is light and saves weight in the structure and its supports, and eliminates to a large extent the slippery surfaces made by snow and freezing in northern climates. There has been some use made of noncorroding steel alloys, but no general use of such materials in bridge construction.

Due to the wide variety of public-works construction almost every material produced and manufactured in the United States has been used in the construction of these projects and in the mechanical and furniture equipment. Brick, lumber, sand, gravel, and broken stone have usually been obtained in the vicinity of a project, while cut stone, lumber, wood trim, steel, metals, cement, plaster, plumbing and electrical supplies, marble, tile, equipment, furniture, etc., frequently have had to be obtained from a distance.

There is very little improvement to be noted in the use of most of the construction materials. Many new materials have been developed and have become available, but in the majority of cases either the material has not been considered to be perfected or else it is a patented product which eliminates it from competitive bidding. The greatest strides have probably been made in the use of concrete.

Paints have not improved much during the past 6 years, but the use of aluminum paint for priming most materials, including wood, has come into much more general use.

## Architects and Engineers

Very few competitions have been held for the selection of architects for the work under discussion. The owners have usually been successful in choosing competent architects, but where the owner or the architect has felt that the architect first selected was not equipped to handle a particular project, a consulting architect was called in to assist. This also applies to engineers.

The P. W. A. programs afforded to many of the architects and engineers employed by the Non-federal public bodies, their first opportunity to do work in which the Federal Government was interested, even though indirectly. The psychological effect of this, on the whole, was to cause them to produce the best work of which they were capable. The resulting improvements in planning, construction, and design were appreciated by the public bodies who employed them, thus bringing about an advance in the requirements of quality in public buildings. Naturally this applies much more to the rural districts than to cities where the standards were already high.

The approximate number of individual architects and engineers in private practice who were employed was 273 on Federal projects and 5,742 on Non-federal projects. The number of architectural and engineering offices employed was 210 on Federal projects and 4,380 on Non-federal projects. The total remuneration paid for these services was $2,294,000 on Federal and $124,068,900 on Non-federal projects. The architects employed on Federal projects, with but few exceptions, served in the capacity of consultants only, the work being done by the organizations of the various Government agencies. Many of the Government bureaus have architectural and engineering divisions and of the 40 bureaus which constructed buildings under the P. W. A. programs, 31 did their own designing and only a few called in consultants.

## Soundness of Construction

As mentioned before, the responsibility for soundness of construction rests with the owner and its architect or engineer. The P. W. A. examines the plans and specifications of projects to make certain that they conform to general standards, but does not as a rule check them for structural soundness. It does, however, as a participant in the financing, reserve the right to make a thorough examination of the plans at any time, and does insist that the owner require the contractor to rectify any mistakes or to correct any conditions of unsound construction that may have been discovered by the resident engineer inspectors in the course of construction. This system works better than if the P. W. A. gave formal approval of all plans and specifications and thereby assumed a responsibility, even if only moral, for the quality of construction, because owners, architects, and engineers use greater care in connection with the structural designing and the preparation of the specifications and plans when the responsibility is placed entirely on them.

It may be definitely stated that the standards and requirements set by the policies of the P. W. A. brought about a marked improvement in the quality and types of construction over those formerly employed by local public bodies without Federal aid. More intelligent planning, and supervision by the architects and engineers were the chief causes of this result. This is borne out by the answers to the questionnaire sent out by the Committee on Architectural Surveys, an analysis of which is shown in Chapter X.

## Check of Costs

Like all Federal organizations, and especially as it was advancing funds, it was imperative that the P. W. A. make a very careful check on all costs. This necessitated a considerable number of reports and forms which had to be filled out by the contractor and approved by the owner.

Many contractors complained of this but there were also many who claimed that the forms and reports had been most helpful to them in keeping better records and in providing them with better information as to how the costs were running during the progress of construction.

## Reduction of Hazards

The buildings constructed during the past 6 years constitute a noteworthy advance in the reduction of hazards to life and property when compared to the buildings of similar types constructed previously. In many parts of the country the problem had not been given much consideration, probably because in the more remote districts risks were considered to be slight. The school authorities often had no requirements or regulations designed to combat fire, or in regions subject to seismic disturbances, to resist earthquakes.

After the 1933 earthquake in the Los Angeles-Long Beach area it was necessary to construct or rehabilitate practically all the schools in the area. Examination disclosed that the schools had been built in ways entirely unsuitable to withstand seismic disturbances, and so the State legislature made it mandatory that all buildings used for public gatherings should be designed to withstand the one-tenth gravity factor, which means that a structure must be able to withstand a horizontal force of over one-tenth of its total weight. The basis of this law was a result of studies made by a Japanese scientist and American engineers. Two types of construction came into use, known respectively as the "rigid frame" and the "flexible frame" types. The "rigid frame" type has proved more satisfactory and is now in general use. This is discussed later under "Region 6" in Chapter V.

After the P. W. A. Extension Act of 1937, the P. W. A. required the owners to design the schools so as to provide all practicable protection against fire. These requirements were based largely on the recommendation of the National Fire Protection Association for the protection of life, and the Building Code recommended by the National Board of Fire Underwriters for protection of property, also on the recommendations of the National Council on School Construction and other authorities, and, to a lesser degree, on State and municipal codes.

The P. W. A. has not compiled requirements regarding the construction of special occupancy structures, such as dormitories, libraries, museums, armories, exhibition halls, hospitals, courthouses, and places of detention and similar institutional buildings. In examining plans it is guided largely by the recommendations of the above-mentioned fire protective associations and applicable local codes.

Some local and State authorities insist that plans be approved by State boards of health. This is a progressive step, and, although the standards of health requirements are low in some localities, the tendency is more and more to approach a high standard throughout the country.

## Craftsmanship and Decoration

The standard of craftsmanship in the use and application of materials has been satisfactory in general on the building projects, being higher in the urban areas and lower in more remote districts where less skilled artisans were available. In the higher types of construction the structural steel work and the masonry, plaster, wood, tile and marble finishes, and the plumbing, heating, and electrical work have usually been of the best standard.

In a good many cases in both Federal and Non-federal work sculptors and painters have been employed to decorate the buildings. This work has varied in character from outstandingly good to very poor. Viewed as a whole the craftsmanship of the sculpture has been excellent.

In Non-federal work the owner employs the artist for sculpture or mural painting, selecting him by competition. This may be done in one of two ways. The architect may carefully draw the outlines of the subject to ensure bidding on an equal basis and then drawings may be submitted by the artists, accompanied by bids, in which case the contract is awarded to the lowest bidder; or else the owner may establish an allowance and then call for drawings either from a number of selected artists or from a number obtained by advertisement. From the designs submitted, the winner is then selected by a jury appointed by the owner. The decision of this jury is final.

In the case of the Federal work carried out by the former Public Buildings Branch of the Procurement Division, a procedure was set up for selecting artists to execute sculpture or painting. Under this procedure programs are provided, describing the nature or subject of the work to be done as well as all necessary data about size, location, etc. A jury is appointed to pass on the designs submitted by the artists and the winning designer is awarded the contract. The Government also has the authority to appoint an artist who had been determined as being in the winning class in some former competition, or who is considered specially qualified for some particular type of work. As a result, a large number of artists were provided with work and many who were previously unknown were discovered and given opportunities.

## Labor

The main purpose of the creation of the P. W. A. was to increase employment of labor in the construction of permanent and useful public projects and in the building industries and the factories which supply building materials. The policy with regard to wages has been that the minimum wage rates of the various classes of labor in each trade must be predetermined by the owners to conform to the prevailing wage rates of the community for work of a similar character. It should be remembered that the P. W. A. does not establish wage rates. Where these rates are not officially established

by law, the owner must establish minimum rates for each trade or occupation, giving consideration to rates established by collective agreements and to rates actually paid for similar work in the vicinity, and then conferring with the labor adviser in the regional office to determine an equitable rate. The hours of labor are required by the P. W. A. to be not more than 8 hours per day nor more than 40 hours per week.

As of December 31, 1938, approximately $380,868,000 had been expended on direct labor on the jobs, *on buildings only*, and approximately $492,683,000 on indirect labor for supplying the materials incorporated in the buildings on Federal and Non-federal projects. The cost of materials used in construction of these buildings was approximately $716,993,000. These costs, especially of direct labor, will be considerably increased when those projects which are still under construction shall have been completed.

In addition to the employment of direct and indirect labor, a large amount of direct employment was provided for legal and financing services and for the architects, engineers, and draftsmen who planned, designed, and supervised construction for the owners, and also for other services of supplies of blueprinting and drawing materials. Building construction affects more different kinds of manufacturers and producers than any other form of work.

The providing of employment produced a valuable psychological effect on direct and indirect labor, in giving employment by which labor could work and earn its own living during these years of slack employment, rather than be forced to accept some form of dole. Undoubtedly, this effect, at least to some extent, must have been reflected in the quality of workmanship produced.

It is not practical to estimate the number of men who have been employed on P. W. A. projects, because in many cases the same men have done different kinds of work under different contractors on the same job and therefore would be listed several times. Often the same men have worked on different projects. The only basis on which such an estimate can be made, and it must be a very rough estimate, is in "man-hours" of work. This means to estimate the total number of hours of employment created in the construction of all the projects. Not including the 1938 program, on direct labor there were approximately 1,697,149,000 man-hours and on indirect labor there were probably about 3,157,000,000 man-hours, making a total of 4,854,149,000.

It is evident, therefore, that the economic effect of the P. W. A. programs on sustaining general industry and the employment of industrial labor has been very great.

# CHAPTER V

# DESIGN

The merit of design has been a much debated question at all times. The judgment of an individual is chiefly a matter of personal taste. What is beautiful to one sometimes is ugly to his neighbor. As, for example, the architecture of India may be too ornate for an Anglo-Saxon. The French have a saying: "Taste and color must never be discussed." Generally, most critics can agree, however, as to whether or not design, stripped of all unnecessary ornament, attains beauty through its line, proportion, and composition, and if it is suitable for its purpose. Therefore, the opinions contained in this book are the expressions of the individual taste of the authors as to the comparative merits of the structures which they have studied and of those which they have selected as outstanding examples of the best work in each of the various types of projects. The projects selected may not always be good architecture, but they appear to be among the best designs that have been produced for a given type of structure.

We use the term design in some cases to mean not only the general architectural and artistic treatment of a building, as distinct from planning, but also, in some cases, to include planning, use of materials, and types of construction.

As has been already noted, probably the greatest improvement in design over that of previous public work has been made in the architectural treatment of sewage-disposal plants, incinerators, and power and pumping stations. Following in order of excellence are dams, courthouses, city halls, auditoriums, post offices, schools, college buildings, and waterworks. Armories have been particularly unsuccessful and very few good architectural examples can be found in this type of work. There have been some extremely well designed and planned prisons and some very bad ones. In general, the quality of design and planning of hospitals and most institutional buildings has not advanced very much.

In connection with penal institutions it may be of interest to note that several years ago the P. W. A. established a routine whereby all plans for prisons were submitted for comment and recommendations to the Bureau of Prisons of the Department of Justice, which made suggestions based on good penology as developed in the Federal penal systems. This has resulted in many changes in plan and design. For example, high walls are often unnecessary, expensive interior cell blocks are being replaced to some extent by detention cottages for women and dormitories for men; and the sizes of employment and exercise areas are being increased. These changes together with various others of less note have altered the whole architectural problem of prisons and the results should be more and more apparent as time goes on.

## Comparisons

Until its reorganization in July 1939, the P. W. A. had seven regional offices in the field. These were located at New York, Chicago, Atlanta, Omaha, Fort Worth, San Francisco, and Portland, and each, respectively, had jurisdiction over regions numbered 1, 2, 3, 4, 5, 6, and 7, respectively. The States included in each region are given below.

In July 1939 Region No. 7 was combined with Region No. 6, with headquarters in San Francisco.

It is possible to compare the architectural progress made in design and construction of the Non-federal work in the different types of structures in the P. W. A. Regions, and to review the nature of the Federal work of the various departments, bureaus, and agencies of the Government. Our opinions are given below.

## NON-FEDERAL PROJECTS

### Region No. 1

The States of Maine, New Hampshire, Vermont, Massachusetts, Connecticut, Rhode Island, New York, New Jersey, Pennsylvania, Delaware, and Maryland are in this region which covers an area of 183,675 square miles. In it are a large number of the ablest architects in the country. More outstanding examples of both traditional and "modern" architecture may be found here than in any other region of the country. The schools and college buildings are nearly all traditional in character. Courthouses, city halls, recreational buildings, bridges, tunnel approaches, hospitals, sewage-disposal and refuse-disposal plants provide many more examples of "modern" design.

In general there is not much change in the planning of buildings but in large scale planning of speed highways and parkways, bridges, and tunnels, there has been enormous progress. Examples of this planning are the Triborough Bridge, the Lincoln Tunnel project, and the network of parkways which radiate from New York City. These are among the outstanding achievements in the country in improving automobile transportation and relieving congested traffic conditions.

The use of materials is relatively standardized in Region No. 1, and those native to the region are all commonly used, such as hardwoods, brick, stone, terra cotta, ceramic tile, cement, gypsum products, metal products, steel, slate, glass, granite, and marble.

The type of construction usually adopted is steel framing with reinforced-concrete floors and with exterior walls faced with brick or stone, backed up with hollow tile. Frames of reinforced concrete are not much used.

## Region No. 2

This region contains the States of Wisconsin, Illinois, Indiana, Michigan, Ohio, and West Virginia. It covers an area of 272,275 square miles. The general quality of architectural design is not as good as that in Region No. 1. Some very good architecture has been done in sewage-disposal plants and waterworks. Examples of good design in other types of building exist in various places, but in general there seems to be little advance in design and a tendency in much of the work to reproduce work done in the past. Traditional and "modern" design both appear without any notable trend toward one or the other.

It does not appear that the region has made much advance in the planning of buildings.

Native materials which are available and much used are hardwoods, limestone, sandstone, brick, clay products, ceramic tile, cement, metal products, and steel. Some use has been made of glass blocks and other new materials.

The most common forms of construction are steel frame or concrete frame with reinforced-concrete floors and exterior walls of brick, stone or terra cotta, backed up with brick or hollow tile. It is of interest that the first tall office building constructed with reinforced concrete framing was built in Cincinnati. This method of construction has been more generally used in this region than in the others.

## Region No. 3

Virginia, North Carolina, South Carolina, Georgia, Florida, Alabama, Mississippi, Tennessee, and Kentucky are in this region which has an area of 425,456 square miles. Traditional architecture of the Colonial period still dominates design here, except in Florida and the Gulf coasts of Alabama and Mississippi where some Spanish influence lingers and where "modern" design has crept in. With the exception of some noteworthy buildings, this area has not contributed much improvement in design. The best work has been done in Florida and Mississippi.

There has not been much advance in planning of buildings, but a good deal has been done in connection with planning of the national parks. An outstanding example of this is the Skyline Drive along the crest of the Blue Ridge Mountains in Virginia which will eventually extend to the Great Smoky Mountains in southwestern North Carolina.

Steel, limestone, marble, granite, cement, brick, clay products, and lumber are native materials and are generally used in construction.

Reinforced concrete, steel and wood framing are all used.

In general, exterior walls are bearing walls. Fireproof or fire-resistive construction is being used more than formerly. Very little has been evolved in the way of new types of construction.

## Region No. 4

This region contains the States of Minnesota, Iowa, Missouri, North Dakota, South Dakota, Nebraska, Wyoming, and Montana, with a total area of 681,132 square miles. The general standard of design has shown little advance. "Modern" design predominates and the largest quantity of the best work is in Missouri, where many of the public buildings are outstandingly successful. In general, the best work has been done in courthouses, penal buildings, recreational projects, and municipal auditoriums.

There has not been much advance in planning except in some projects such, for example, as the Kansas City and St. Louis auditoriums, which are of considerable interest.

Native materials are granite, marble, limestone, cement, brick, and some lumber. A good deal of the material used in construction is imported from other regions.

The common types of construction are steel frame, concrete frame, and wood with exterior walls of brick, stone, or stucco. Glass blocks have been installed to a considerable extent in schools and courthouses, and parts of the walls of the Floral Conservatory in St. Louis are of structural glass.

## Region No. 5

This region contains the States of Louisiana, Oklahoma, Arkansas, Texas, New Mexico, Colorado, and Kansas, covering an area of 746,534 square miles. The climate varies from semitropical on the Gulf coast to severely cold in winter in the mountain regions. As a result, the native styles of architecture show a wider variation than in any other region. Much interesting work, influenced by the Indian adobe architecture, has been done in New Mexico. The work in Texas and Louisiana shows the influence of the Spanish and French traditions. In Kansas, Oklahoma, Arkansas, and Colorado, design has conformed more to the work of the Middle West. The "modern" type of design has appeared occasionally and sometimes, as in the Exposition Building and the rubbish-disposal plant at Shreveport, Louisiana, has been done extremely well. The best designing has been in connection with dams, waterworks, courthouses, and hospitals.

Climate has been the controlling factor in the development of plans. In the coastal regions southern exposure to take advantage of the Gulf breeze is of primary importance. In New Mexico, Colorado, and northern Texas, small windows and thick or well-insulated walls must provide protection against the heat of the sun in summer and the extreme cold in winter. Such varying conditions of climate have resulted in a considerable variety of plans.

Much of the building material used in the region is produced locally. Brick, clay products, limestone, marble, granite, lumber, hardwoods, and cement are all available. Most metal products and steel must be brought from other States.

Reinforced concrete and steel are both used for frames in construction. Exterior walls are most frequently of brick, stone, or stucco facing on either brick or hollow tile walls.

## Region No. 6

The States of California, Utah, Nevada, and Arizona are included in this region, which is climatically divided into the northern and southern sections differing completely from each other. It has an area of 467,933 square miles. Most of the buildings in Utah, Nevada, and Arizona do not show very great advances in design but in California it is fair to say that almost a new school of architectural design has been evolved. The "Field Bill," enacted in the State legislature following the earthquakes of 1933, and discussed in Chapter IV of this volume, was primarily responsible for this. It caused the abolition of all types of veneer construction and the elimination of projecting cornices and free or loose ornamental features. Furthermore, it confined all construction to three types: All concrete, combined concrete and steel, and wood, and required that all three types be designed to resist seismic disturbances. The architectural traditions of California are confined generally to the Spanish and the American architecture of the first half of the nineteenth century. Out of this tradition and with the aid of probably the best work in concrete finish done in the entire country, a type of architectural design has been evolved which is neither traditional nor very "modern" but which is thoroughly satisfactory aesthetically.

New features have appeared in planning, especially in the large schools due to the requirements for protection against earthquakes. These schools are separated into a series of individual buildings connected with each other by means of metal slip joints or by arcades or passageways.

Almost all of the building materials are produced in the region, with the exception of steel and structural wood.

The use of gunite for the construction of walls has been developed extensively in California. Gunite is a mixture of dry sand and Portland cement which is shot through a hose at a pressure of 60 pounds per square inch, water being added at the nozzle of the hose. The material is shot onto a wall or onto single-faced forms in a semiplastic state and is equally as strong as the usual form of concrete but of greater density and may be used under conditions where concrete cannot be successfully poured. It considerably reduces the cost of form work.

## Former Region No. 7

This region included the States of Oregon, Washington, Idaho, and the Territory of Alaska, which are now included in Region No. 6 and which have an area of 836,114 square miles. Architectural tradition has not been deeply rooted in these States, and there seem to be no definite trends in architectural design. There are wide variations in climate, which is warm and humid on the sea coast, severely cold in winter in the eastern and mountain regions, and almost arctic in most of Alaska. The coastal bridges of Oregon and the Grand Coulee Dam on the Columbia River are much more than mere feats of engineering and their aesthetic value ranks high.

These States appear to have made but few new contributions to the planning of buildings.

Native materials which are in general use are lumber, sandstone, and brick. Metal products, steel, and cement are imported. Marble exists in large quantities in Alaska, and in inaccessible places in Washington, but due to transportation costs and lack of finishing facilities it is not in common use.

Construction is usually of steel, reinforced concrete, or wood, with no particular innovations except that along the seacoast a good deal of stucco is being used for exterior walls, applied directly to concrete. It seems to withstand the very damp climate extremely well.

One very curious condition exists in northern Alaska. In this region ice is present throughout the year at certain distances below the surface of the ground. During the summer, if rain water is allowed to penetrate the soil around a building it will melt the ice, thus causing the structure to settle. This makes it of vital importance to carry away rain water from the walls of the buildings. Also, as the upper soil, down to the permanent ice bed, is generally frozen in the winter in the extremely cold sections, as in Nome, the problem of water supply and sewage disposal is a very serious one.

## FEDERAL PROJECTS

There have been 40 departments, bureaus, and agencies of the Federal Government which have constructed buildings under the P. W. A. By far, the largest number of these buildings have been carried out by the former Public Buildings Branch of the Procurement Division of the Treasury Department, the Bureau of Yards and Docks of the Navy Department, the Quartermaster Corps and the Corps of Engineers of the War Department, and the National Park Service of the Department of the Interior. Practically every type of structure used by man has been planned, designed, and built by the Government.

The former Public Buildings Branch of the Procurement Division, now the Public Buildings Administration of the Federal Works Agency, built post offices, courthouses, Federal office buildings, quarantine and immigration stations, Coast Guard stations, border inspection stations, marine hospitals, and in addition carried out work for the State Department, the Department of Justice, and the Public Health Service.

The Bureau of Yards and Docks of the Navy Department built hospitals, air and radio stations, submarine bases, navy yards, etc.

The Quartermaster Corps of the War Department built army posts, hospitals, garages, magazines, and warehouses, while the Corps of Engineers constructed bridges and dams.

The National Park Service built shelters, houses, and a multitude of buildings of all types that have to do with the national parks. The Bureau of Reclamation built Boulder Dam, Grand Coulee Dam, and many others for irrigation and power.

A great variety of buildings and structures were erected by the remaining 34 departments, bureaus, and agencies.

The average quality of the design of these many and varied structures is high. Local tradition has been observed as far as possible. The "modern" influence is less pronounced in Federal than in Non-federal work.

The buildings are designed with great simplicity and a very sparing use of ornament, emphasis being placed on line, good composition, scale, and proportion. The rather rigid requirements in space and arrangement of Federal projects have made innovations in plan rare. In general, however, the buildings are well and economically planned, with emphasis placed on proper light and ventilation and elimination of waste space, together with economy in cost.

Most of the materials used were obtained, as far as possible, from the State in which the project was located. Very few new materials have been used.

The great majority of these Federal buildings are fireproof, constructed with steel or reinforced-concrete frames, reinforced-concrete floor slabs, and exterior walls of brick or stone. Most of the exceptions to this are in many of the structures built for the national parks, which are often of frame and frequently of log construction. Innovations in construction are almost entirely confined to dams, which have already been discussed.

From the records of the Bureau of Labor Statistics of the Department of Labor it appears that the costs of Federal projects constructed from plans and specifications prepared by the Government are probably from 2 percent to $2\frac{1}{2}$ percent higher than similar projects constructed from plans and specifications made by private architects and engineers. Federal specifications are very detailed and, in addition, contain frequent references to other standard specifications on materials and their installation. Furthermore, the Government is the owner of Federal projects and, therefore, its supervision of construction is generally more meticulous than that of smaller public bodies, and the requirements of the plans and specifications are generally more rigorously enforced.

*CHAPTER VI*

# SOCIOLOGICAL RESULTS

In this chapter we make a general summation of most of the sociological benefits to our national life brought about by the construction of the public structures during the past 6 years. These benefits have been far reaching.

Transportation and communication have benefited by larger and better highways and modern bridges and tunnels, and loans to the railways have enabled them to improve their rights-of-way, electrify their lines, and to recondition and add to their rolling stock. Airfields, constructed for commercial use and for the defense forces of the Nation, have not only added to the efficiency of the defense forces but have provided means by which transportation by air may be further perfected.

Opportunity for outdoor life and exercise for the public has been increased by the work carried out in the national parks, the community centers, and the schools. Water supply, electric light, and power have been provided for many communities for the first time in their histories. The restoration of old and historic buildings has added to the general culture of the Nation.

The construction of dams has not only provided flood control and electric power but has opened vast areas of land for settlement and agriculture by providing irrigation.

Government departments were given the opportunity, lacking for many years, of constructing buildings and projects for the use of the public. The Army and the Navy were able to replace many disgraceful and insanitary temporary buildings in their posts with adequate hospitals, barracks, and housing facilities.

Throughout the country, hospitals and State institutions have been able to build or greatly improve their plants for the insane, the sick, the aged, and the crippled. Notable advances have been made in the design, planning, and operation of prisons, enabling them to put into effect the new procedure whereby an effort is made to rehabilitate prisoners rather than merely to lock them up.

Sewage, garbage, and rubbish disposal plants have added greatly to the purification of rivers and beaches and to the sanitation of towns and cities.

The advances made in our school systems and in the cause of education by the added facilities made possible by libraries, museums, laboratories for research work, and other rooms for special studies, athletics, dramatics and public gatherings, are discussed in Chapter VIII, prepared for this book by a specialist in school-building problems, of the Office of Education, Federal Security Agency.

XV

*CHAPTER VII*

# OBSERVATIONS

In order that the P. W. A. programs should provide immediate benefit in employment and the stimulation of industry, it has been found necessary up to the present time to establish a time limit within which all construction under each program must be completed. Through this policy the P. W. A. programs have accomplished their purpose, but the process naturally necessitated too much haste by the owners' architects and engineers in the study of problems, in the design of buildings and structures, and in the preparation of plans and specifications. As an outgrowth of this haste many later changes in plans were required, inaccuracies in estimating cost occurred, necessary and important items were omitted from contracts, and errors were found which had to be corrected during construction.

As an example of the haste with which projects were begun, all of the working drawings for one project, consisting of 25 buildings, were completed by the owner's architects in only 26 working days. The best design of which architects and engineers are capable can be obtained only when they have sufficient time to study their problems thoroughly. Considering the necessary haste in getting projects under way, the results have been splendid on the whole.

The difficulties cited above imply the need for long-range comprehensive planning and programming of public works by the majority of the public bodies of the country. This applies to the departments of the Federal Government and is provided for by the Federal Employment Stabilization Act of 1931. Only by such long-range advance planning and programming can the needs of a community be ascertained and coordinated far enough in advance to allow architects and engineers time to study each problem properly.

It is true that most cities with a population of over 100,000 already have city-planning organizations of some kind. Few of these cities have been able as yet, however, to develop well-worked-out comprehensive plans for future civic development, although the majority do have long-range plans for their schools. As discussed in chapter VIII, only 21 of the States have State school-planning boards, and the majority of the counties and small cities have practically no facilities for the study of these problems. The general tendency is, therefore, to build for immediate needs only and to give consideration to projects individually, without relation to the broader aspects of community needs.

The development of a long-range program of public works for a community involves among other things a survey of all of the requirements and anticipated wants related to its growth and probable resources. Such a survey, to be of real value, must be more than a mere inventorying of the various projects which appear at the moment to be desirable. The projects of the several departments of the community must be related to each other in a comprehensive plan of development and must, also, be related to ability to finance. Furthermore, a long-range plan and program, to have meaning, must include an element of flexibility in order to allow for changing conditions or unforeseen circumstances which may arise from year to year. It should anticipate the needs of the community for as much as 5 or 6 years in advance and should be reviewed annually and brought up to date.

With such a program in operation, a community would be in a better position to undertake engineering and architectural studies and preparation of plans a year or two in advance of actual construction. There would thus be created a reservoir of easily available and well-prepared projects, which could be drawn upon as the need for any of them arose or as the need for emergency employment might occur.

While many cities and other State and local governments would be willing to embark upon the preparation of long-range programs and plans, few of them have either the understanding of the processes involved or the financial resources required. It seems appropriate, therefore, to suggest that the State and local public bodies should be encouraged in the study of advance planning for their public works needs through appropriations made for this purpose. The National Resources Planning Board has done much pioneering on this subject through its regional offices and with the cooperation of State and local planning boards. When in the future an economic situation arises that makes Federal aid in construction necessary, such aid should include immediate advances for detailed planning of projects. It is obvious, however, that these communities which have planned and programmed public works ahead will be able to get started earlier and those which have failed to plan may fail to receive grants for their projects.

The building industry is subject to wide fluctuations from varying causes and in times of depression is among the first to suffer. Even in times of normal business prosperity, depressions may occur generally or in certain sections, which may increase if not offset in some manner. Such building depressions often may start a widespread general depression. This can be understood when it is remembered that the building industry, besides providing direct employment, involves the use of practically all of our manufactured materials.

It is not possible, of course, to forecast periods of depression or to forecast the financial condition of the States or of the industries at any given time. If Congress should make annual appropriations which would be set aside to assist the States and other governmental bodies, to be drawn upon only at times of threatened depression, a reserve fund could be built up which would make it possible to use previously planned projects for quick construction work in order to maintain the normal level of the building industry. The States should be encouraged to institute a similar policy. Such a procedure would constitute a powerful weapon with which to combat depressions.

Serious consideration should be given to the subject of building codes. There is today much confusion and lack of standardization in this field. There are only 10 States which have building codes, namely, California, District of Columbia, Indiana, Louisiana, Massachusetts (limited), New Jersey (limited), North Carolina, Ohio, Pennsylvania (limited), and Wisconsin. New York and Texas are preparing State codes. Of the 3,165 towns and cities with over 2,500 population in the country, 1,887 have some form of building codes. But few of the 3,071 counties have codes. There appears, therefore, to be the need of a much greater adoption and unification of codes. It is suggested that much could be accomplished by a complete study of the situation and the Federal Works Agency would be the natural department for such a study in the field of public buildings.

It appears that in undertaking public works, it would be advisable to have a wider distribution of work among more architects and engineers than has been made by the owners in the recent years of emergency. Due to the emergency and the resulting necessary speed required in the execution of the work, in many cases a large number of projects have been given to one architect or engineer. Sometimes when an owner learned that an architect had executed a particular type of building, it employed him in the belief that he could get the project or the numerous projects started quickly. This, of course, was a mistake, as it resulted in many cases in the duplication of very bad architecture.

To improve the quality of design of public buildings, properly conducted competitions for the selection of architects should be encouraged throughout the country. It is the best method yet devised to stimulate architects to do the best work of which they are capable and in addition has the advantage of giving the younger men a chance to prove their ability.

There exists in Washington an organization known as the Commission of Fine Arts, whose function is to review and approve for the Government all designs of public buildings, parks, and works of art in the District of Columbia. This advice *must* be given but need not necessarily be followed. It is suggested that this Commission or a similar body act in this way in connection with *all* Federal work and furthermore that its advice be made available to any communities and States *if they desire it*. This might help greatly to improve the quality of architectural and engineering design throughout the country. The function of such a commission might be enlarged further to include a continuous study of new materials, new forms of construction, and new equipment, thus creating an impartial source of information on matters pertaining not only to the esthetic side of building but to the practical side as well.

As to the general consideration of design of the public buildings constructed in the past 6 years, however, it may be stated definitely, in summation, that although naturally there has been a considerable amount of bad architecture, the general result has shown great improvement over the work of the past 100 years.

# CHAPTER VIII

# SCHOOLS

by

ALICE BARROWS

of the

Office of Education

FEDERAL SECURITY AGENCY

---

*A study of school buildings erected with P. W. A. aid
on which construction was completed or substantially
completed before 1939*

---

The P. W. A. has been a lifesaver for the schools.

During the World War period (1914–22) thousands of children were housed in old insanitary school buildings and were on part time and double sessions, and very little construction was carried out.

During the period following the war (1922–28) an effort was made to catch up on the construction of buildings and in these years the average capital outlay per year per pupil was $15.27.

After 1929 the depression put a stop to this recovery and construction fell off even more than during the war years. In 1930 the capital outlay per pupil was $14.44, in 1932 it had fallen to $8.03, and in 1934 it had reached the low figure of $2.24. This meant that the capital expenditure dropped from $370,877,969 in 1930 to $210,996,262 in 1932, and to $59,276,447 in 1934. Since normally it takes approximately 2 years to plan, finance, and erect a school building, this last figure represents appropriations made in 1932.

During the 4 years from 1934 to 1938 the P. W. A. made grants and loans for school building amounting to $113,155,766 per year. These grants and loans, together with funds supplied by the applicants, made possible an expenditure of $232,405,061 per year, or $8.80 per year per pupil. In other words, the average expenditure each year per pupil for school buildings, with P. W. A. aid, from 1934 to 1938, has been almost four times as great as for the year preceding the organization of the P. W. A., but less than three-fifths of the amount per pupil per year in the period preceding the depression (1922–28).

## Number of Completed Buildings Erected With P. W. A. Aid

According to the records of the Public Works Administration, applications were made by 3,179 owners for grants and loans for 5,406 public-school buildings and additions during the period from September 1933 to October 1938. In answer to questionnaires sent to 3,179 school districts by the Office of Education in connection with the Survey of the Committee on Architectural Surveys in May 1939, information was secured for 1,965 completed school buildings. These school buildings were distributed over the 48 States. They were found in all types of communities. That the construction was not confined to cities is shown by the fact that nearly two-thirds of them were erected in school districts outside of cities. Furthermore, 47 percent of the buildings erected in cities were in communities under 25,000 in population. This is important because the communities outside of the larger cities are the ones which have been severely handicapped for years due to lack of funds in their school-building programs.

## Buildings Erected With P. W. A. Aid Eliminated or Replaced Many Existing Buildings

One of the most pressing problems in the modernization of our school system is the elimination of small school districts and the reorganization of schools into larger administrative units so as to provide modern educational programs for children in both elementary and high schools. For years one of the chief stumbling blocks in the way of such reorganization has been the existence of too many small buildings and lack of funds for the construction of the larger centralized schools.

The P. W. A. has materially advanced the reorganization of schools into the larger administrative units by making possible the erection of the larger units which are essential for such reorganization. For example, each of 150 buildings erected with P. W. A. aid eliminated 2 to 3 existing buildings; each of 29 buildings eliminated 4 buildings; each of 20 buildings eliminated 5 existing buildings; each of 28 buildings eliminated 6 to 9 buildings; and each of 17 buildings eliminated 10 buildings or more.

Furthermore, 47 percent of the 1,965 new buildings and additions eliminated fire-hazard buildings.

Examples of school buildings erected with P. W. A. aid which replaced old buildings are the high schools at Leland, Miss., and at Columbia, Miss., the Jonathan Dayton Regional High School in Springfield, N. J., the Elliot Grade School, Natick, Mass., and the Carl F. Bailey School at Hillsdale, Mich.

## School Buildings With Modern Facilities Made Possible by P. W. A. Aid

P. W. A. aid for the construction of school buildings not only made possible the elimination of fire-hazard buildings and the reorganization of schools into larger administrative units, but it also made possible the erection of school buildings with the educational facilities now considered essential in a modern educational program. Because of the complex conditions of modern life it is necessary to give children a much richer and more varied educational program than formerly in order that they may develop the intelligence and resourcefulness to meet the conditions of a changing civilization. This means that elementary schools as well as high schools must provide opportunities for work in science, art, music, nature study, shop work, and facilities for play and recreation, dramatics, and motion pictures. The erection of school buildings with P. W. A. aid greatly increased the number of buildings with these modern educational facilities.

For example, 72 percent of the 1,965 new buildings and additions had auditoriums, and 76 percent had either gymnasiums or combined auditorium-gymnasiums. Furthermore, in addition to 13,273 class-rooms in these new buildings and additions, there were 1,122 libraries, 1,625 science laboratories, 860 social-science rooms, 593 art rooms, 834 music rooms, 1,425 home-economics laboratories, 1,054 industrial-art rooms, 373 agricultural laboratories, and 2,825 other special-activity rooms.

The fact that since 1933 hundreds of school buildings containing art and music rooms, science laboratories, auditoriums, and gymnasiums have been erected all over the country cannot help having a lasting effect in encouraging the type of school building which makes possible a modern school program. The P. W. A. officials would doubtless be the first to point out that they had nothing to do with determining the kind of facilities which went into the buildings. Such matters were rightly left to the school officials. But the point is that if the P. W. A. had acted in the bureaucratic fashion in which those who are opposed to centralization of activities in the Federal Government assume that Federal agencies will act, then the P. W. A. would have insisted on having control over the determination of the educational contents of the buildings. It did nothing of the kind. It left the schools free to plan their educational programs, but at the same time by giving them the money which made possible the type of building which every progressive

school wants, it helped to spread knowledge of, and interest in, the modern type of school building.

One-third of the 1,965 school buildings erected with P. W. A. aid were elementary school buildings. It is often assumed that because of the decline in the birth rate new buildings for elementary schools are not needed. This assumption is not correct. Most of the elementary-school plants need modernization. Many elementary school children are still housed in 1-room schools which need to be eliminated and supplanted by centralized school plants with modern equipment. Many elementary schools, even of 8 or 12 rooms, do not come up to modern standards of heating, ventilating, lighting, and sanitation. Furthermore, a recent study by the Office of Education shows that 39 percent of all school buildings in 506 cities of 10,000 population and over are more than 30 years old. The majority of these buildings are elementary school buildings, and they are as appropriate for children of 1939 as would be the log cabin for adults of 1939.

An excellent example of a modern elementary-school building erected with P. W. A. aid is the Burgwin Elementary School in Pittsburgh, Pa. This building is functionally planned to provide modern educational facilities for elementary-school children, such as an auditorium, gymnasium, library, nature-study room, music room, handwork room, etc.

Of the other buildings erected through P. W. A. aid 30 percent were planned for combined elementary and high schools. Examples of these combined elementary- and high-school buildings are those of Algoma, Wis., Moose Lake, Minn., Saybrook, Conn., and Jackson, Miss. Thirty-three percent of the buildings were planned for either high schools, junior high schools, or junior-senior high schools. Some examples of this type of building are the high schools at Palm Springs, Calif., the Hollywood High School at Los Angeles, Calif., the high school at Ansonia, Conn., the Western High School at Detroit, Mich., and the high school at Ogden, Utah.

## Cost of New Buildings and Additions

Of the 1,965 new buildings and additions, the cost data were obtained for 1,324 new buildings and 529 additions. The cost of 1,324 new buildings was $213,242,442, and the cost of 549 additions was $47,153,031. The total cost of the 1,873 buildings was $260,395,473. This figure does not include the cost of equipment and land.

## Importance of Long-Range Surveys of School Plant Needs

Apparently, few of the buildings erected with P. W. A. aid were based upon long-range studies of school plant needs which took into consideration a building program for a wide area. For example, the need for 1,152 school buildings was based upon a study of the individual districts only, rather than upon a comprehensive survey of building needs of a whole State or group of counties.

Such long-range studies of building needs are often carried

on by cities, but only 21 State departments of education have school building divisions and very few of these have made State-wide long-range studies of school plant needs. Such studies should be carried on in every State department of education, in cooperation with State planning boards, as has already been done in Virginia and Florida. They are essential if the reorganization of small school districts into larger centralized districts is to keep pace with the needs of children and adults. Furthermore, it has already been proved that State departments of education which have based their building programs on long-range State-wide studies of school plant needs have been able to show conspicuous savings because of such studies. For example, the State Department of Education in Virginia estimates that the State school building survey recently conducted in that State by the director of the school building division, in cooperation with the State Planning Board, has saved the State $2,000,000 by preventing unnecessary building through careful population studies, elimination of many small schools, and housing of pupils in centralized schools. But State departments of education do not have the funds for making such studies. They can only be made if the Federal Government should make grants to the States for the specific purpose of conducting long-range, scientific surveys of school plant needs.

Such surveys are particularly important because an investigation conducted recently by the Office of Education showed that there is need for a continuation of large Federal grants to the States for school building construction. For example, a study conducted in 1937 showed that superintendents of schools in 62 percent of cities of 10,000 population and over, estimated that $496,000,000 was needed immediately for the construction of school buildings. This estimate did not include the needs of any of the rural areas or of communities under 10,000 population.

## Opinions of School Superintendents in Regard to the Construction of School Buildings Under P. W. A.

School superintendents in each of the 48 States have now had experience with the planning and construction of school buildings erected with P. W. A. aid over a period of 6 years. Some superintendents have had official relationship with a great many buildings so constructed, others with only one or two buildings, but some superintendents in each of the 48 States have had some experience with the erection of school buildings with the aid of P. W. A. Consequently, it seemed desirable to get the reaction of these superintendents to the work of the P. W. A. so far as school buildings are concerned. It was obvious, however, that their judgment would not be worth much unless they had had experience both with buildings erected with P. W. A. aid and also with buildings which had not been so financed in part. Therefore, superintendents were asked to give their opinion only in case they had had experience with construction of school buildings of both types.

On this basis, 817 school superintendents replied to a questionnaire giving their opinion of school building construction under P. W. A. as follows:

Of the 817 school superintendents, 47.4 percent said that school building standards were higher under P. W. A., 47.2 said they were about the same, and only 2.7 said they were lower.

Forty-eight percent said that in their opinion the construction of school buildings under P. W. A. was better than that for buildings erected without this aid, 44.7 percent said it was the same, and 4.4 percent said it was poorer.

Forty-eight percent said that the plans and specifications were better under P. W. A., 46.4 percent said they were the same, and 2.9 percent said the plans and specifications were less complete.

Twenty-two percent said that the competition for contracts under P. W. A. was fairer, 70.0 percent said it was about the same, and 4.2 percent said they were not so fair.

A larger percentage of both city and county superintendents agreed upon the superiority of accounting methods developed under P. W. A. than was the case in any of the preceding four answers. For example, 59.2 percent of all the superintendents said that the accounting methods under P. W. A. were better than in the case of buildings erected without P. W. A. aid, 33.8 percent said they were the same, and 2.9 percent said they were poorer.

This information is given in detail in the statistics at the end of this publication.

## Comments Upon the School Buildings Erected With P. W. A. Aid

No attempt will be made in this report to appraise, from an architectural standpoint, the school buildings erected with P. W. A. aid. But a few comments on several present tendencies in the functional planning of school buildings may be of interest to architects. The comments are in the nature of general conclusions and suggestions arising out of a study of a large number of buildings erected with P. W. A. aid.

Plans of school buildings depend upon the kind of education to be carried on in the buildings. In the days of the all-study school, the planning was comparatively simple since all that was needed was a given number of classrooms under one roof. But in the last quarter century rapid changes in social and economic conditions have necessitated far-reaching changes in the curriculum and program of both elementary and high schools. As has already been pointed out, these changes in curriculum are reflected in a demand for buildings that contain not only classrooms but auditoriums, gymnasiums, music rooms, art rooms of various types, science laboratories, libraries, shops, home economics, and sewing rooms. Moreover, the number of these rooms, their location, size, and equipment depend upon the particular educational program carried on in the building.

School superintendents who have carried out extensive school building programs during the last 20 years realize that if they are to get the full value of every dollar invested in their buildings it is important that they plan their educational program before the plans are drawn so that they can give the architect the following information as a basis for preliminary plans: (1) The maximum number of pupils per academic classroom and the dimensions which have been found to be the most satisfactory; (2) the maximum number of pupils per period who will use such special rooms as libraries, art rooms, and music rooms, and the kind of equipment to be used in these rooms; (3) the dimensions of the gymnasium based on the number of pupils using it at one time; and (4) the capacity of the auditorium and its dimensions, and the equipment of the stage. In other words, the school cannot be planned satisfactorily from a functional standpoint unless it is the result of the joint efforts of the school people and the architect. Failure on the part of the school superintendent and staff to tell the architect how each unit is to be used and the maximum number of pupils likely to use it, and what kind of equipment is to be put into the rooms, often results in tragic waste.

## Modern Trends in Functional Planning of School Buildings

Since the efficient planning of a school building depends upon the kind of educational program to be used in it, and since there is a great amount of experimentation in curricula and programs at the present time, it is obvious that no hard and fast standards can be made in regard to the planning of different units in a building. If a school is operating on one type of educational program, a given number of rooms of certain sizes will be needed. But if there is a different type of program, rooms of entirely different kinds and dimensions may be needed for a school of the same number of pupils.

For example, in an elementary school where many different kinds of activities are carried on in each classroom, classrooms of 22 by 35 feet or larger may be required. On the other hand, in an elementary school where only academic work is taught in the classrooms and where there are separate rooms for a library, for nature study, art, music, etc., the tendency is to make the classrooms 22 by 30 feet and the special rooms 22 by 40 feet or 22 by 45 feet. In a combined junior-senior high school, the classrooms may be 24 by 26 feet or 24 by 28 feet and there may be a great variety of special rooms. For example, a music course may require a choral room, orchestra room, band room, and instrumental music room. The planning of these rooms should be carried on in close cooperation with the director of music, and the dimensions of the rooms will vary with the program of the school. The same procedure applies to all other special activity rooms.

Furthermore, it should be remembered that school curricula and educational programs are always in process of change to meet the needs of youth in a complex and constantly changing civilization. For this reason it is essential that modern school buildings should be erected, as office buildings are, with nonsupporting walls between rooms. If this is done then the type and size of room can be changed without necessitating any change in fundamental structure.

One of the units in the school building that is essential for a modern educational program is the gymnasium, but the number and sizes of gymnasiums, locker rooms, and showers will depend upon the program of play and physical education. If that program provides for two classes using the gymnasium each period of the day, either two separate gymnasiums may be required or there may be one gymnasium unit so constructed that by the use of a folding door on runners two gymnasiums may be provided for the daily work. By throwing open the folding doors the total space is made available for intramural basketball games. Too often there is a tendency to plan gymnasiums on the basis of their occasional rather than their daily use. That is, they may be planned primarily for intramural basketball games without sufficient regard to daily use. When this is done the gymnasium is likely to be far larger than is necessary for one class, and yet cannot be used by two separate classes. It should be remembered that the greatest waste in school building planning lies in providing rooms for occasional rather than regular use.

The location of the gymnasium is very important. Sometimes it is located on one wing at the front of the building, and the auditorium on the corresponding wing. From an architectural standpoint this is attractive but from a functional standpoint there are some grave objections to it. In the first place, outside light is not necessary for a gymnasium. Therefore, it is a waste to use space for the gymnasium that can better be used for classrooms. In the second place, it is desirable to place the gymnasium toward the rear of the building so that there may be easy access to the playground which is usually behind the building.

The auditorium is one of the most important units in the school building and yet it is usually the most poorly planned. The reason is that until lately there has been considerable confusion as to how the auditorium should be used. Originally it was merely an assembly hall where the whole school met in the morning for opening exercises. In recent years, however, it has come to be recognized that the school should be the community center of the neighborhood and that the auditorium should be constructed for use both by the school and by the community as a school theater in which plays, concerts, lectures, and motion pictures may be presented. Unfortunately, the use of the auditorium as a school and community theater is of such recent growth that school officials and architects are only just beginning to realize that the modern school auditorium must be planned on altogether different lines from the old assembly hall.

The first essential in planning an adequate school auditorium is to recognize that the old tradition that the school auditorium should be large enough to house the entire school at one time not only is not necessary in a modern school program but actually prevents the planning of the kind of auditorium needed for both school and community use. A school auditorium with a seating capacity of 1,500 to 2,000 is too large for the presentation of plays. Most professional theaters in New York City have a capacity of 1,000 seats or less. Very few professional actors can project their trained voices or "get across the footlights" in a 1,500-seat auditorium. Much less can this be done by amateurs.

The greatest fault in the planning of school auditoriums is usually found in the planning of the stage. It is recommended that the stage should be not less than 25 feet in depth, that the proscenium arch should be not less than 24 feet or more than 32 feet in width, and that the off-stage space from side wall to side wall should never be less than twice the width of the proscenium. Yet a recent study of the Office of Education shows that in 30 auditoriums only 2 stages had a depth of 25 feet, in only 13 did the width of the proscenium arch conform to the above standards, and none of the stages had off-stage space equal to the width of the proscenium arch.

When auditoriums are planned as just described, they cannot be used for the proper presentation of plays and concerts because, first, the stage is not large enough for more than two or three persons to move around owing to the furniture, and, second, there is not enough off-stage space in which to place property between acts. Without doubt the slow development of the school building as a community center has been due in large part to the failure to construct the auditorium in accordance with the technical requirements of the well-planned modern theater. For this reason the recent bulletin of the Office of Education entitled "The School Auditorium as a Theater" should be of prac-

tical value both to school superintendents and architects.

In the past there has been a tendency to build what is called a combined auditorium-gymnasium instead of a separate auditorium and gymnasium. This tendency is decreasing. It is generally recognized by educators that a combined auditorium-gymnasium is undesirable both from a functional and an administrative standpoint. They admit that such a unit is not satisfactory either as a gymnasium or an auditorium because a room constructed for the purpose of throwing a basketball from one end of it to the other cannot be designed satisfactorily to have the character needed for a theater. In most cases the usual argument advanced for a combined auditorium-gymnasium is that it is cheaper than building them as separate units. Fortunately, recent studies have shown it is not necessarily true that a combined auditorium-gymnasium is cheaper. If auditoriums are constructed to provide for 33 to 50 percent of the capacity of the school, which is now the general tendency, then it is possible to construct a separate auditorium and a separate gymnasium, the total cubage of which is no greater, in fact often less, than the cubage of the combined auditorium-gymnasium.

# CHAPTER IX

# TYPES OF SELECTED PROJECTS

The projects illustrated on the following pages are representative of the best work of different types of architecture completed, or substantially completed, up to January 1, 1939, with the financial assistance of the Public Works Administration.

The different types are classified into 24 different kinds of projects, as follows:

Local government buildings:
- *a.* Municipal buildings.
- *b.* Courthouses.
- *c.* State capitols.
- *d.* Miscellaneous State buildings.
- *e.* Police and fire.

Auditoriums and armories.
Libraries.
Memorials and museums.
Elementary schools.
High schools.
Combined elementary and high schools.
Junior colleges.
Colleges and universities.
Social and recreational buildings.
Hospitals and institutions.
Jails and penal institutions.
Warehouses and docks.
Sewage-disposal plants.
Garbage and rubbish-disposal plants.
Waterworks.
Light and power plants.
Dams.
Airfields and hangars.
Bridges and highways.
Army and Navy posts.
Post offices.
Miscellaneous.
Housing projects.

## City Hall, *Pawtucket, Rhode Island*

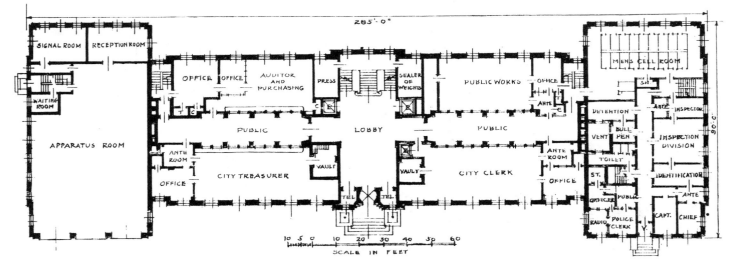

The city of Pawtucket is situated on the Seekonk River at the head of Narragansett Bay. As early as 1790 it began its industrial career with the construction of the first textile plant built in America, and today it has over 300 mills, plants, and factories manufacturing cotton textiles, woolens, silks, wire, machinery, etc.

The city departments were housed previously in rented quarters. The new city hall provides quarters for all of the municipal departments and is part of a civic center group which includes the Central High School and the Memorial Bridge.

Its over-all dimensions are 285 by 90 feet and the tower is 156 feet high. It was completed in March 1936 at a construction cost of $393,460 and a total project cost of $448,042.

1

## Municipal Building, *Town of*

## Stratford, Connecticut

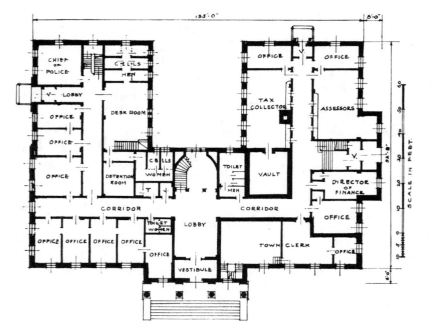

This municipal building is in the town of Stratford, east of Bridgeport, and on the west bank of the Housatonic River, near its mouth. It is on a triangular plot of ground with streets on all sides and is placed well back from the apex of the triangle.

The building is of fireproof construction up to the roof. With the exception of the portico, the exterior walls are of red face brick. The floor slabs are concrete of bar-joist construction, and the roof is wood covered with slate. The cupola is wood.

Offices and a garage for the police department are in the basement. The upper floors provide quarters for the town clerk, the tax assessors and collectors, the town manager, a courtroom, council chambers, and drafting rooms for the chief engineer.

The dimensions of the building in plan are 99 by 143 feet. The height to the top of the cupola is approximately 60 feet. The project was completed early in 1937 at an approximate cost of $225,000.

Town Hall, *West Hartford, Connecticut*

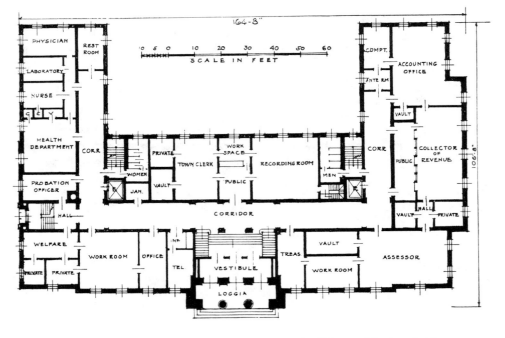

West Hartford, a suburb of Hartford, Connecticut, had a population of 25,000 in 1930. The new town hall, which replaces a small and obsolete frame building, is on a main thoroughfare in a district which is partly residential and partly business. It houses all the town offices, including the police department, the court, and a jail.

The exterior walls are red face brick with trim and base of limestone. Doors, windows, cornices, and the cupola are wood. The roof is slate laid on gypsum plank.

The building is U-shaped in plan, is two stories and a basement in height, and has a volume of 628,000 cubic feet. The over-all dimensions are 107 by 165 feet and each wing is 33 by 43 feet. The space between the wings is occupied by a one-story garage. It was completed during February of 1937 at a construction cost of approximately $260,600 and a project cost of approximately $321,000.

3

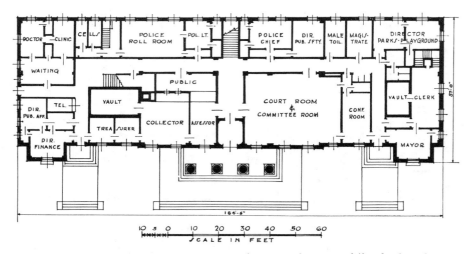

## Municipal Building

### *West Orange, New Jersey*

West Orange is a suburban community in the New York Metropolitan area, a short distance west of Newark. In general it is residential in character.

The new municipal building replaces an old and obsolete structure which was inadequate in size and had no proper facilities for the storage of records. Some of the municipal offices were in temporary buildings, some in rented quarters and there were no garage facilities with the result that the city-owned automobiles had to be stored in public garages. The new building houses all of the city departments. The basement contains a garage, storage space, and a block of six cells. On the first floor are the police headquarters, courtroom, and offices for the mayor, clerk, treasurer, and others. The second floor has offices for the engineer, director, building inspector, the street department, and a drafting room.

The structure is fireproof throughout, the exterior walls being of red face brick with limestone trim.

The overall dimensions are 57 x 165 feet and the building was completed during July 1937, at a construction cost of $209,279. The total project cost was $226,093.

City Hall, *Medford, Massachusetts*

Medford is a residential suburban community a short distance north of Boston and its population has increased from 23,150 in 1910 to 59,174 in 1930.

The history of Medford is recorded on two tablets at the main entrance of the new city hall and reads as follows:

> Settlers were reported "upon Mysticke" in 1629. A larger group in 1630 settled near the square and named the place "Meadford." The first recorded town meeting was held in 1674. In 1676 the first selectmen were elected and in 1689 the first representative was sent to the General Court. Town form of government continued until Medford was incorporated a city in 1892.
>
> Medford's first town meetings were held in private homes, later in meeting houses until a town hall was erected in 1833. That building was partially burned and rebuilt in 1835 and 1850 and remodeled in 1893 to accommodate the new city government. It was razed in 1916 and from that date offices were leased until the completion of this building in 1937.

The building is T-shaped in plan and three stories in height, and its over-all dimensions are 180 by 131 feet. It is fireproof throughout, the exterior walls being of water-struck brick and limestone.

The project was completed in September 1937 at a cost of approximately $450,000.

5

## City Hall

*Cranston, Rhode Island*

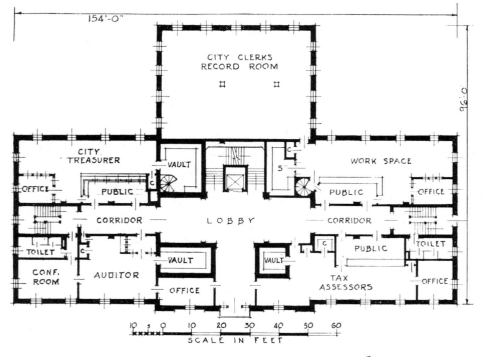

Cranston, which adjoins Providence on the southeast, is the fourth city in size in the State, its population having increased from 21,107 in 1910 to 42,911 in 1930.

The new city hall, which houses all of the municipal offices, replaces the old frame town hall built in 1885 which was considered to be a firetrap, and, in addition, made it possible to eliminate three other buildings which were used as annexes to the town hall and for which a yearly rent of $1,080 was paid.

The new city hall is T-shaped in plan and is three stories in height, including the basement. The exterior materials are granite, red face brick, and buff limestone. The sloping roofs are covered with slate the windows are part wood and part steel, and the exterior doors are part wood and part bronze. The structure is fireproof.

The ground-floor area is 11,271 square feet and the volume of the building is 509,550 cubic feet. It was completed in June of 1937 at a project cost of $271,464.

## Town Hall

*Berwick, Maine*

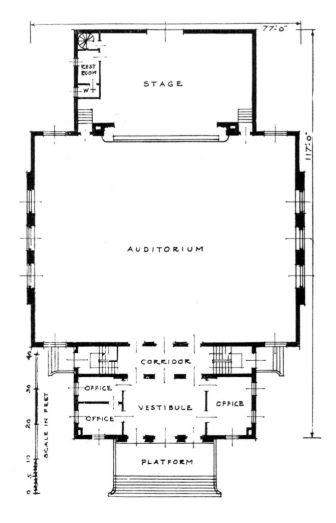

Berwick, which has a population of about 2,000, is on the Salmon Falls River, about 12 miles from Portsmouth, New Hampshire, in the extreme southwestern part of the State. It is in an agricultural area, but has a small cannery and two woodworking plants.

A bequest of securities was made to the town which was intended to provide funds for the building. Due to a decrease in the value of these securities it was necessary to obtain P. W. A. aid, and even with this aid a smaller building was constructed than the one originally contemplated.

The over-all dimensions of the building are 117 by 77 feet and it is two stories high with a basement. It houses all of the town offices, the fire department, a library, an auditorium, a kitchen, and a social room.

It has a steel frame, concrete floors, and wood roof. The exterior walls are brick with wood trim and the cupola is wood. It was completed in January 1939 at a construction cost of $67,557 and a project cost of $85,385.

7

Municipal Building, *Warren*, *Pennsylvania*

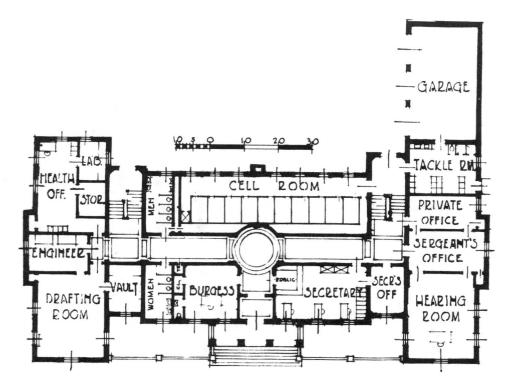

This structure replaces a municipal building which was 70 years old, which had been remodeled several times, and had passed the point of economic usefulness.

The new building contains offices for the burgess, borough clerk, city engineer, police department, health department and welfare clinic, and the council chambers. There is a pistol range in the basement, a jail with eight double cells, a dormitory for transients, and some unfinished space for future expansion.

The structure is fireproof. Foundation and basement walls are concrete, floors are reinforced concrete slabs supported by steel beams, and the roof is slate over wood sheathing supported by steel trusses. The exterior walls are faced with sand-finished handmade red brick with limestone trim except that the cornices and cupola are wood.

The plan is H-shaped, 137 by 101 feet over all. The construction was completed in January 1937 at a construction cost of $92,307 and a project cost of $119,274.

## Municipal Building

### *Lewistown, Pennsylvania*

Lewistown is the county seat of Mifflin County and is situated on the north bank of the Juniata River, 61 miles west of Harrisburg. This new building replaces a structure 70 years old which was obsolete and past the point of economic usefulness.

The property is 100 feet wide by 65 feet deep. The building houses all of the municipal agencies and has in addition general storage space and a scale large enough to weigh the heaviest trucks.

It is fireproof throughout with steel frame, and floors and roof are constructed of truss steel joists and concrete slabs. The front and side walls are variegated limestone backed with brick and tile and the rear wall is face brick. Windows are steel and exterior doors white metal.

The office floors are wood, all doors are walnut, all ceilings acoustically treated, and the stairs are steel. A complete ventilating system is included in the equipment.

The building is rectangular in plan with extreme dimensions of 42 by 81 feet. It was completed in March 1937 at a total project cost of $67,321.

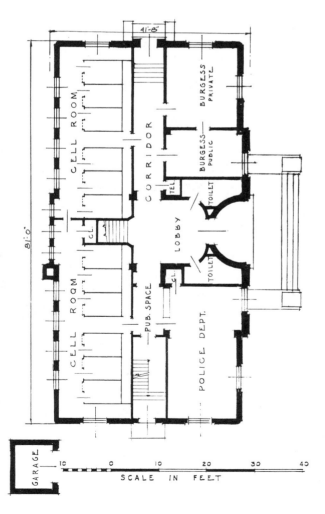

## Municipal Building, *Crafton, Pennsylvania*

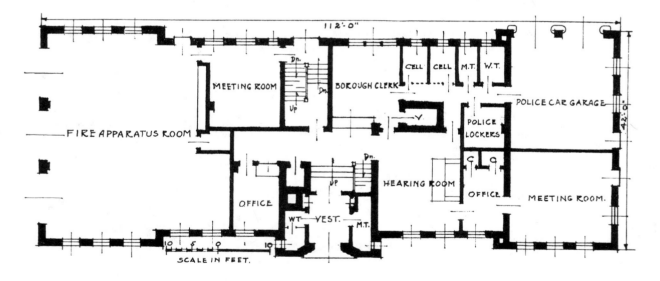

The Borough of Crafton, originally called Killiman and later Brodhead, is a residential community with a population of 7,500, lying just outside of Pittsburgh.

The building is part two stories and basement in height and has over-all dimensions in plan of 112 by 42 feet. It houses the municipal offices, the police and fire departments. There is space for the fire apparatus and a police-car garage, reading and billiard rooms for the firemen, police hearing room, detention cells, council chamber, offices for the borough secretary and tax collector, and a room for social gatherings.

The construction is fire-resistant. The exterior walls are limestone backed up with hollow tile and the floors are reinforced concrete on steel joists.

The volume of the building is 140,000 cubic feet. It was completed in August 1938 at a construction cost of $75,382 and a project cost of $75,382, the costs being identical for this project.

## Municipal Building
### *Saddle River, New Jersey*

The Borough of Saddle River is a high-class residential community with an area of about 5 square miles, chiefly devoted to large estates. It is located in northern New Jersey, about 22 miles from New York by way of the George Washington Bridge. Previous to the completion of the new building an old frame building without improvements other than electric light was rented as a town hall and for the storage of fire apparatus.

The first floor of the project contains an entrance foyer, the mayor's office, council room, offices for the assessor and collector, and an auditorium seating 225 people. The second floor contains a balcony to the auditorium, seating 125, and a library. In the basement are a fire-apparatus room, firemen's recreation room, police and recorders' room, detention room, and community kitchen.

The building is of fireproof construction with reinforced concrete floors, steel trusses, and gypsum plank roof. This building, the old Dutch Reformed Church, and the school-house in the immediate vicinity, form a community center. The exterior walls are native brownstone on the front portion of the building. The trim is wood and the roof is slate.

The dimensions are 69 by 84 feet. The completion date was December 15, 1937, and the total project cost $59,256.

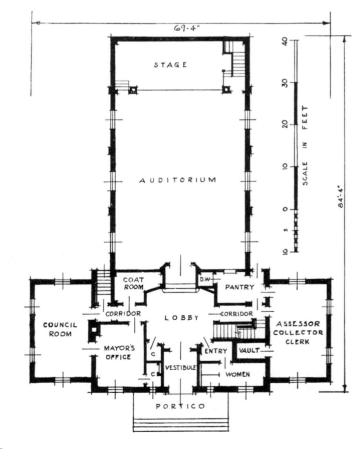

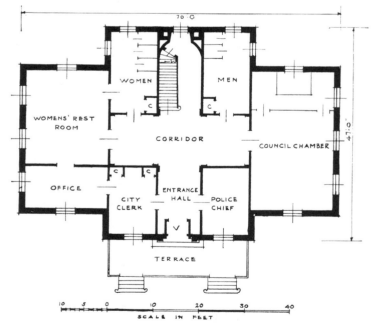

## Municipal Building

### *Pocomoke City,*

### *Maryland*

stands has an area of 9,000 square feet and is in the center of the business district.

The structure provides quarters for the city officials and contains, in addition, a rest room and toilets, and space for the Pocomoke Library.

The exterior walls are red face brick with a cut-stone belt course at the first-floor level. Sash and trim are wood and the roof is slate. There is a masonry terrace at the entrance with a wrought-iron rail.

The building was completed in April of 1937 at a total project cost of $46,939.

Pocomoke City, with a population of 2,609 in 1930, is in Worcester County in the extreme southeastern part of the State. The property on which this municipal building

Town Hall, *Seymour, Connecticut*

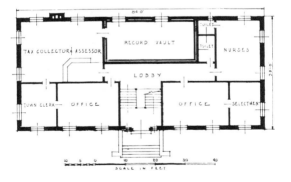

Seymour, with a population of 6,890 in 1930, is on the east bank of the Naugatuck River, a short distance north of its junction with the Housatonic River.

The new town hall is in the commercial center and opposite the post office. It provides quarters for the town clerk, the tax collector, the selectmen, the nurses, and a record vault on the first floor, and quarters for the police department and a jail in the basement.

The building is semifireproof, the first floor being concrete and the ceiling beams and roof of wood. The exterior walls are selected common brick, windows, doors, cornice, and cupola are wood, and the roof is covered with slate. The over-all dimensions in plan are 84 by 38 feet.

It was completed in October 1936 at a construction cost of $35,873 and a project cost of $38,662.

## Town Hall, *Chester*, *Massachusetts*

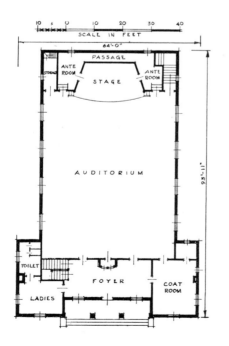

The town of Chester is midway between Springfield and Pittsfield on the main line of the Boston & Albany Railroad. Its population in 1930 was 1,400. It has some small manufacturing plants and is a center of education in that it possesses the only high school within a radius of 30 miles.

The new town hall replaces an older building which was destroyed by fire in 1935. It is T-shaped in plan and, due to a sloping site, is two stories high in front and three in the rear.

In the basement are three social rooms and all utility rooms. The first floor has an auditorium 46 by 58 feet with a stage and two anterooms. On the second floor are rooms for town officers, the tax department with a waiting room, two private offices, and a moving-picture projection booth.

The wall construction below the first floor is concrete and above the first floor is brick backed with terra-cotta block. The floor construction is wood joists on steel girders. The trim is wood and the walls of the recessed porch are faced with wood.

The building was completed in February of 1937 at a construction cost of approximately $36,600.

## City Hall

*Delaware, Ohio*

The new city hall at Delaware replaces a building which was built in 1873 and which was destroyed by fire in 1934. Following the fire, the city offices were housed in an abandoned school building, the fire department occupied rented quarters, and municipal prisoners had to be confined in the county jail.

The new building was erected on the old site, which has been suitably landscaped.

The first floor provides quarters for city offices, the fire department, and a police garage. The second floor houses council chambers, conference rooms, the office of the city engineer, a jail, and quarters for the jailer.

The construction is reinforced concrete with exterior walls of red face brick and stone trim.

The volume of the building is 280,000 cubic feet. It was completed in February 1937 at a project cost of $95,047.

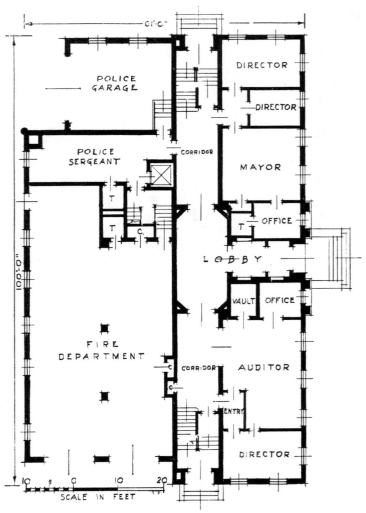

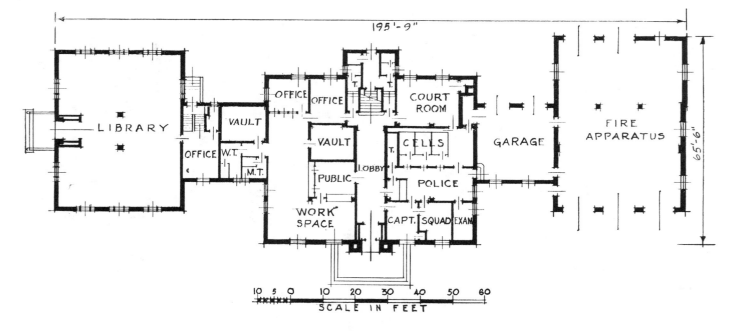

## Municipal Building, *Des Plaines, Illinois*

This building is unusual in that it houses both the city hall and the public library of Des Plaines, Illinois. The old city hall had become obsolete and it was sold, together with its property, thus providing funds to help finance the new project. The old public library was inadequate and was demolished in order to provide a site for the new municipal building.

The first floor of the new structure contains, in addition to city offices, a large room for the use of the city council and municipal court, which can also accommodate about 150 people at minor civic meetings. The east wing houses the fire and police departments and the west wing, with a separate entrance on the side street, houses the public library.

The exterior is red brick with brick quoins at the corners and stone trim.

The building has a usable floor area of 10,000 square feet and was completed at a total project cost of $91,567.

## Municipal Building
### *Marietta, Ohio*

The river-port city of Marietta, at the junction of the Muskingum and Ohio Rivers, was one of the first settlements of the "Northwest Territory." Today it is a city of 15,000 people with many minor manufacturing industries.

Before 1935 the municipal government was housed in an obsolete nonfireproof building with an auditorium seating 900 on the top floor, necessitating unsightly fire escapes.

The new municipal building occupies an ample site and the project included, in addition, a connecting wing to a relatively new and modern fire-department building and the landscaping of the entire site.

The new building contains quarters for all of the departments of the city government and also an auditorium seating 1,400 and a banquet hall with kitchen facilities. The construction is steel and reinforced concrete, and the exterior walls are red face brick with stone trim. The principal rooms are acoustically treated, and mechanical ventilation is provided throughout. Many walls are decorated with mural paintings depicting the pioneer history of Marietta.

The building has a volume of approximately 210,000 cubic feet and the project cost was $123,808.

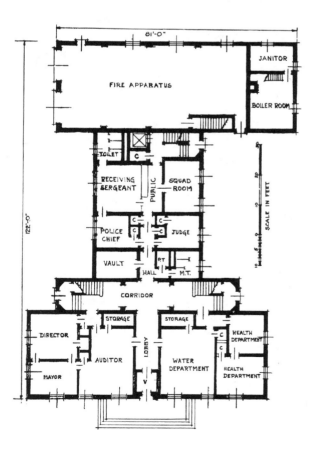

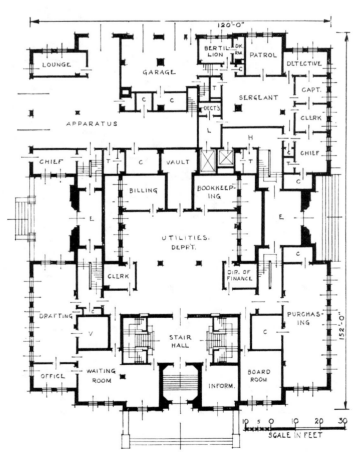

## Municipal Building

### *Hamilton, Ohio*

This project included, in addition to the construction of the municipal building, the purchase of a site which was selected in the business district of the city, facing the Miami River.

The building provides space for the city council, all of the offices for the departments of the city government, municipal courts, a jail, the police department with a rifle range for their use, and a unit of the fire department.

The structure is fireproof throughout and its exterior walls are faced with limestone relieved by a small amount of carved ornament and decorative metal spandrels between the windows.

It was completed in April 1936 at a construction cost of $419,783 and a project cost of $573,690.

## City Hall

### *Saginaw, Michigan*

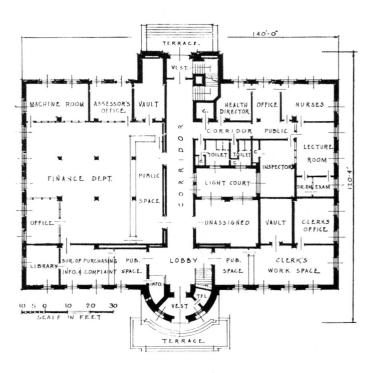

This city hall occupies the site of a former building which was destroyed by fire on April 9, 1933. It is approximately 120 by 140 feet over-all in plan and is two stories and a basement in height. As it is on sloping ground, the basement windows are above grade on the rear.

The basement provides space for the public-welfare department and for a small courtroom. On the first floor are most of the city offices and space for record storage. The council chamber, the mayor's offices, and the department of public works are on the second floor.

The building is fireproof, of reinforced concrete, and the exterior walls are faced with slightly rough native stone in narrow courses laid irregularly with flush mortar joints. The trim is of sawed limestone and a small amount of marble at the main entrance.

The volume of the structure is approximately 545,000 cubic feet. It was completed in November 1937 at a construction cost of $294,349 and a project cost of $312,526.

## City Hall and Auditorium

### *Montgomery, Alabama*

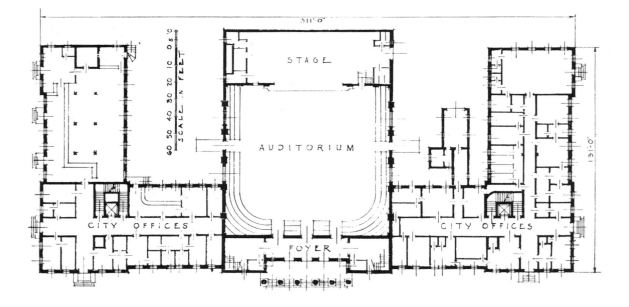

The population of Montgomery, the capital city of Alabama, was 66,079 in 1930. Its city hall was destroyed by fire in 1932 and shortly thereafter a grant from the P. W. A. made possible the construction of a new building, which was placed on a site adjoining the State capitol.

It is two stories in height and accommodates the water department, police department, tax collector, health department, engineering department, and the mayor and his staff.

In addition, it provides an auditorium with a seating capacity of 2,300, a stage, and miscellaneous offices.

The exterior walls are red brick trimmed with stone, and the building is fireproof throughout and air-conditioned. It is E-shaped in plan with over-all dimensions of 131 by 311 feet.

It was completed at a construction cost of $623,815 and a project cost of $687,493.

## Municipal Building

### *Roanoke Rapids, North Carolina*

The city of Roanoke Rapids, in the northeastern part of the State, consolidated with the city of Rosemary in 1931, thereby increasing its population from 3,400 to 9,400. Hydroelectric development on the Roanoke River made electric power available at a low rate, thus inducing six large textile plants to establish themselves nearby. At that time the city was without a municipal building and rented quarters were used for the various city departments.

A loan and grant from the P. W. A. made possible the erection of a fire-resistant building, 83 by 102 feet over all, and two stories and a basement in height, which houses the fire department, sanitary department, tax collector, the mayor, and a court.

The exterior walls are brick with stone trim except the cornice and cupola, which are wood. The pitched roofs are covered with asbestos shingles.

The structure was completed at a construction cost of $32,334 and a project cost of $37,697.

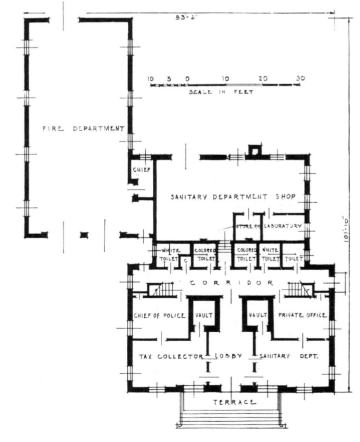

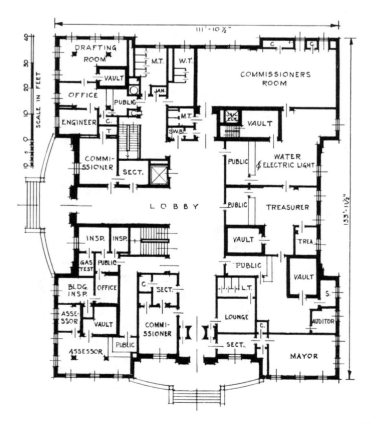

## City Hall Building
### *Sioux Falls, South Dakota*

Sioux Falls is in the extreme eastern part of the State on the Big Sioux River and its population of 33,362 in 1930 makes it the largest community in South Dakota.

The new city hall is three stories and a basement in height and houses all of the municipal offices, including the police, health, and water departments, as well as the judicial offices, a jail, a garage, and an auditorium seating 400.

The structure is fireproof throughout, with a steel frame and reinforced concrete floor and roof slabs. The exterior walls are face brick trimmed with stone and granite. All sash are metal. Small spots of carved stone ornament are used over the first-floor windows and over the main-entrance door.

The building was completed at the end of July 1936 at an approximate project cost of $432,000.

## City Hall

### *Kansas City, Missouri*

Kansas City has a well-studied plan for its civic center and the city hall takes its place in the group. It occupies an entire city block in area and consists of a rectangular base six stories high from which a tower rises to a height of 429 feet above the basement floor.

The building is planned not only to meet the space requirements of the present city government but to meet increased future requirements based on the expected normal growth of the city.

The construction is fireproof throughout and consists of steel framing adequately wind-braced and encased in concrete. The exterior walls are carried on spandrel beams and are faced with limestone. The walls at the top of the rectangular base are decorated with sculptured panels depicting the history and progress of the civic government.

The landscaping is simple but in character to conform to the city hall plaza and the disposition of the entire civic center.

The base of the structure measures 128 by 201 feet and the main shaft above the base is 97 by 124 feet. The total expenditure for the city hall building was $4,121,768 and an additional $308,724 was required for the construction and landscaping of the city hall plaza.

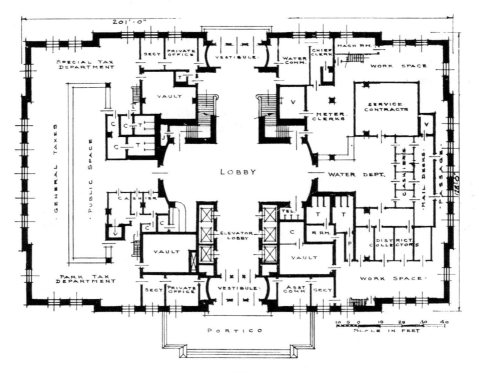

23

## City Hall, *Brentwood, Missouri*

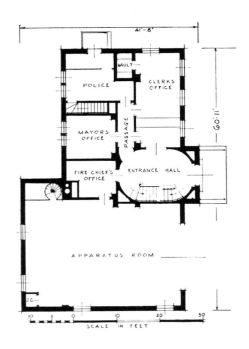

Brentwood is a suburb of St. Louis, a short distance west of the city, and had a population of 2,819 in 1930. Its new city hall is erected in a residential district and provides space for a council chamber, offices for the mayor and the aldermen, the police department, including a small dormitory and a jail, two fire trucks, and the necessary storage and utility room.

The building is two stories and a basement in height and is of fireproof construction throughout. The exterior walls are red face brick trimmed with stone. The roof is covered with slate and is surmounted by a small cupola of wood which contains the fire siren.

The project was completed in December 1935 at a construction cost of $45,016 and a project cost of $54,035.

## Courthouse and City Hall, *Fort Smith, Arkansas*

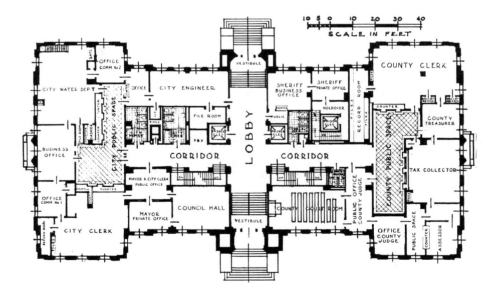

The new Sebastian County Courthouse at Fort Smith has six floors, counting the semi-basement and the central penthouse of two floors devoted entirely to the jail. On the basement floor is a large assembly hall, the police department, miscellaneous offices, and storage space for supplies and for cars. The first, or main floor contains the council room and offices for the mayor, tax collector, assessor, clerk, engineer,

and local utilities. The circuit, municipal, and chancery courts are on the second floor with offices for the judges, clerks, and reporters. The third floor has offices for attorneys and officials connected with the county.

The building is fireproof and faced with ornamented limestone. The project was completed in October 1937 at a construction cost of $462,804 and a project cost of $495,548.

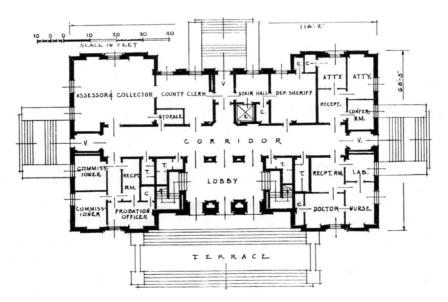

## County Office Building

### *Port Arthur, Texas*

Port Arthur was selected for the location of the Jefferson County Office Building as being the place from which county affairs could be most economically carried on.

The building is 116 by 68 feet in over-all dimensions and is two and part three stories in height. The first floor pro-vides offices for the assessor and collector of taxes, commis-sioners, county health officer, sheriff, county attorney, and a conference room. On the second floor are a large assembly room seating 235, two small courtrooms for justices of the peace, and a jury room. With the exception of the jail office and a guard room, the partial third floor is devoted entirely to cell blocks for prisoners.

The exterior is limestone and the property is large enough to be well landscaped. The project was completed in August 1936 for a total cost of $240,000.

## Municipal Building

### *Austin, Texas*

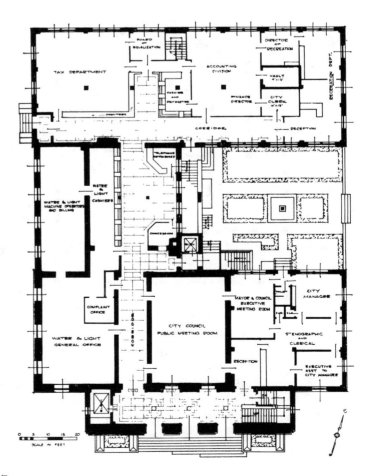

It was decided to remodel the municipal building at Austin rather than to build a new one because the old structure had sound masonry walls and also because it contained some relatively modern equipment in excellent condition. The walls of the addition are brick and tile and the entire exterior is veneered with 4 inches of limestone.

The first floor provides space for the water, light, tax, and accounting departments, and the permanent files of these departments are easily accessible by a stairway to the basement. The second floor is occupied by the engineering and legal departments and the purchasing agent, while the third floor houses the police department.

Construction consists of reinforced concrete columns and floor slabs while the roof slab is supported on steel joists. The building is equipped with a complete summer and winter air-conditioning system. The ground floor area is approximately 14,800 square feet. The structure was completed in January 1939 at a construction cost of $276,846 and a project cost of $296,636.

## Municipal Building, *Oklahoma City, Oklahoma*

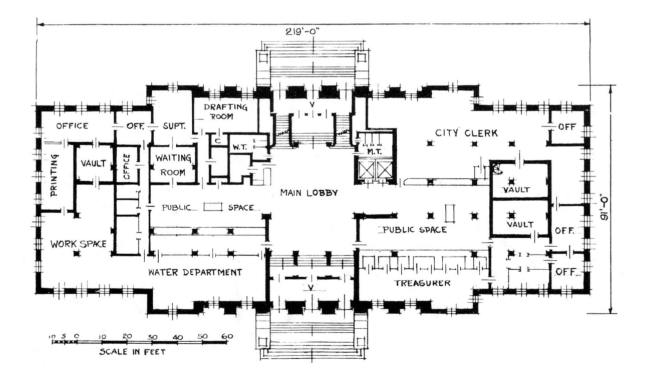

Oklahoma City is the capital and largest city of the State, having a population of 185,389 in 1930.

The new municipal building provides quarters for all of the commissions and departments of the city government except the police department and the court which are housed in a new jail building, which was built at the same time and as part of the same P. W. A. docket.

The structure is fireproof throughout with a steel and concrete frame, the exterior walls being select buff limestone, backed up with brick, and a considerable quantity of ornamental metalwork appears on the main-entrance facade.

It was completed during February 1937 at an approximate cost of $663,000. The jail building, constructed at the same time, brought the cost for the two buildings to $853,000.

## Municipal Building

### *Santa Fe, New Mexico*

The population of Santa Fe was 11,176 in 1930. The Spanish tradition, which is strong in New Mexico, is reflected in many of the public buildings erected in the State. This municipal building has stucco walls and loggias in this character.

It is a two-story structure with a small basement for the heating plant. The first floor is occupied by the usual administrative offices for the mayor, clerk, treasurer, attorney, and inspectors, as well as the police court and large council rooms. The second floor is largely devoted to the jail.

The building is of fire-resistant construction, with reinforced concrete floors and roof slabs and masonry exterior walls.

It was completed in December 1937 at a construction cost of $121,131 and a project cost of $129,501.

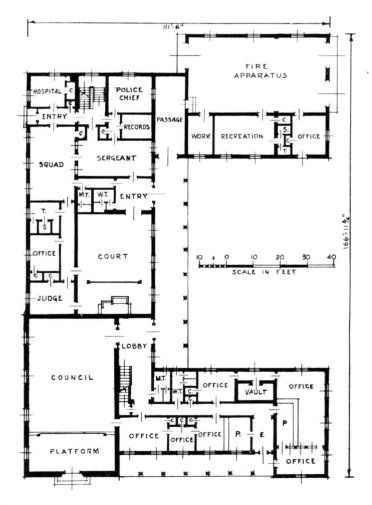

Municipal Building, *Ardmore, Oklahoma*

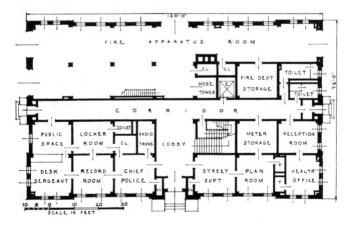

The new Municipal Building at Ardmore replaces two old structures, one of which was used as the city hall and one as the police station, and makes possible the concentration of all of the municipal departments under one roof.

The building is three stories in height and is 72 by 120 feet in plan. The police department, offices for the street superintendent and health officer, and space for the fire-department apparatus are on the first floor. The second floor is devoted to the council chamber, water department, city manager's office, city engineer's office, and a dormitory for the firemen. Half of the third floor is occupied by the municipal court and judge's offices and the other half houses the jail.

The structure is fireproof with exterior walls of light-colored brick trimmed with stone. It was completed in September 1937 at a construction cost of $110,093 and a project cost of $116,699.

## Municipal Building
### *Refugio, Texas*

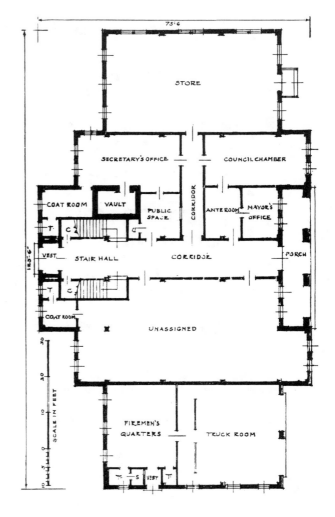

Refugio is one of the oldest towns in Texas, having been in-corporated by an act of the Congress of the Republic of Texas on February 1, 1842. It has a population of approximately 3,000 people.

Before completion of the new municipal building, the town was making use of a temporary sheet-iron structure in which not only the fire apparatus but the permanent municipal records were kept.

The new building is two stories in height with hollow-tile walls and partitions. Its stucco exterior, the arcaded entrance, and the tile roof give it the Spanish character which is native to the region.

The first floor contains offices, a meeting room for State officials, garage for two fire trucks, firemen's quarters, and a hall for the use of civic organizations. The second floor is given up to a ballroom with a band platform and concession spaces.

The project was completed in March 1936 for a total cost of $42,952.

City Hall, *Santa Maria, California*

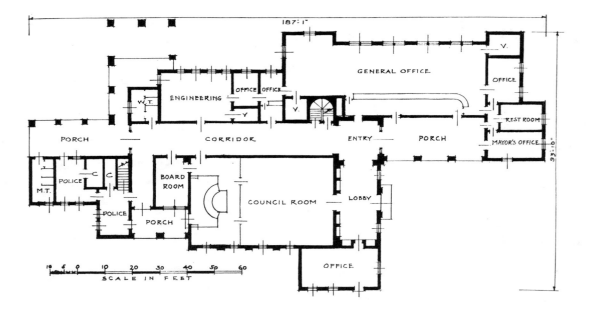

Santa Maria, the second largest community of Santa Barbara County, had a population of 7,057 in 1930.

The new city hall centralizes the municipal departments and houses the council, the engineering department, the city court, jail, police and fire departments.

The plan is irregular in shape, approximately 94 x 187 feet, and contains 17,200 square feet of usable floor area.

All of the exterior and bearing walls are reinforced concrete. The roof is wood-truss construction and is covered with handmade mission tile. The building is designed to resist adequately normal earthquake shocks.

The structure was completed during 1934 at a total cost of $68,200.

City Hall, *Canby, Oregon*

The city hall at Canby is a good example of a municipal building designed to accommodate most of the departments of a small community.

The structure provides quarters for the council chamber, light and water departments, police and fire departments, and adequate storage space.

The construction consists of concrete foundation walls, brick exterior walls above grade, and frame floors, partitions, and roof. All trim is wood.

The building was completed in March 1937 at a construction cost of $10,850 and a project cost of $11,642.

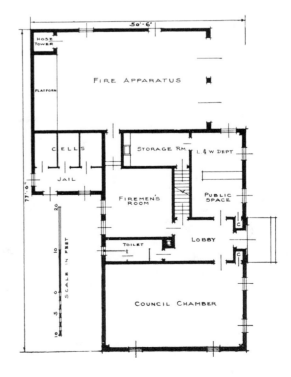

City Hall, *Santa Cruz, California*

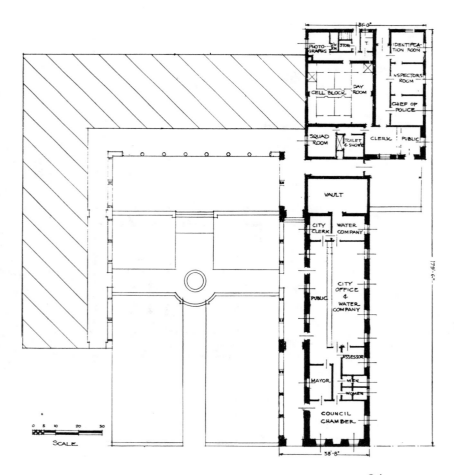

Santa Cruz is 60 miles south of San Francisco on Monterey Bay. In 1930 it had a population of 14,395.

The various departments of the city government are housed in the new city hall around a court on one floor. This project added space to the existing building for the water department, police department, office of the mayor, and council chamber. In the basement there is a rifle range for the police department, storage space, and the heating plant.

The building is semifireproof with concrete exterior walls trimmed with local stone. It is designed to resist seismic disturbances. The roof is covered with shingle tile molded to resemble redwood shakes.

It was completed in September 1937. The cost of construction was $57,674 and the project cost was $61,184.

## City Hall, *Lindsay, California*

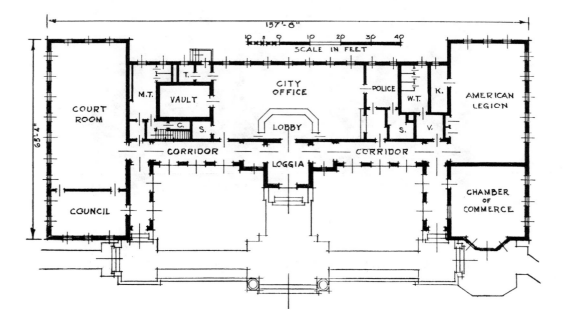

The new city hall in Lindsay is a U-shaped structure with over-all dimensions of 158 by 65 feet. The wing on the left is used as a hall for public meetings and for sessions of the court. The wing on the right contains rooms for the chamber of commerce and the American Legion. The central part of the building has a room used for a city office with smaller rooms for the chief of police, a record storage vault, and necessary toilet facilities. All of the offices and rooms are reached from an open corridor around the courtyard.

The construction is reinforced concrete and is designed to withstand earthquake shocks. The total floor area is approximately 7,800 square feet. The building was completed in 1936 at a construction cost of $57,804 and a project cost of $65,932.

## Suffolk County Courthouse, *Boston, Massachusetts*

Suffolk County has an area of 55 square miles and in 1930 had a population of 879,536.

The new courthouse is located in the downtown business section of Boston. It is rectangular in plan with over-all dimensions of 120 by 158 feet and is 309 feet (25 stories) in height. The basement and basement mezzanine are occupied by 108 cells, 8 padded cells, and kitchen facilities. The building contains 21 courtrooms, a grand-jury room, petit-jury rooms, and offices for the probation department, the clerk of court, sheriff, attorney, and judges. There is a library on the twelfth and another on the thirteenth floor. In general, the courtrooms are 2 stories in height and the mezzanines on the intermediate floors are devoted to jury rooms and other space necessary for the conduct of the courts.

The construction is fireproof throughout. The exterior walls are granite up to the fourth floor, above which they are gray glazed brick trimmed with granite. In addition to the public elevator service there are two elevators for prisoners and one for judges. The corridors and lobbies throughout

*Continued on following page*

## Suffolk County Courthouse

### *Boston, Massachusetts*

*Continued from preceding page*

have marble wainscots and the courtrooms are finished variously in oak, walnut, or mahogany.

The building was completed in April 1939 at an estimated construction cost of $4,483,083 and an estimated project cost of $4,997,027.

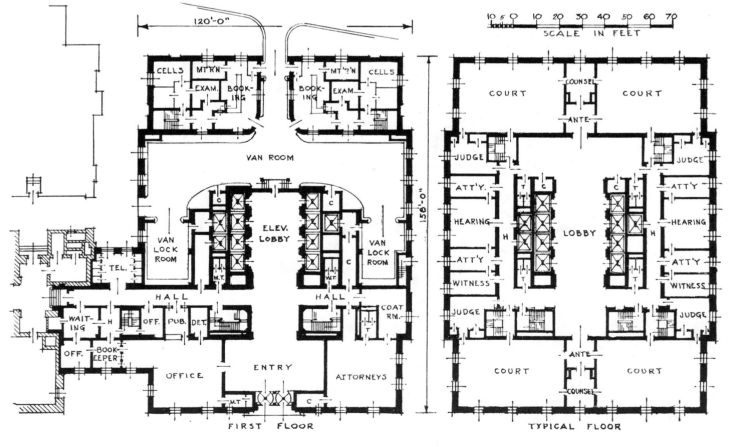

FIRST FLOOR          TYPICAL FLOOR

Courthouse, *Brooklyn, New York*

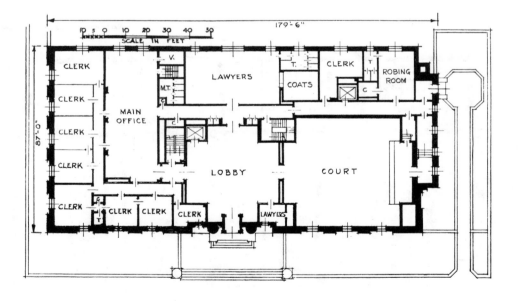

This building houses the Appellate Division of the Supreme Court, Second Division, State of New York, and is in the Borough Hall section of the city, near other city and State buildings. On the first floor it contains a courtroom 55 by 57 feet which extends through the second story in height. The judge's chambers, court officials' rooms, and a large library, 38 by 58 feet, are also included.

The plan is rectangular in shape with over-all dimensions of 180 by 87 feet. The structure is fireproof, the exterior walls are light gray granite backed with brick, windows are steel, and exterior doors are copper-covered. There is air conditioning throughout.

The building was completed in October 1938 at a construction cost of $1,044,405 and a project cost of $1,452,162.

## Courthouse, *Jamaica, New York*

This structure houses the 23 civil courts of Queens County and provides quarters for the judges, the clerk of the city court, the grand jury, the district attorney, and the county clerk. In addition, it provides offices for the naturalization bureau, the motor-vehicle bureau, the bar association, the supreme-court board, and the law library.

The building is fireproof, of steel-frame construction, and the exterior is of limestone. The courtrooms are air-conditioned. It is seven stories in height, with two mezzanine floors, and has a basement and sub-basement. The building was completed in June 1939 at an estimated construction cost of $4,960,717 and an estimated project cost of $5,637,189.

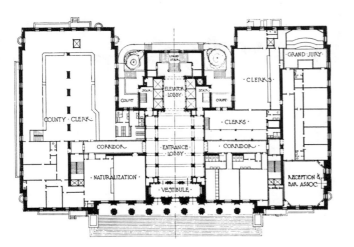

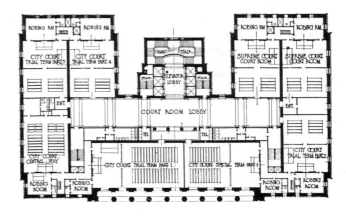

## Kalamazoo County Building, *Kalamazoo, Michigan*

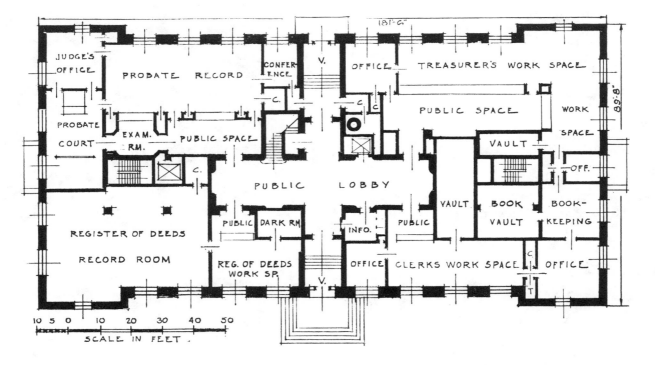

The first county building at Kalamazoo was erected in 1835 and was a frame structure 42 by 55 feet and two stories in height. The second, built in 1882, was an ornate, three-story, brick and stone edifice with a central tower and four corner turrets. The new county building is six stories and a basement in height and 90 by 182 feet in plan. Its size reflects the growth, over a century of time, of the area it serves.

It houses two courtrooms with accessory offices and jury rooms, all of the county offices, record vaults, the county jail, and the sheriff's quarters.

It is fireproof throughout, of steel and reinforced concrete, and the exterior walls are faced with limestone. The high base is granite. It was completed in October 1937 and has a volume of 1,400,000 cubic feet. The construction cost was $710,817 and the project cost $742,590.

## Courthouse, *Covington, Indiana*

This building, in addition to housing the county court and its officers, provides space for the county clerk, treasurer, welfare department, county nurses, agricultural department, school departments, record storage, and for certain bodies of the Federal Government.

It is a fireproof structure throughout and the exterior walls are limestone from nearby quarries. A limited amount of decorative stone carving is used on the outside, and the foyers and corridors of the first and second floors are decorated with mural paintings.

The building was completed in July 1937. It has a volume of about 500,000 cubic feet. The construction cost was $228,822 and the project cost $241,545.

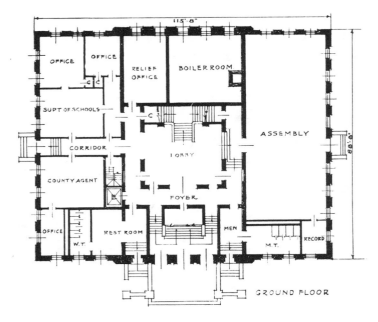

GROUND FLOOR

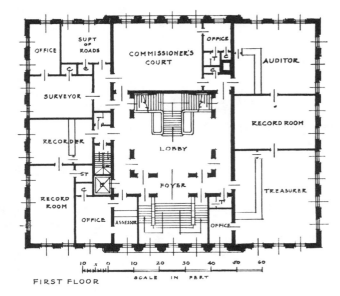

FIRST FLOOR
SCALE IN FEET

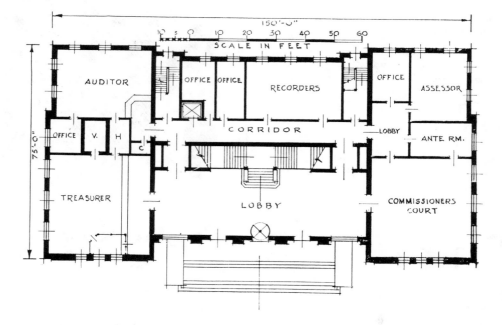

## Shelby County Courthouse

### *Shelbyville, Indiana*

The new courthouse at Shelbyville was erected on a public square in the center of the town on the site of an old pre-Civil War building.

It is a two-story and basement structure with a partial third floor which houses jury rooms and a few offices. In the basement are record offices and record-storage vaults, a community social room with a stage, and various accessory rooms. The first floor contains the commissioner's court and offices for the county treasurer, auditor, assessor, and recorder. On the second floor are the courtrooms and offices for the county clerk and county surveyor.

The construction is fireproof throughout, of steel and reinforced concrete with exterior masonry walls faced with limestone. A considerable amount of carved-stone ornament is used.

The building was completed in April 1937 at a construction cost of $238,868 and a project cost of $253,584.

## Bureau County Courthouse, *Princeton, Illinois*

The new courthouse is 114 by 109 feet in plan. It encloses and makes use of the walls of the old courthouse which was 56 by 92 feet and provided space for the courtroom and accessory quarters.

The new building provides space for the county clerk, county treasurer, county court, circuit court clerk, State attorney, board of supervisors, county superintendent of schools, highway commissioners, tuberculosis clinic, old-age pension board, police, work-relief agencies, and rooms for the grand jury and petit jury.

The structure is fireproof throughout, including the old building where the wood floors were replaced by concrete slabs. The exterior walls are faced with limestone with a minimum amount of restrained ornament.

The building was completed in September 1937 at a construction cost of $204,878 and a project cost of $221,476.

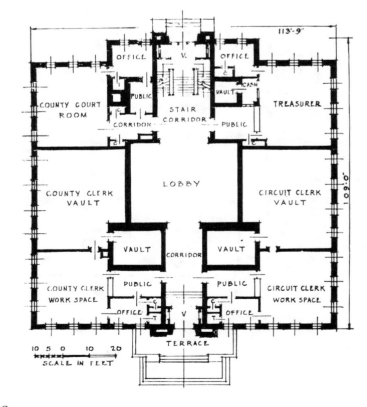

## Tennessee Supreme Court

*Nashville, Tennessee*

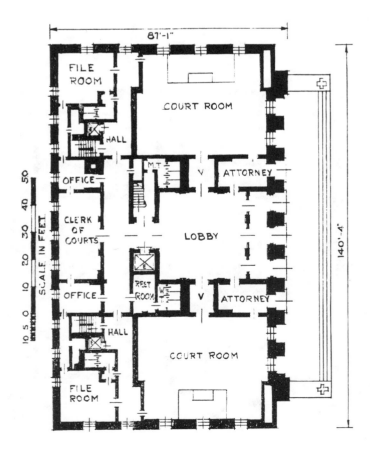

Before the erection of this building the supreme court was housed in the State capitol and its offices were located in rented quarters in various parts of the city. The new structure houses the Tennessee Supreme Court, the Tennessee Court of Appeals, the legal department of the State government, the attorney general and his staff, and an extensive library.

The building is 140 by 87 feet over all and four stories in height. It is fireproof throughout and the exterior walls are faced with marble backed up with brick and tile. The basement contains a garage connected directly with the upper floors by elevators. A complete air-conditioning system was installed. The structure was completed in April 1938 at a construction cost of $629,267 and a project cost of $654,104.

## Davidson County Public Building and Courthouse, *Nashville, Tennessee*

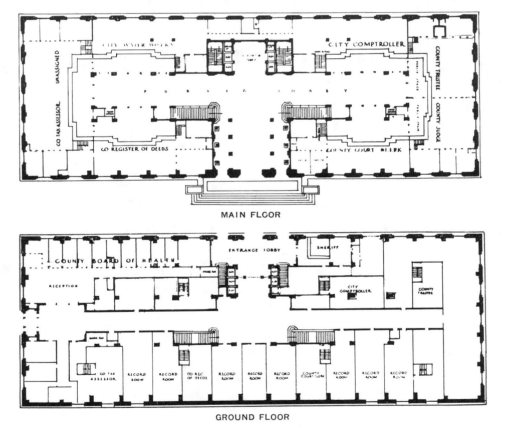

**MAIN FLOOR**

**GROUND FLOOR**

This is one of the few P. W. A. projects for which an architect was selected by competition.

The building occupies an entire block in the city of Nashville and is seven stories and a basement in height. It houses all of the county and municipal offices, as well as four courtrooms with accessory rooms, and in addition, the county jail which occupies the entire seventh floor.

The construction is fireproof, with steel framing and reinforced concrete walls and roof. The exterior walls are faced with limestone and granite.

It was completed in March 1938 at a construction cost of $2,074,869 and a project cost of $2,167,911.

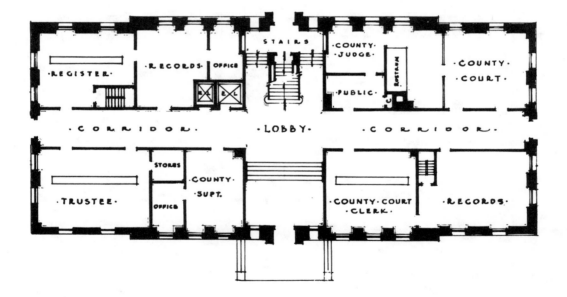

## Courthouse and Jail

### *Jackson, Tennessee*

This project consisted of a building 160 by 65 feet in plan and 4 stories and a basement in height. The basement contains offices for the county agent, farm welfare, the Red Cross, the health department, and a receiving room for the jail. On the first floor are the offices for the county clerk, registrar, county superintendent, tax assessor, sheriff, and county judge. The second floor is occupied by 2 courtrooms each 35 by 50 feet and by offices for the clerk of the court, the chancellor, circuit court clerk, and jury rooms. On the third floor, in addition to the upper parts of the 2 court rooms, are offices for the election commissioner and the attorney general as well as additional jury rooms. The fourth floor houses the jail with cells for 80 men and 24 women, and the necessary hospital facilities, kitchen, pantry, and jailer's rooms.

The construction is fireproof, with reinforced concrete frame and exterior walls of brick faced with stone. It was completed in March 1936 at a construction cost of $282,674 and a project cost of $307,798.

## Mitchell County Courthouse and Jail
### *Camilla, Georgia*

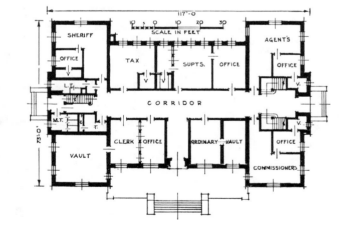

Mitchell County is a prosperous agricultural district. Its sound financial condition aided by a grant from the P. W. A. enabled it to erect a court house building and a jail building both much needed in the county. The upper picture shows the court house which is two stories high with partial basement, and the lower picture shows the jail.

The plan is the first floor of the court house. The first floor accommodates the various county officials and the second floor houses the courtroom, judges' offices, jury room, and witness rooms. The exterior brick walls are faced with marble.

Both structures are fireproof. They were completed in January 1937 at a construction cost of $177,792 and a project cost of $189,348.

Courthouse and Jail, *Snow Hill, North Carolina*

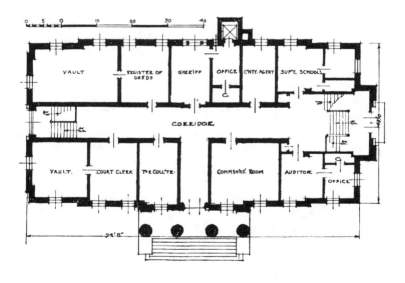

The new courthouse at Snow Hill is three stories and a basement in height, 95 by 45 feet in plan, and replaces an obsolete structure built in 1876. The basement provides two offices in addition to the necessary service rooms; the first floor houses all of the county officials; on the second floor are the courtroom and jury rooms; and the third floor is given up entirely to the jail which can house 24 prisoners.

The building is fireproof throughout, the exterior walls being faced with brick, trimmed with stone. It was completed in January 1936 at a construction cost of $101,855 and a project cost of $109,159.

## County Courthouse

### *Vero Beach, Florida*

In order to provide quarters for the court, the county officials, and the proper storage of records, Indian River County secured a loan and grant from the P. W. A. with which a two-story courthouse, 116 by 70 feet, was built.

The first floor contains offices for the recorder, auditor, engineer, commissioners, board of health, assessors, school board, and treasurer. The second floor is occupied by the courtroom, the judge's chambers, jury rooms, and the county clerk. Adequate vaults have been provided in connection with each department for the storage of records.

The building is fireproof throughout and the exterior walls are brick, backed with clay tile and trimmed with cast stone.

It was completed in March 1937 at a construction cost of $65,657 and a project cost of $71,396.

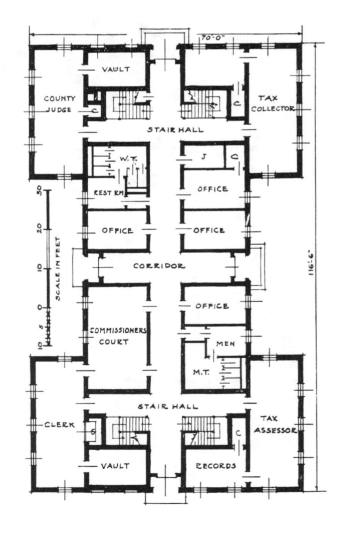

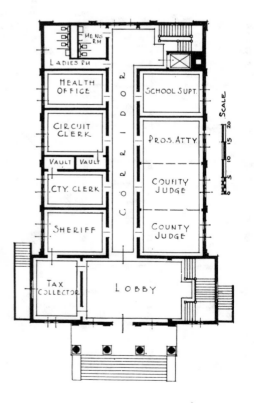

## Grant County Courthouse
### *Williamstown, Kentucky*

The county commissioners of Grant County secured a grant from the P. W. A. which enabled them to construct this new courthouse to replace an old and outgrown structure.

The new building is 2 stories, a partial third story, and a basement in height and 98 by 60 feet in plan. Offices for the county engineer, county agent, and social security are in the basement. The various county departments are on the first floor. The second floor is occupied by a courtroom together with jury and witness rooms. The partial third story is entirely given over to the jail which accommodates 24 male and 8 female prisoners.

The building is fireproof throughout, with exterior walls of face brick trimmed with limestone. It was completed in January 1939 at a construction cost of $100,694 and a project cost of $106,933.

## Peach County Courthouse

### *Fort Valley, Georgia*

Peach County was formed in 1924, its area being taken from several adjoining counties. Its form of government is unusual in that it is entirely managed by one man who is called the county ordinary.

There had been no courthouse and no proper place for the storage of records until the completion of the new courthouse in December 1936.

The building is two stories in height and houses all of the county offices, the court, jury rooms, and record-storage vaults. It is fireproof and the exterior walls are red face brick trimmed with wood. The construction cost was $64,391 and the project cost $74,371.

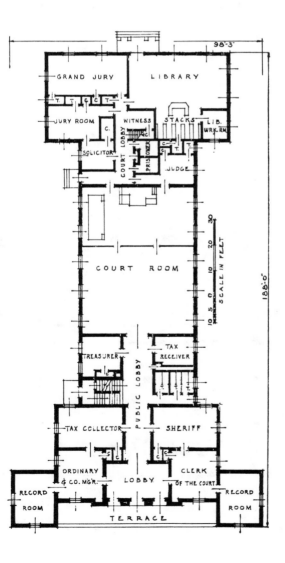

## Clay County Courthouse

### *Liberty, Missouri*

The site of the Clay County Courthouse is bounded by four important city streets allowing a wide main entrance approach, an entrance to the first floor from the rear, and an entrance to the ground floor on one side.

The building is rectangular in plan and three stories in height. On the ground floor are offices for the superintendent of schools, the welfare department, the coroner, the county engineer, the supervisor, the county agricultural agent, an assembly room with a platform, a women's lounge, and the necessary utility rooms. The first floor is occupied by the probate and county court rooms, offices for the probate judge, clerk of court, recorder, assessor, and county judges. On the second floor are a circuit court, library, two petit jury rooms, witness rooms, and offices for the clerk of the court, county attorney, judges, and sheriff. There is a small jail in connection with the sheriff's office.

The structure is fireproof and the exterior walls are faced with limestone. It was completed in October 1936 at a construction cost of $263,410 and a project cost of $283,928.

## Village Hall, *Bovey, Minnesota*

This small village hall has a distinct Scandinavian flavor and might almost be standing in some Swedish village rather than in Bovey, Minnesota. It is two stories and a basement in height and in the basement houses a garage for the fire department, a large dining room, kitchen and pantry, storage space, and the heating plant. On the first floor are offices for the police department, the council room, a library, and a club room. The second floor is occupied by a large auditorium with a stage and dressing rooms.

The building is steel and reinforced concrete with exterior walls of brick and a roof covered with copper. It was completed in June 1935 at a construction cost of $65,775 and a project cost of $71,000.

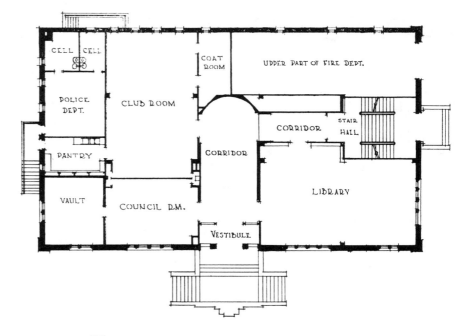

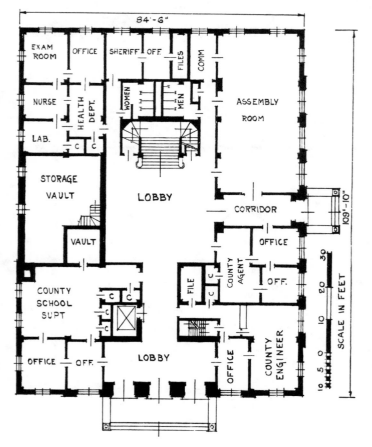

## Gallatin County Courthouse

### *Bozeman, Montana*

This building is three stories and a basement in height and is 85 by 110 feet in plan. The courtroom and offices for the court officials, jury rooms, etc., are on the top floor. The second floor houses most of the county departments and the first floor provides a large community room as well as offices for the county engineer, superintendent of schools, the health department, county agent, and sheriff.

The building is fireproof throughout and the exterior walls are faced with limestone. It was completed in September 1936 at a construction cost of $224,313 and a project cost of $243,951.

Stark County Courthouse, *Dickinson, North Dakota*

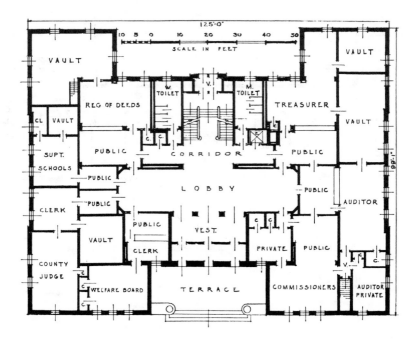

This structure is three stories and a basement in height and is rectangular in plan. The second and third stories are set back from the outer walls of the first story, except at the main entrance.

The basement contains an auditorium, committee and recreation rooms, office for the county engineer, vaults, and storage space. On the first floor are offices for the county judge, auditor, commissioners, treasurer, superintendent of schools, registrar of deeds, county nurse, and work space and

vaults. A large courtroom and offices for the district judge, clerk, sheriff, attorney, and court reporter are on the second floor as well as jury rooms and vaults. On the third floor are separate cell blocks for men and women, rooms for the matron and jailer, and a kitchen.

The building is of fire-resistive construction and the exterior walls are light-colored brick with stone trim. It was completed in June 1937 at a construction cost of $191,708 and a project cost of $207,487.

55

This structure is immediately opposite the present State Capitol Building and is an important unit of a well-developed plan for the State and municipal group, occupying a square which is landscaped and surrounded by streets.

The building is three stories in height and rectangular in plan, and contains the supreme court room, judicial and administrative offices, and a law library as well as the State library.

It is fireproof throughout and the exterior walls are faced with limestone. It was completed in March 1937 at a construction cost of $160,454 and a project cost of $170,642.

## Supreme Court and State Library, *Cheyenne, Wyoming*

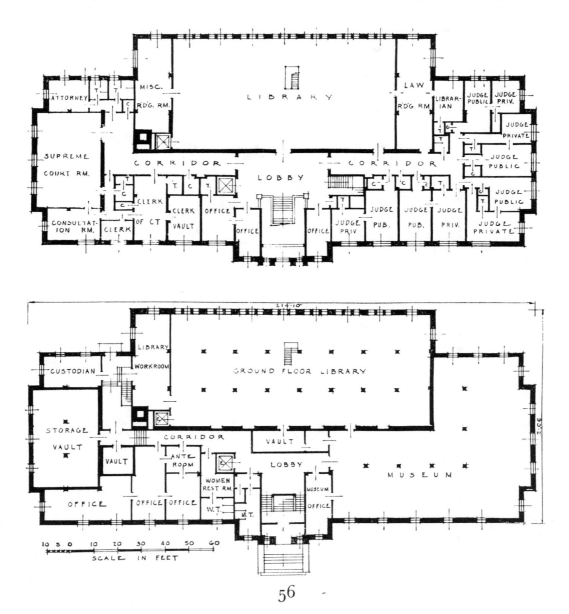

Cass County Courthouse, *Atlantic, Iowa*

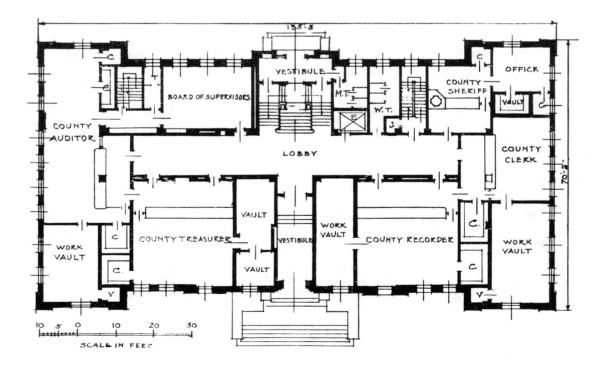

Atlantic, the county seat of Cass County, had a population of 5,585 in 1930. It provided a large piece of property bounded by four important streets on which to erect the new courthouse.

The building is three stories and a basement in height and houses all the county officials on the first floor. The second and third floors are occupied by the courtroom, offices for the court officers, and the jail.

The structure is fireproof throughout, with exterior walls of brick trimmed with stone. It was completed in June 1935 at a construction cost of $141,274 and a project cost of $152,872.

## Garfield County Courthouse, *Enid, Oklahoma*

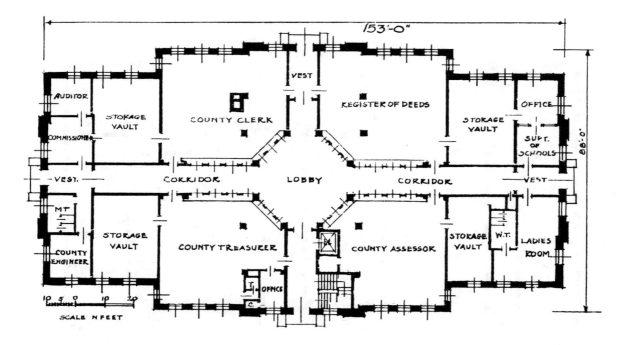

This new four-story and basement structure, with a partial fifth story, replaces an old courthouse which was destroyed by fire.

The basement contains offices for the justice of the peace, an assembly room, ladies' parlor, and the necessary utility rooms. The first floor is occupied by the offices of the county treasurer, clerk, assessor, recorder, county engineer, auditor, and superintendent of schools. The district and county courtrooms, with offices for the judges, reporter, and attorneys, are on the second floor. The third floor contains the jury rooms and the upper parts of the courtrooms. The jail occupies the fourth and partial fifth floors.

The building is fireproof and is faced with limestone. It was completed in April 1935 at a construction cost of $199,560 and a project cost of $207,575.

## Courthouse and Jail

### *Oklahoma City, Oklahoma*

The new county courthouse at Oklahoma City replaces a structure erected in 1905 which had been outgrown and also had been condemned by the State fire marshal.

It is approximately 132 by 204 feet in plan and 10 stories in height, the jail occupying the 2 top floors. The rest of the building is occupied by courtrooms with the necessary space for the court officials, offices for the county departments, and the vault and storage space. The jail can accommodate 365 prisoners and is entirely modern in lay-out and equipment.

The project was completed in February 1937 at a construction cost of $1,139,699 and a project cost of $1,208,838.

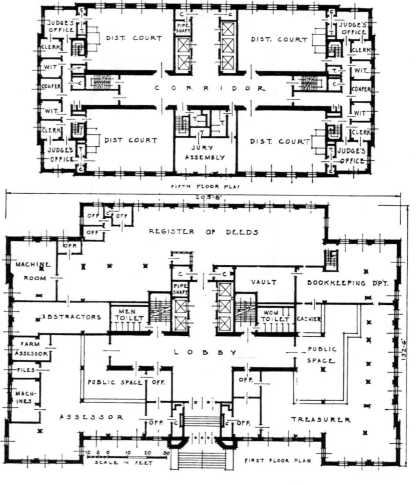

## Courthouse, *Portales, New Mexico*

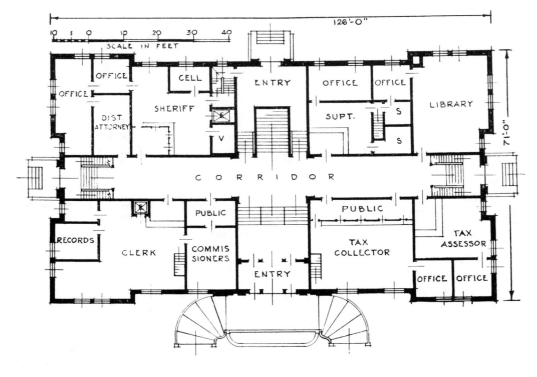

The new Roosevelt County Courthouse replaces a courthouse and a jail which were 37 years old and in poor condition.

On the ground floor are offices, record vaults, an assembly room, and storage and utility space. The first floor is occupied by the sheriff, tax assessor and collector, county clerk, and other public officials. The courtroom, offices for the court officers, jury and witness rooms are on the second floor.

The top floor in the central part of the building houses the jail.

The construction is reinforced concrete and structural steel, and the exterior walls are light buff face brick trimmed with cast stone.

The building was completed in January 1939 at a construction cost of $187,756 and a project cost of $197,381.

Contracts were awarded on December 15, 1934, for the construction of the Grayson County Courthouse. It is a four story and basement building, 140 by 87 feet in plan, and contains on the first floor an assembly room, the tax department, county clerk, auditor, sheriff, the county courtroom, judge's chambers, and a jury room. On the second floor are two large district courtrooms, offices for the district judge and court reporter, and jury rooms. The third floor contains the upper parts of the courtrooms and jury dormitories, while the top floor is entirely occupied by the jail which is arranged to accommodate 150 prisoners, separated into various classifications.

The building is fireproof throughout, with a reinforced-concrete skeleton frame. The exterior walls are faced with light cream-colored cordova stone. A set-back of 7 feet between the walls of the top floor and the parapet wall screens the jail windows from the street.

The project was completed in July 1936 at a construction cost of $298,047 and a project cost of $315,762.

## Grayson County Courthouse

*Sherman, Texas*

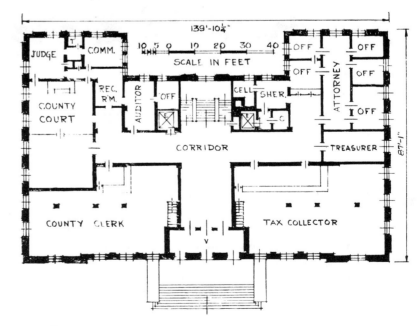

Alameda County Courthouse, *Oakland, California*

The Alameda County Courthouse is in the city of Oakland across the bay from San Francisco.

The project consisted of the erection of an 11-story building to house the courts and county government. The building occupies the site of the old hall of records and provides approximately 300,000 square feet of floor area.

It houses the superior courts which include 12 court rooms, etc., the justice's court, offices of the district attorney, library,

offices of the tax collector, county board of supervisors, clerk, civil-service commission, recorder, treasurer, county library, and other agencies of the county government.

The building is fireproof throughout and is constructed of steel and reinforced concrete. The base and the masonry terrace walls and steps are granite and the walls above the base are finished in concrete.

*Continued on following page*

## Alameda County Courthouse

### *Oakland, California*

*Continued from preceding page*

Project Calif. 1100–R consisted of an addition to the original contract for the granite base, terrace walls, steps, and steel sash.

The structure was completed in 1936 at a construction cost of $1,657,890 and a project cost of $1,657,890.

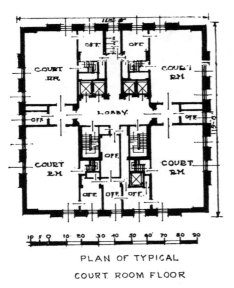

PLAN OF TYPICAL
COURT ROOM FLOOR

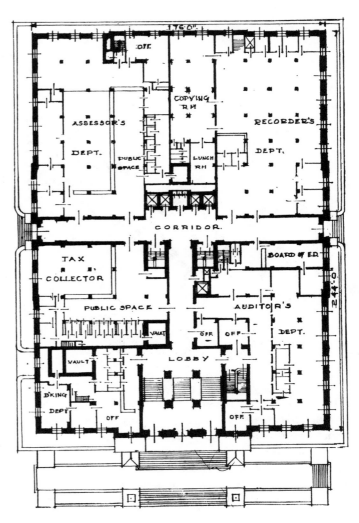

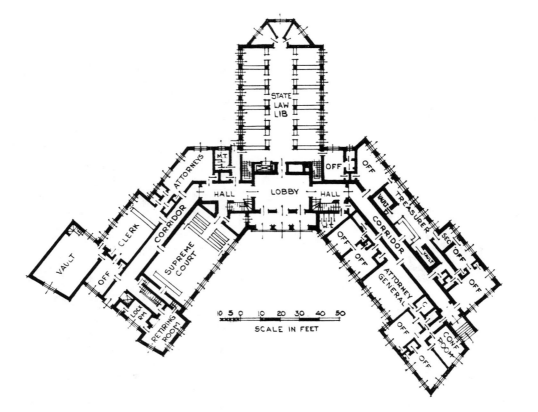

Supreme Court Building, *Santa Fe, New Mexico*

The Supreme Court Building was built to relieve the congestion that existed in the State capitol where the supreme court had always been housed.

The new building is occupied by the supreme court with its accessory offices, the attorney general, the State treasurer, and the State law library. The necessary vaults and storage spaces are provided for each department.

It is a semifireproof structure provided with a sprinkler system. The floors are concrete on steel joists, sash are steel, and exterior walls are brick covered with cream-colored stucco. Copings and window sills are brick.

It was completed in August 1937 at a construction cost of $282,443 and a project cost of $316,233.

## Courthouse and Jail

### *Las Cruces, New Mexico*

The Dona Ana County courthouse and jail is a part two- and part three-story building, U-shaped in plan, with a large patio formed by the walls of the building on three sides and a stucco wall on the fourth. It is designed in the "Pueblo" type of architecture frequently used in the State.

On the first floor are offices for the county clerk, commissioners, sheriff, school superintendent, tax assessor and collector, a library, and record-storage vaults. The courtroom which is two stories in height, is on the second floor together with the judge's chambers, jury room, consultation rooms, witness rooms, and offices for the court recorder, county agent, health officer, and county nurse. The third floor has jury dormitories and a jail which accommodates 24 prisoners.

The construction is reinforced-concrete framing, and the exterior masonry walls are stuccoed. The building was completed in February 1938 at a construction cost of $171,302 and a project cost of $181,594.

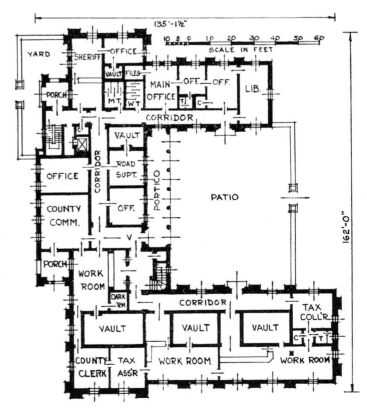

## Supreme Court and Library, *Carson City, Nevada*

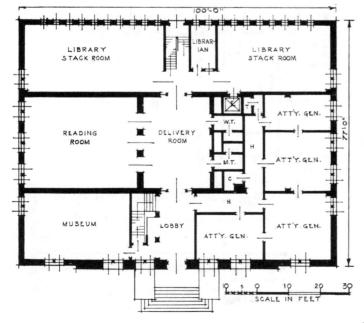

The Supreme Court of Nevada was formerly housed in the State Capitol Building in quarters which were small, inconvenient, and entirely inadequate for the proper and dignified conduct of the court proceedings. The State library, also in the capitol, was in a small annex in the rear of the building.

The new building, two stories and a basement in height and 77 by 100 feet in plan, contains a museum, the library reading room, stacks, an office for the librarian, and offices for the attorney general on the first floor. The second floor contains the supreme court room, 30 by 50 feet in size, as well as offices for the three justices, their secretaries, and clerks.

The construction is reinforced concrete, the exterior walls being terra cotta backed with brick. The building was completed during 1937 at a construction cost of $156,406 and a project cost of $163,433.

## State Capitol

### *Salem, Oregon*

The Oregon State Capitol replaces a structure which was destroyed by fire in 1935. It occupies the site of the former building and is the dominating feature of a well-designed city plan. A mall has been laid out from the main facade of the capitol, cutting through several city blocks, which will be flanked on each side by future buildings of the State government, one of which, the State library, has already been constructed.

It is one of the few P. W. A. projects for which an architect was selected through competition.

The first floor is occupied by offices and work space for the land board, State treasurer, the board of control, department of motor vehicles, general office, and a large rotunda from which wide stairways ascend to the floor above on which are the senate chamber and the house chamber. The various offices for the State departments and the Governor's suite are accommodated on the second, third, and fourth floors.

The building is fireproof throughout. The exterior has a granite base, and the walls are faced with Vermont marble. The sculpture and mural paintings are noteworthy. It was completed in June 1939 at an approximate construction cost of $2,294,000.

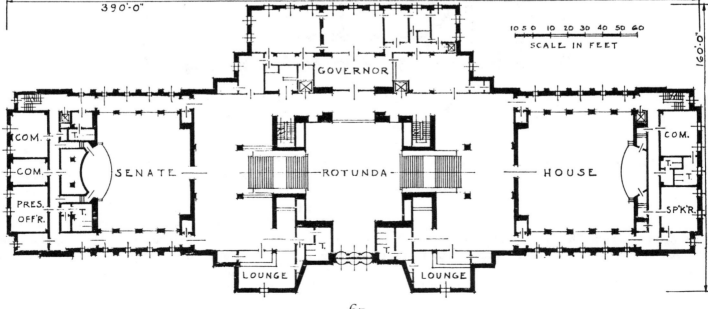

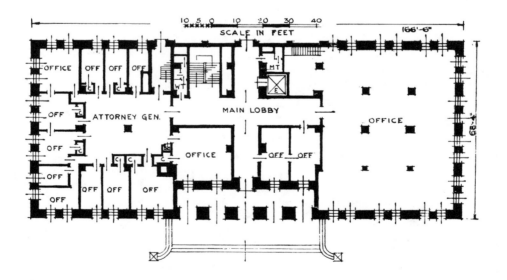

## Addition to State Capitol

### *Phoenix, Arizona*

The addition to the State capitol at Phoenix is a separate building connected to the existing structure by means of a corridor.

It is rectangular in plan, 68 by 167 feet, and is four stories and a basement in height. It is occupied by the supreme court, the superior courts, the law library, the offices of the attorney general, the State historian, and necessary vaults and stacks for the storage of records.

The building is fireproof throughout, with reinforced concrete framing and a steel-truss roof. The exterior walls are brick with tufa stone trim, except the first story which is granite. It was completed in 1938 at a construction cost of $570,717 and a project cost of $605,575.

## Hall of Records

### *Annapolis, Maryland*

This building was erected on one end of the campus of St. John's College to provide proper storage for the State records and also to commemorate the three hundredth anniversary of the founding of the Maryland colony. It conforms in character to the colonial architecture of Annapolis both on the exterior and on the interior, in the details of cornices, paneling, stair rails, and other features.

In addition to the stack space, the building provides offices for the archivist, a clerical force, and rooms for repairing old books and manuscripts.

The structure is fireproof with masonry bearing walls, steel beams, and reinforced-concrete floor and roof slabs. The exterior walls are faced with handmade red brick trimmed with limestone and wood. Doors and windows are wood. The stack space is air conditioned to better preserve the old records and parchments.

There are 6,718 square feet in the ground-floor plan and the volume of the structure is 303,400 cubic feet. It was completed in the spring of 1935 at a construction cost of $203,018 and a project cost of $212,780.

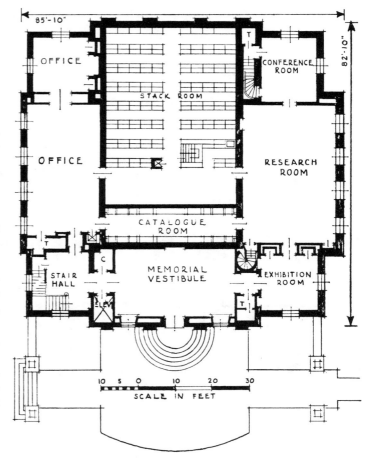

## Hall of Records

### *Dover, Delaware*

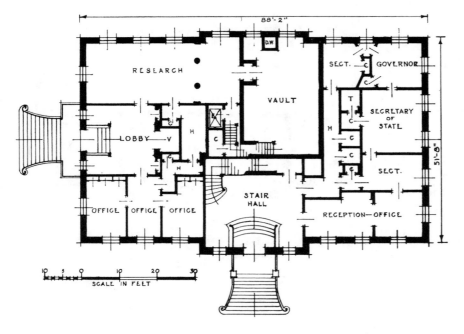

The Hall of Records is a much needed addition to the group of State buildings at Dover. It contains offices for the governor and the secretary of state, the research room, the archives lobby, and a vault 19 by 24 feet for the storage of records, on the first floor. On the second floor are offices for the motor-vehicle department and the franchise-tax department.

The building is fireproof throughout. The exterior walls are red brick laid in flemish bond and the trim is marble and wood. The roof is covered with slate. The finish throughout the interior is in keeping with the eighteenth century character of the structure and a considerable use is made of wood paneling, cornices, and stair rails. Stairs are of marble and the floor of the research room is cork.

Each floor, including the basement, has approximately 4,500 square feet of usable space and the over-all dimensions of the building are 88 by 52 feet. The work was completed in December 1938 at a construction cost of $145,693 and a project cost of $159,785.

## State Administration Building, Finance Department, *Harrisburg, Pennsylvania*

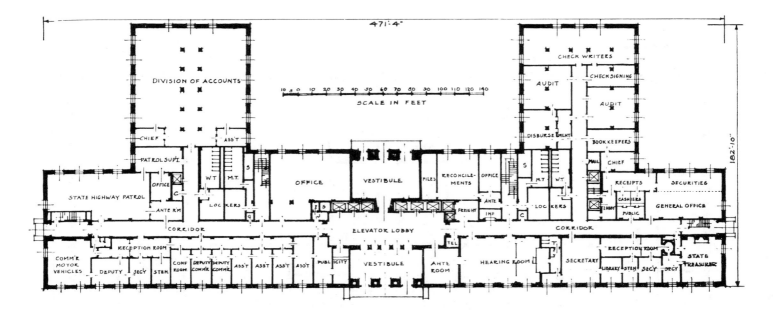

The new Finance Department Building of the State capitol group at Harrisburg makes possible the gathering into one building of related units of the State government which were formerly widely scattered.

The monumental character of the structure and the use of stone for the entire exterior was dictated by its position opposite the Educational Building at the northeast end of the Capitol Plaza.

It provides quarters for the departments of the auditor general, revenue, and State treasurer.

It has a volume of approximately 6,800,000 cubic feet and its estimated cost is $4,736,270. It is expected to be completed toward the close of 1939.

### State Office Building, *Baton Rouge, Louisiana*

ment. This proved to be incorrect and due to urgent need, the State Office Building, often called the Capitol Annex, was erected about 400 feet distant from the capitol.

It is a part four and part six-story building, rectangular in plan, with over-all dimensions of 130 by 260 feet, and in addition to a large amount of office space, houses the official board room and library.

It has a reinforced-concrete frame and exterior masonry walls faced with limestone which matches as closely as possible the limestone used on the capitol building. The windows are aluminum, ceilings are

At the time the Louisiana State Capitol was constructed, it was considered large enough to house virtually all of the administrative offices and departments of the State government. acoustically treated, and the whole building is air-conditioned.

It was completed in August 1938 at a construction cost of $1,104,395 and a project cost of $1,190,525.

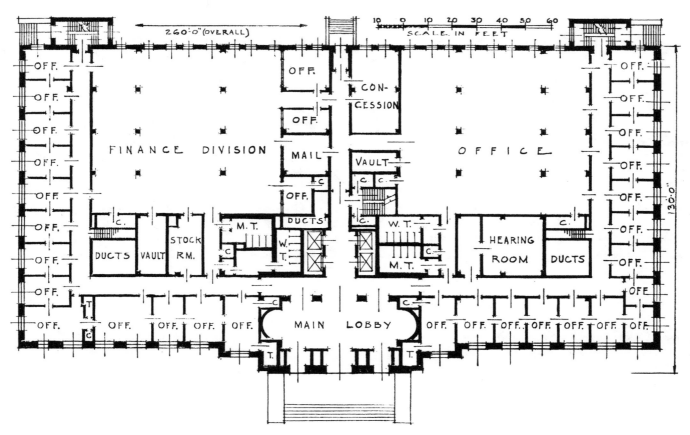

## Materials Research Laboratory, *Carson City, Nevada*

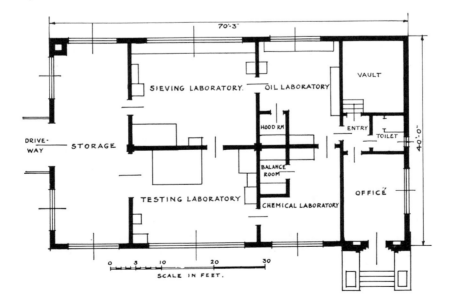

The research work carried on by the department of highways involves the use of highly explosive and inflammable gases and reagents and it was obviously desirable that the laboratory be separated from the other agencies of the department.

The new building is rectangular in plan. It houses the oil, chemical, and sieving laboratories, an office, and ample storage space. The equipment includes electric ovens, water-distillation apparatus, carbon-combustion furnaces, cylinder-braking machines, and other necessary apparatus.

The construction is semifireproof, with exterior walls of concrete, steel-bar floor joists, and steel roof trusses. All sash are metal.

It was completed during 1936 and the project and construction costs were the same, being $38,182.

State Police Substation, *Topsfield, Massachusetts*

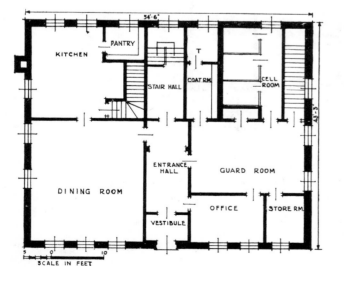

This P. W. A. project consisted of the erection of a Troop Headquarters Building at Framingham and of four substations in Concord, Hyannis, Shelbourne Falls, and Topsfield. These buildings are similar in architectural character and the substation at Topsfield illustrates them satisfactorily.

The Topsfield Substation is two stories, an attic and a basement in height and 54 by 43 feet in plan. It provides quarters for 12 troopers, as well as the necessary offices. The design is a simple adaptation of Georgian architecture with red brick exterior walls, wood trim, and a slate roof.

The project was later consolidated into and became a part of Project 875 (Mass.). The total estimated cost of the five buildings was $234,190 and the Topsfield Substation was completed in October 1935.

## Central Fire House and Police Station, *Greenwich, Connecticut*

This new structure replaces old and inadequate quarters for the police and fire departments which had been located in the basement of the Greenwich town hall. It faces on three main streets and is separated from the town hall by a private street so that it is entirely free standing.

The building is trapezoidal in plan and three stories in height. It provides the fire department with an apparatus room, a dormitory, a recreation room, a banquet hall, and a kitchen. The police department has a sergeant's room, police-car garage, a pistol range, a police court with its necessary office space and jail facilities. There is also a recreation area provided on the roof.

It is a fireproof structure with a skeleton steel frame, concrete floor and roof slabs, and the exterior walls are faced with limestone above the high base which is granite. An elevator serves the police quarters. The project was completed in February 1939 at a construction cost of $304,748 and a project cost of $326,788.

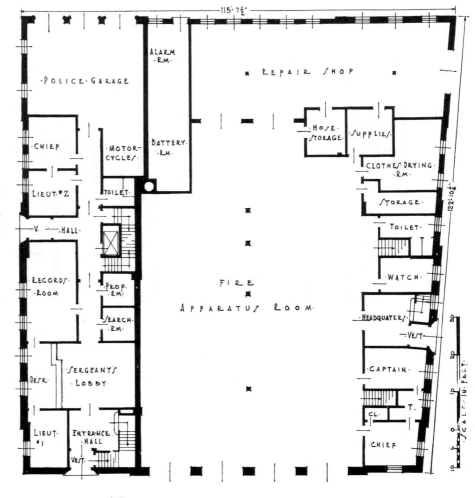

Fire Headquarters, *Greenfield, Massachusetts*

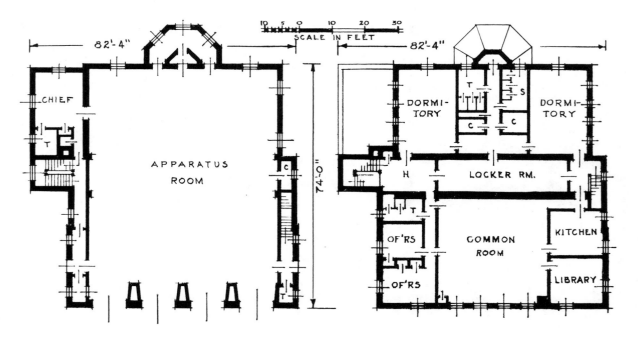

The city of Greenfield, with a population of 15,500 in 1930, had not only outgrown its old fire headquarters but the location of the old building in the business district had become undesirable due to traffic congestion.

The new building has space for seven pieces of apparatus, as well as the chief's quarters and a watch room on the first floor. On the second floor are a recreation room, two dormitories, locker room, kitchen, library, officers' rooms, and the necessary toilets, showers, etc.

The exterior walls are water-struck red brick; the cornices, windows, doors, and cupola are wood; and the roof is slate.

The building is 74 by 82 feet in plan. It was completed in March 1937 at a construction cost of $89,761 and a project cost of $97,503.

Fire Department Building, *Ansonia, Connecticut*

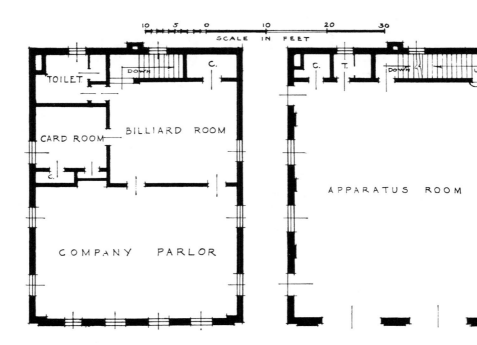

The Webster Hose, Hook and Ladder Company No. 3 is a unit of the fire department of Ansonia. Its new building is located in a residential area of the city. The first floor houses the apparatus and the second floor a recreation room, cardroom, and lounge.

The building is two stories and a basement in height, 36 by 46 feet in plan, and is built of red brick with limestone trim and wood floor construction. It was completed in May 1937 at a construction cost of $25,830 and a project cost of $29,780.

State Highway Patrol Barracks, *Cambridge, Ohio*

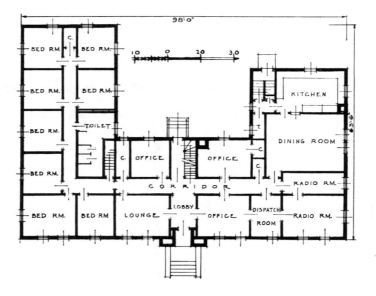

The Ohio State Highway Patrol operates from the city of Columbus and has four district headquarters, all radio-connected. Three of these units are in permanent buildings. The Cambridge headquarters has been provided with this new building through the P. W. A., replacing their temporary quarters which had been destroyed by fire.

It stands on a 4-acre site at a high point on the national highway, the site having been selected after tests to determine the best location for radio transmission. The project included, besides the building, the radio tower with its network of buried ground lines.

The barracks building is 64 by 98 feet in plan and is two stories and a basement in height. The basement contains a recreation room, 27 by 62 feet, in addition to space for the utilities. On the first floor are offices, public space, a dining room, a kitchen, the radio dispatch room, and eight bedrooms. The second floor is unfinished at present.

The exterior is brick with stone trim. The roof is covered with slate. The project was completed in November 1937 at a construction cost of $58,432 and a project cost of $62,701.

## Central Fire Station
### *Louisville, Kentucky*

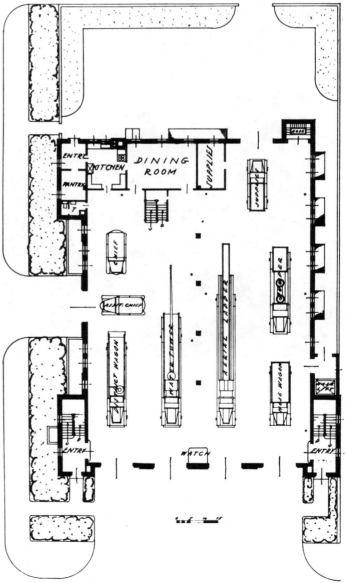

The rapid growth of the city of Louisville, population 307,745 in 1930, necessitated additional facilities for the fire department. A grant was secured from the P. W. A. with which this central fire station was built, as well as a hospital annex, an extension to the sewerage system, and some park recreational improvements. The total cost of all of these projects was $1,665,230.

The fire station is three stories and a basement in height, approximately 90 by 120 feet in plan, and has a volume of 564,322 cubic feet. In the basement is a swimming pool, 30 by 60 feet. The first floor houses the apparatus and in the rear it has a dining room and kitchen. Offices and dormitories occupy the second floor, and the third floor, which is set back and not visible from the street, houses the fire-alarm system.

The building was completed in June 1937 at an estimated construction cost of $171,198 and an estimated project cost of $190,220.

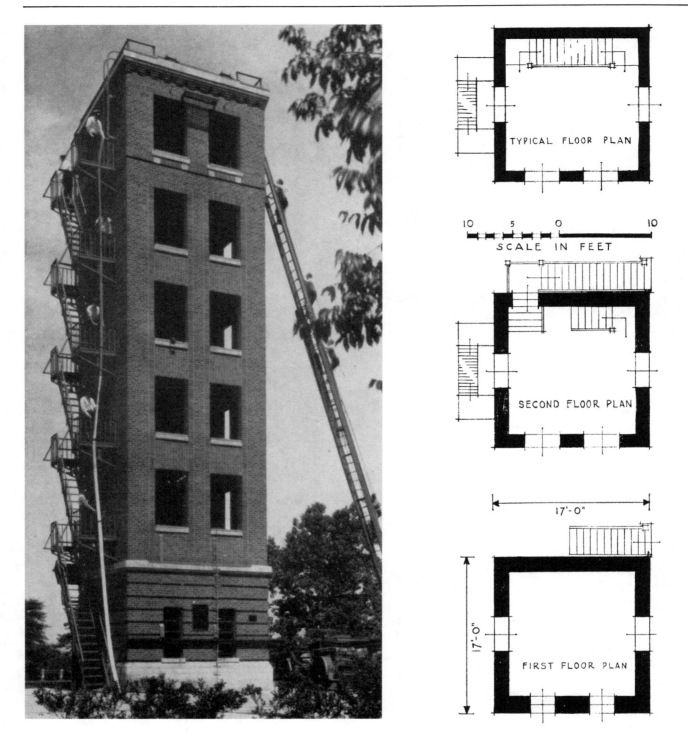

TYPICAL FLOOR PLAN

10    5    0    10
SCALE IN FEET

SECOND FLOOR PLAN

17'-0"

17'-0"

FIRST FLOOR PLAN

## Fire Drill Tower, *Memphis, Tennessee*

Memphis is the largest city in Tennessee, as well as being one of the largest inland water ports in the world. Its population in 1930 was 253,143.

An old wooden tower for the training of the fire department had become unsafe and this new masonry structure, six stories in height, has replaced it. The exterior walls are brick, trimmed with limestone, and the floors are concrete. It has an interior stairway and an exterior fire escape and also facilities for drying and storing fire hose.

The structure is 17 by 17 feet in plan and 67 feet in height. The funds for its erection constituted a loan and grant from the P. W. A. and the project cost was $10,055.

## Fire Station

*Shreveport*

*Louisiana*

This fire department substation is one unit of a large project in Shreveport for modernizing the fire and police department stations and equipment.

The building provides space on the first floor for the motorized and other equipment and on the second floor, sleeping quarters for the employees. The hose tower is on the left side. The simple design combined with effective landscaping harmonizes with the residential district in which the station stands. It was completed in January 1935 at a construction cost of $18,933 and a project cost of $19,990.

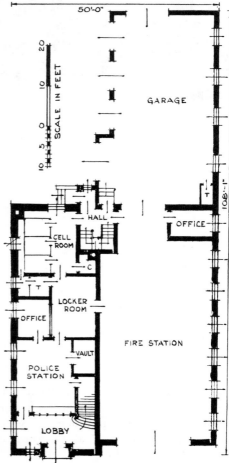

## Fire and Police Station

### *Hinsdale, Illinois*

This building was part of a municipal project which consisted not only of the construction of the fire station and the remodeling of the police station, including the addition of the second story, but the improvement of two city parks.

The completed fire and police station is Georgian Colonial in design. It is built of red brick with slightly projecting brick quoins and the trim and cupola are wood. It houses the fire and police departments, including a cell room. The increased facilities of the police station provide a fireproof garage.

The building was completed in April 1935 at a construction cost of $26,188 and a project cost of $28,598. The project cost, including the work on the two parks, was $51,789.

## Fire Department Headquarters, *Des Moines, Iowa*

This is a modern fire station which includes not only all the necessary facilities for the fighting of fire but also provisions for training, recreation, housing of personnel, and maintenance of all equipment. The building is located in the business district of the city at the intersection of two important streets which are not, however, arteries of excessive traffic. In addition to the building illustrated, the project includes a shop building and a drill tower.

The headquarters building is rectangular in plan, 128 by 117 feet. The apparatus room provides space for five units of rolling stock besides space for cars for the chief and assistant chief. The signal room is completely protected by a fire stop. A large storage room and the captain's office are also on the ground floor. On the second floor are a dormitory, dining room, kitchen, rooms for recreation and instruction, and a handball court, as well as living quarters and an office for the chief and his staff. A hose tower is an integral unit in the building, of sufficient height to accommodate standard lengths of hose.

The building is fireproof, with exterior walls of brick trimmed with stone and some terra cotta. It was completed in January 1938 at a construction cost of $260,778 and a project cost of $281,700.

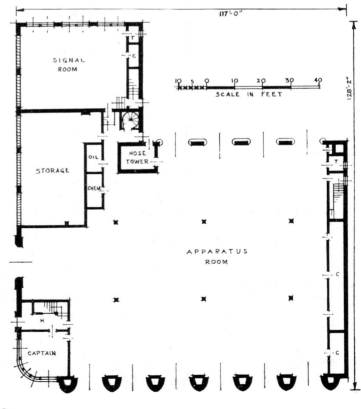

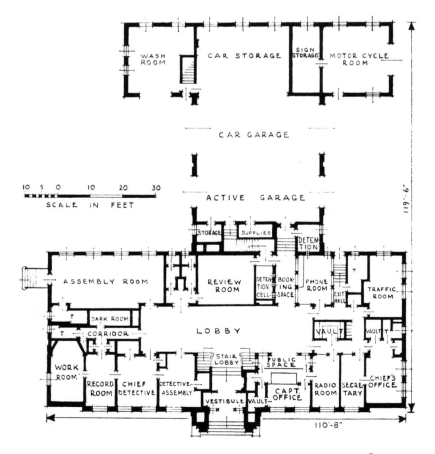

## Police Department

### *Cedar Rapids, Iowa*

The construction of this building provided Cedar Rapids with adequate and modern quarters for its police department.

The structure is two stories and a basement in height and includes a large lobby, offices for the chief of police and detectives, a pistol range, and a motorcycle patrol room, together with a complete modern radio communication system, as well as the necesssary record vaults and other quarters required for the proper functioning of the department.

The building is fireproof throughout. The exterior brick walls are trimmed with stone. It was completed in February 1938 at a construction cost of $113,966 and a project cost of $132,405.

## Central Fire Station

### *Austin, Texas*

This building is part of a project which also included the addition of two new wings of approximately 16,500 square feet to the existing city hall, its renovation, the wrecking of an old fire station, and the construction of concrete walks and drives.

The fire station occupies one fourth of a city block and is provided with wide entrances on two streets. It is two stories in height and contains space on the ground floor for fire trucks and equipment, a recreation room, and offices for the fire chief, fire marshal, and the radio broadcasting unit. The second floor is devoted to sleeping quarters for the employees, a kitchen, an assembly room, and a guest room. The hose-drying rack, gasoline pump, and handball court are outside the building.

The fire station has reinforced concrete footings, and solid brick walls, with face brick on the exterior and in the apparatus room. Other rooms have plaster finish. The roof is 20-year composition. It was completed in January 1939 at a construction cost of $43,779 and a project cost of $46,945.

## Fire Department

### *Petaluma, California*

The site of this building is 100 by 150 feet and is on the corner of two streets. The building is approximately 80 by 88 feet and is one and part two stories in height. The foundations are concrete and the superstructure is frame with a stucco surface.

The first floor houses seven pieces of fire apparatus, contains a recreation room, office, kitchen, storage room, toilet facilities, and alarm and battery rooms. Dormitories for the firemen, quarters for the fire chief, toilet and locker facilities are on the second floor.

The building was completed in 1938 at a construction cost of $39,403 and a project cost of $43,858.

Armory, *Jersey City, New Jersey*

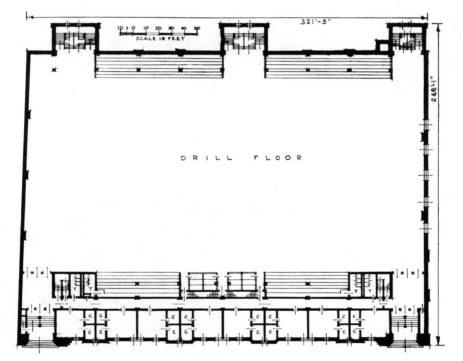

This armory provides quarters for one battalion of infantry, one battalion of engineers, two medical units, and one division of the naval militia. The large drill hall is on the street level and has banks of seats on two sides. Under these seats are eight company rooms and equipment storage rooms, and on two mezzanine floors are four more company rooms and individual space for future rooms.

The structure is fireproof and is supported on piles. The exterior walls are brick with a granite base and terra cotta trim.

The building is 248 by 321 feet in plan. It was completed in February 1936 at a construction cost of $1,038,276 and a project cost of $1,098,330.

102d Cavalry Armory, *West Orange, New Jersey*

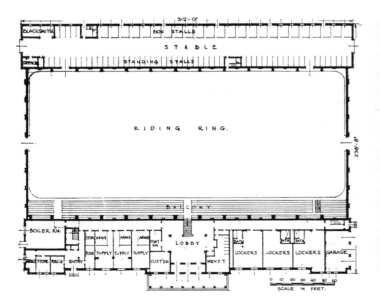

This city is a residential suburb near New York. It has a population of approximately 25,000. The building contains a large riding ring, stable quarters, rifle range, machine shop, repair shop, caretaker's quarters, company rooms, officers' lounge, grill room, and administrative section.

It is fireproof throughout with structural steel frame and concrete floor construction. There are 74,256 square feet on the ground floor. The volume is 2,598,690 cubic feet.

It was completed in November 1938 at a construction cost of $458,469 and a project cost of $498,757.

## Farm Show Arena, *Harrisburg, Pennsylvania*

The annual farm show in Harrisburg has the support of about 30 State farm organizations and attracts an attendance as high as 125,000 people per day.

The new arena is of sufficient size to accommodate all livestock judging, with several classes being judged at the same time. The building is 346 by 230 feet in plan and the arena is 240 by 120 feet, with semicircular ends. The permanent seating, which rises in an unbroken ring around the arena, accommodates 8,250. The arena itself, when the hall is being used for conventions, seats 4,250 in temporary seats, thus providing a maximum capacity of 12,500. When the hall is used for boxing or wrestling exhibitions, the seating capacity is 12,000. Temporary seats are stored underneath the permanent seats.

The construction is fireproof. The steel bow trusses are 224 feet between walls and support precast concrete slabs on which composition roofing is applied. The exterior walls are face brick trimmed with rubbed concrete. The volume of the building is 6,760,000 cubic feet. The project, except for the Meeting Rooms, was completed in December 1938 at a construction cost of $1,105,423 and a project cost of $1,196,343.

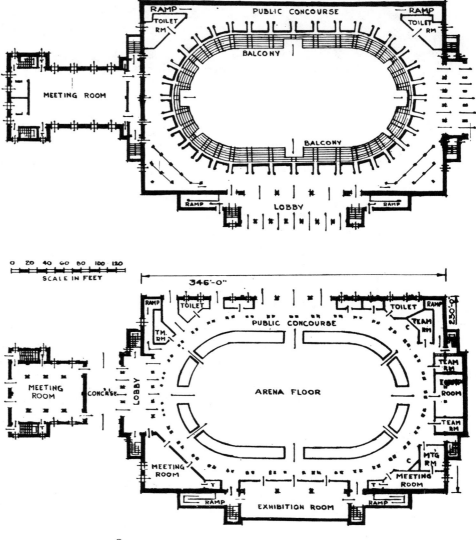

## National Guard Armory

### *Ligonier, Pennsylvania*

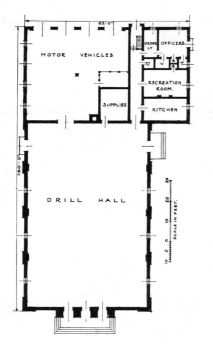

The Ligonier Armory is the headquarters of Company F, One Hundred and Third Medical Regiment of the Pennsylvania National Guard, and was part of a general program to house properly the military forces of the State.

The building provides a drill hall, 60 by 90 feet, a quartermaster's supply room, a troop room, an orderly room, several officers' rooms, and a six-car garage.

Its design is extremely simple, the exterior walls being red face brick with parapet coping, sills, and trim of stone.

It was completed in June 1938 at a construction cost of $56,942 and a project cost of $64,378.

## Armory Addition
*Mount Holly, New Jersey*

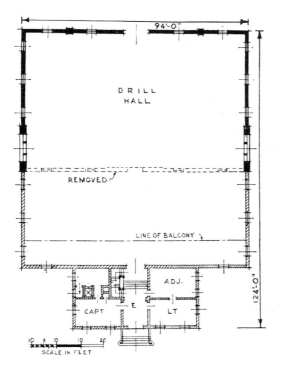

The addition to the armory at Mount Holly provided quarters for an additional company of infantry and for battalion head-quarters. It also provided additional garage facilities, storage and recreation space, and classrooms for officers and men.

The construction is fireproof with exterior walls of brick trimmed with wood. Floor slabs are reinforced concrete and roof trusses steel. The recreation room is finished in knotty pine.

The project was completed in October 1936 at a construction cost of $47,715 and a project cost of $52,748.

## National Guard Armory

### *Canonsburg, Pennsylvania*

This armory is the headquarters of Company H, One Hundred and Third Medical Regiment of the Pennsylvania

tion and locker room for enlisted men, a kitchen, and a mobilization room 20 by 60 feet. The second floor, entered from a street on a higher level, is occupied by the main lobby, storage rooms, and the drill hall 70 by 100 feet. The mezzanine forms a balcony overlooking the drill floor.

The building is fireproof. The foundations are concrete, and the frame, columns, and roof trusses are steel. The

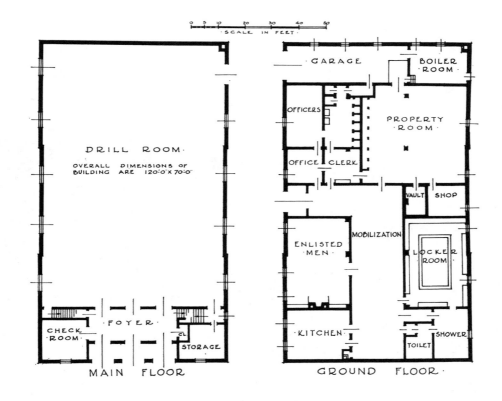

National Guard. The building is also extensively used for public meetings and entertainments.

The structure is two stories and a mezzanine in height. The first floor contains two offices, officers' recreation and locker room, the company property room, a garage, recrea-

exterior walls are sand-finished red brick and wood trim with a base of native sandstone. The drill hall floor is designed to carry loaded trucks parked over its entire area.

The project was completed in October 1938 at a construction cost of $85,548 and a project cost of $94,497.

## Civic Center, *Hammond, Indiana*

This structure stands in a 37-acre tract of land which includes a park, a high-school site, fields for baseball, football, and tennis, and extensive automobile parking space.

The building contains a gymnasium-auditorium with 3,156 permanent balcony seats and 2,200 additional removable seats, Boy and Girl Scout headquarters, camera clubs, practice rooms for drama, offices for the recreational director, and a complete lay-out for exercise and minor sports, including a swimming pool.

It is fireproof throughout, faced with brick, trimmed with limestone. Its volume is 2,250,000 cubic feet. It was completed in May 1938 at a construction cost of $448,237 and a project cost of $476,446.

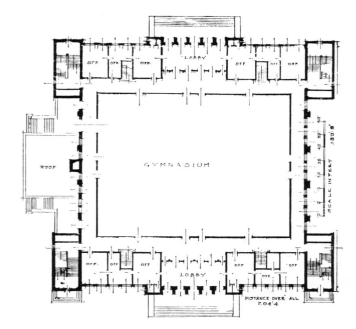

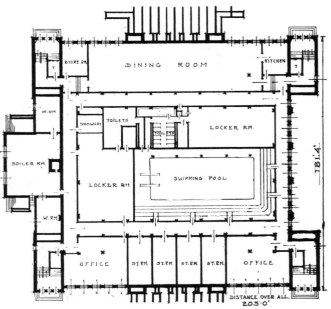

## Armory and Office Building

### *Springfield, Illinois*

This is a dual-purpose building which houses three companies of the Illinois National Guard and provides much-needed office space for the State government.

The new building is 5 stories and a basement in height and approximately 189 by 299 feet in plan. In the basement is a large exhibition hall, a rifle range, an ordnance shop, quartermaster stores, and miscellaneous storage space. The drill hall, 118 by 169 feet, is on the first floor. It has a stage, 45 by 110 feet, and with the balconies which seat 3,000, can accommodate 6,500 persons when used as an auditorium. On this floor is also office space for the National Guard, as well as club rooms, committee rooms, a banquet hall, and a

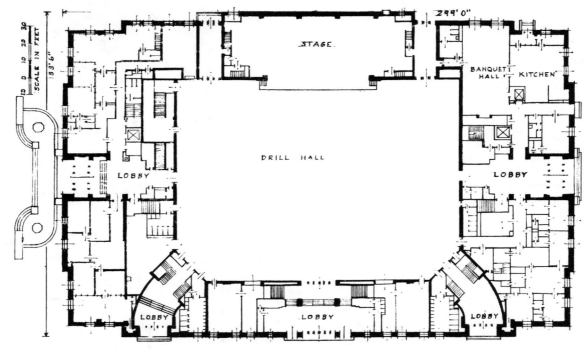

The site is an entire square, approximately 350 by 350 feet, opposite the State Capitol group of buildings, and the armory and office building occupies half of the area. The central heating plant for the capitol group occupies part of the other half, and as future requirements necessitate expansion of the armory and office building, the heating plant will be removed elsewhere.

kitchen. The second, third, fourth, and fifth floors, on the street sides around the drill hall, provide 13,000 square feet of office space for use of the State government.

The construction is fireproof, of structural steel and reinforced concrete. The exterior walls are limestone. The building was completed in October 1937 at a construction cost of $1,254,460 and a project cost of $1,259,618.

## National Guard Armory

### *Rockford, Illinois*

The Rockford Armory is one unit of a program to house adequately the National Guard of the State of Illinois. Up to 1938, 15 armories had been constructed in the State and at present three more are under construction in the Chicago area.

The building at Rockford has over-all dimensions of 246 by 183 feet, and it has a total floor area of 69,840 square feet. The drill hall, 180 by 120 feet, has a balcony seating 1,000. It also is provided with a stage, 26 by 57 feet, and around the drill hall are clubrooms, general property and equipment rooms, and a kitchen, in addition to the necessary lobbies, stairs, etc.

The structure is fireproof. The exterior walls are faced with brick of two shades trimmed with limestone.

It was completed in January 1937 at a construction cost of $225,464 and a project cost of $251,478.

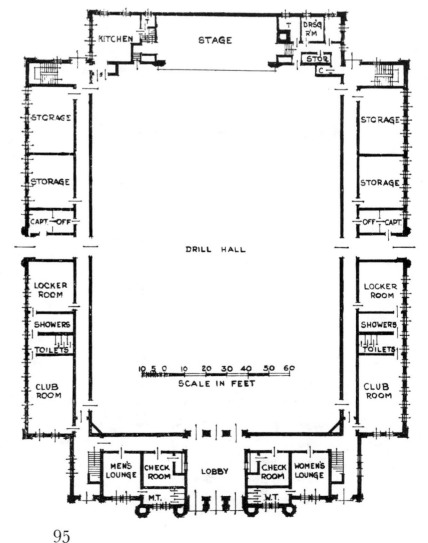

## National Guard Armory, *Tallahassee, Florida*

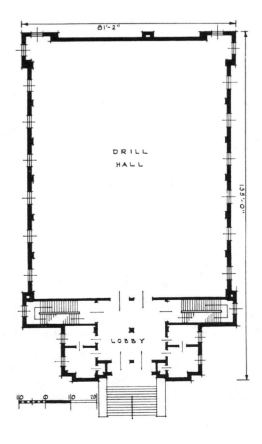

This armory houses Company M, One Hundred and Twenty-fourth Infantry, and the headquarters of the Second Battalion of the One Hundred and Sixth Quartermaster Regiment of the National Guard of Florida. These units were formerly housed in quarters over a grocery store in Tallahassee which were neither burglar-nor fireproof, and as a result of an inspection by representatives of the Army, the units were placed on probation until new quarters could be provided.

The armory was erected by the city of Tallahassee with P. W. A. aid, but since the county of Leon was obligated to provide quarters for the National Guard, the county obligated itself to repay the city over a period of 25 years.

The building is two stories and a basement in height and 81 by 135 feet in over-all dimensions. The basement contains a rifle range, locker rooms, and storage space. On the first floor is the drill hall and offices for the commanding officer. Offices and a gallery for spectators are on the second floor.

The construction is semifireproof, with exterior walls of brick trimmed with limestone. The drill-room floor is wood on a reinforced-concrete slab.

The project was completed in June 1935 at a construction cost of $66,197 and a project cost of $74,365.

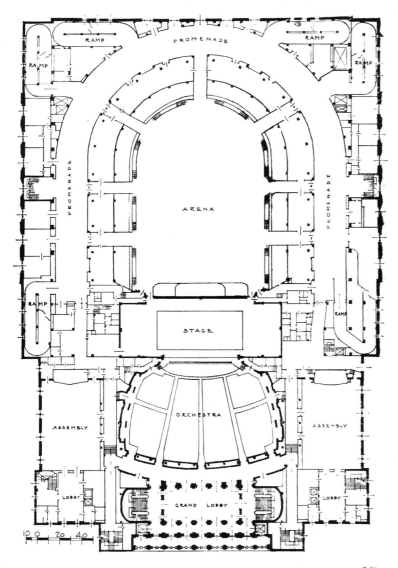

## Municipal Auditorium
### St. Louis, Missouri

This auditorium forms an important unit of the St. Louis "plaza group." It faces a large park around which are grouped the city hall, the municipal courts building, the civil courts building, and the soldiers' memorial. It includes 3 main assembly centers, a music hall seating 3,500 with its stage, an arena which can be opened to the stage by raising a 30-ton steel soundproof and fireproof curtain and which has a seating capacity of 12,500, and an exposition hall with an area of 91,000 square feet, providing space for 500 exhibition booths. These assembly centers are served by ticket lobbies, foyers, and a cafeteria and refreshment bar. There are in addition 4 large assembly halls, each with a stage, committee rooms, and offices.

The arena, or convention hall, is U-shaped in plan and may be entered directly from the street by means of 6 ramps. It is served by stairs and elevators as well. The means of exit make it possible to clear the hall of 12,500 people in 10 minutes.

The building is fireproof throughout and is faced on the exterior with limestone. Air conditioning is provided for the entire structure and in summer a 1,200-ton refrigeration plant maintains a temperature differential between the outside and inside air within a range of 15°. The structure had been built before P. W. A. was organized but was unfinished. It was completed in April 1938 at a total construction cost of approximately $6,000,000 of which $2,218,635 was provided by P. W. A. for the finishing and decorating.

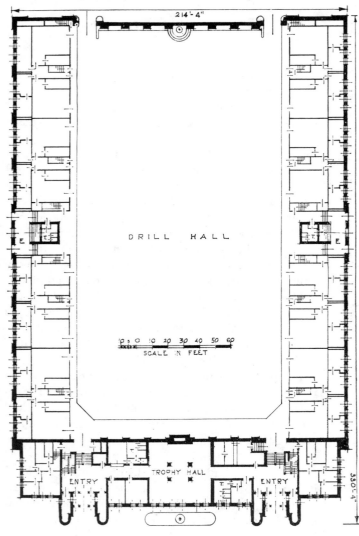

## Armory

### *Minneapolis*

### *Minnesota*

This armory at Minneapolis provides quarters for 16 artillery, infantry, and naval units of the National Guard and Naval Militia.

The main drill hall is flanked on each side by balconies underneath which are 16 supply rooms, each with an office and orderly room. There are also a trophy room, medical-examination rooms, officers' rooms, recreation rooms, and storerooms.

The building is 215 by 330 feet in plan and is constructed of reinforced concrete, steel, and brick. The exterior walls have a high granite base above which they are brick with stone trim. The curved roof is supported by hinged steel arches. It was completed in January 1936 at a construction cost of $698,202 and a project cost of $932,453.

Hibbing Memorial Building, *Hibbing, Minnesota*

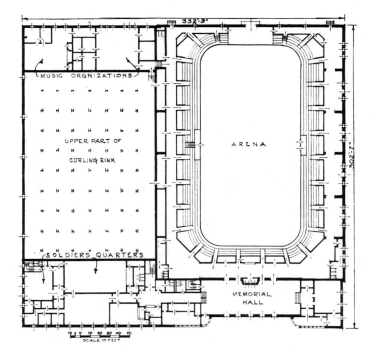

This structure is in reality a community center and provides for athletics and for social and educational activities.

The arena, which is approximately 100 by 200 feet, is surrounded by bleacher seats. There are rooms for the American Legion and the Ladies' Auxiliary, lounges, billiard and card rooms, and administrative offices. A large curling rink approximately 130 by 200 feet has a small gallery for spectators, a curlers' clubroom, lobby, and locker room.

The building is constructed of reinforced concrete and the exterior walls are faced with light-colored brick. The roof of the arena is arched and supported by hinged steel trusses, thus providing a clear floor area.

The project was completed in December 1935 at a construction cost of $528,293 and a project cost of $549,438.

## Community Building

*Ely, Minnesota*

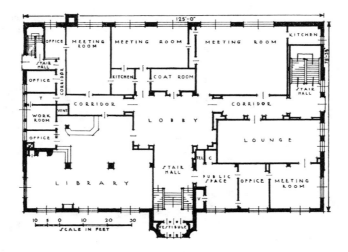

This building serves the city of Ely as a community and recreation center. It is three stories and a basement in height and 125 by 78 feet in plan. In the basement are a meeting room, a cafeteria, serving room, and kitchen. The first floor is occupied by a library, a lounge, meeting rooms, a kitchen, office, and work space.

The large auditorium with its stage, meeting rooms, a kitchen, and storage space are on the second floor. The third floor contains the fan room, a projection booth, and storage space.

The floor slabs and stairs are reinforced concrete, and the auditorium is spanned by steel trusses. All exterior walls are faced with stone. An air-conditioning and cooling system made possible the use of glass block panels in lieu of windows.

The building was completed in February 1938 at a construction cost of $208,748 and a project cost of $229,416.

## Municipal Auditorium

### *Valley City, North Dakota*

Valley City is on the Sheyenne River in the southeastern part of the State. It had a population of 5,268 in 1930.

The new auditorium provides a large foyer from which one enters the main auditorium, which is provided with a stage and gallery. There are, in addition, meeting rooms, a dining room, a kitchen, and the necessary utility rooms. The main floor of the auditorium seats approximately 1,200 people, and the balcony accommodates approximately 400 more.

The building is semifireproof. The exterior walls are brick with a small amount of limestone trim.

It was completed in July 1937 at a construction cost of $99,470 and a project cost of $115,332.

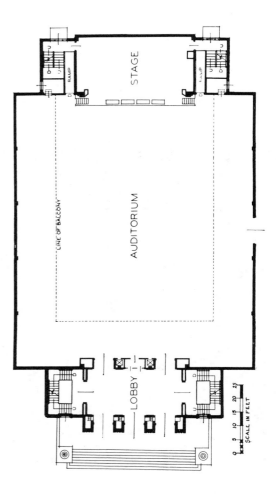

## Municipal Coliseum, *Fort Worth*, *Texas*

At the time of the Centennial Exposition held in Fort Worth in 1936, the city officials determined to erect several permanent buildings that would maintain their civic usefulness after the closing of the exposition. Among the most important of these were the Coliseum and the Memorial Tower.

The Coliseum provides an area 125 by 250 feet in which

horse and stock shows can be held, as well as rodeos and athletic exhibitions.

The building is 232 by 405 feet in over-all dimensions. The arena is surrounded by tiers of seats under which is a concourse 17 feet wide extending around the building and connecting with the seating space at short intervals, thus assuring easy circulation. Near the performers' entrance are a stock chute and cattle pens.

The construction is semifireproof. The walls and partitions are masonry, the balcony is reinforced concrete, and the wood roof is supported on steel trusses. The arena is enclosed by a concrete wall and its floor is earth. The exterior walls are faced with a light-colored brick trimmed with stone and terra cotta.

The Memorial Tower is midway between the Coliseum and the auditorium building and is connected with both by covered passageways.

The project was completed in February 1937 at a construction cost of $581,580 for the Coliseum and $116,836 for the Tower. The project, of which the Coliseum and the Tower were a part, included seven major buildings and had a total cost of $1,902,808.

## Exposition and Convention Hall

### *Houston, Texas*

The rapid and continuous growth of Houston and its surrounding territory was accompanied by an increased demand for facilities to care for the numerous conventions and expositions held there each year.

The large exposition and convention hall constructed by the city with P. W. A. aid is T-shaped in plan and 402 by 426 feet in its over-all dimensions. It contains the exposition hall with a seating capacity of 6,500 and an arena 150 by 285 feet, a music hall seating 2,500, a large stage between these 2 halls with a proscenium arch 50 feet wide on the music hall side and one 70 feet wide on the side of the exposition hall, and numerous conference and committee rooms.

The building is semifireproof. It is framed with steel and reinforced concrete, and the exterior walls are a light-colored face brick trimmed with stone. The arena has a mastic floor on concrete for use during horse shows and rodeos and is provided with a sectional wood floor in panels, 5 by 10 feet, which can be put down when the hall is used for conventions.

The project was completed in May 1938 at a construction cost of $1,189,811 and a project cost of $1,329,508.

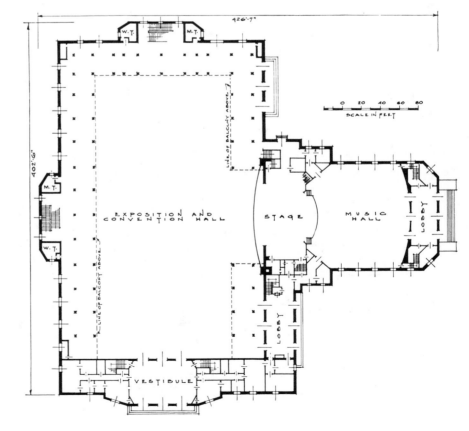

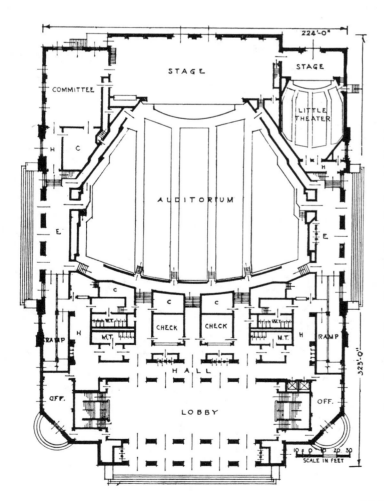

## Municipal Auditorium, *Oklahoma City,*

## *Oklahoma*

Before the erection of this auditorium, Oklahoma City had no place which could seat more than 2,000 people where public meetings could be held.

The new municipal auditorium has remedied this condition. It contains an auditorium with a seating capacity of 6,000, a small theater seating 400, a convention hall seating 900, 22 small committee rooms, and an exhibition hall with a floor area of 38,000 square feet. The auditorium stage is sufficiently large and well equipped to permit the production of plays and operas and to accommodate large orchestras and can be used also for convention purposes.

The building is semifireproof. The exterior walls are faced partly with limestone and partly with brick trimmed with limestone. All the ceilings of the auditorium, committee rooms, and the basement exhibit space are acoustically treated.

The project was completed in August 1937 at a construction cost of $1,146,783 and a project cost of $1,205.000.

## Memorial Auditorium

### *Fresno, California*

The city of Fresno has a long-range program of civic develop-ment and this auditorium is an important unit of this plan.

The building is approximately 170 by 236 feet in over-all dimensions. The auditorium is 100 by 140 feet and is pro-vided with a stage, 35 by 100 feet, and a gallery around three sides. A large foyer, committee rooms, and the necessary services are included in the facilities.

The construction is reinforced concrete designed to resist seismic disturbances, and the exterior finish is in concrete. The project was completed in December 1936 at a construc-tion cost of $406,292 and a project cost of $517,903.

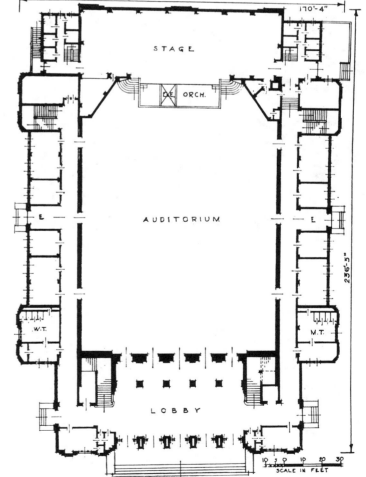

## Municipal Auditorium
### *San Jose, California*

The auditorium at San Jose is an adaptation of the Spanish colonial architecture of California, and its stucco walls and red-tile roof harmonize with its semitropical setting.

The building has an area of 50,000 square feet and consists of the auditorium which seats 3,500, a small theater seating 597, a meeting hall seating 400, 2 exhibition halls, 5 committee rooms, quarters for the chamber of commerce, and the necessary service rooms. The auditorium has a large and well-equipped stage. The project was completed in April 1936 at a construction cost of $422,628 and a project cost of $530,515.

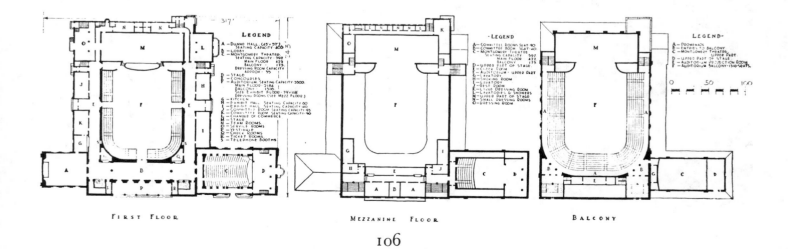

FIRST FLOOR                    MEZZANINE FLOOR                    BALCONY

Klamath Armory, *Klamath Falls, Oregon*

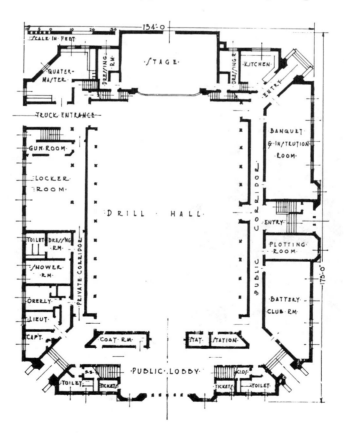

The Klamath Armory houses units of the National Guard and is used also as an auditorium for large gatherings.

The over-all dimensions of the building are 134 by 173 feet, and it contains the drill hall 70 by 110 feet, a stage, a battery club room 22 by 52 feet, a banquet hall 22 by 52 feet, kitchen, quartermaster's supply and ordnance rooms, officers' rooms, and locker rooms.

The exterior walls are brick trimmed with cast stone. It was completed in September 1935 at a construction cost of $93,731 and a project cost of $126,238.

Free Public Library *Teaneck, New Jersey*

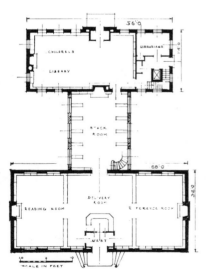

Teaneck is a rapidly growing residential community in the metropolitan area of New York City. The former library building became inadequate. Alterations were made to the present building and two end wings were added. The old portion is shown in the middle of the photograph.

The wing at the left is divided by low shelving into three spaces for delivery, reading, and reference. The lower portion of the walls is covered with continuous book shelving. The wing at the right contains the children's room, document vault, toilets, and the librarian's room, office, and kitchenette.

The exterior walls are brick with wood cornices and stone insets. The roof is slate. The interior partitions are cinder or terra-cotta block. The floors are covered with linoleum. The left wing is 32 by 68 feet and the right wing is 24 by 56 feet.

The building was completed in December 1936 at a construction cost of $55,865 and a total project cost o $60,246.

## Public Library

### *Harrison, New Jersey*

The town of Harrison is in an industrial section immediately to the east of Newark. It was well supplied with public schools but had no public library facilities. This building is in a residential neighborhood.

The over-all dimensions of the building are 94 by 60 feet. In the basement there are a community room, staff room, workroom, boiler room, and toilets. On the first floor are a reading room, a stack room, and librarian's office. There is an exhibit room on the mezzanine floor.

It is fireproof with concrete floors, steel trusses, and brick bearing walls. The roofing is slate.

It was completed in February 1938 at a construction cost of $79,041 and a total project cost of $112,273.

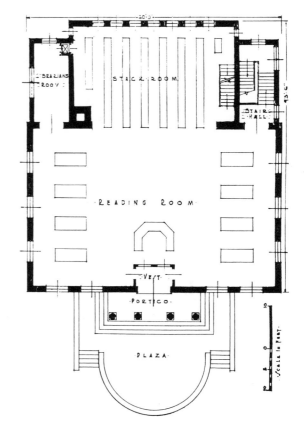

Public Library, *Allenstown, New Hampshire*

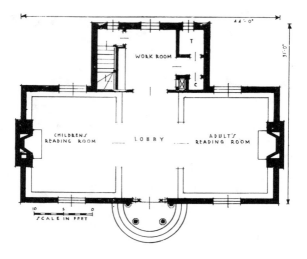

Allenstown, with a population of 1,549 in 1930, is on the Suncook River about 6 miles southeast of the city of Concord. Before the erection of this building the public library had been housed in a private home.

The library is located in a residential section of the town. It is a T-shaped structure and contains an entrance lobby, a workroom, and a reading room for adults and one for children. Each reading room has a fireplace and book shelves all around the room.

The building is semifireproof. Its exterior walls are brick backed up with hollow tile, the trim is wood, and the roof is covered with slate. Its over-all dimensions are 44 by 31 feet.

It was completed in October 1934 at a construction cost of $11,822 and a project cost of $13,138.

## Roselle Memorial Library

*Roselle, New Jersey*

Roselle is a borough situated approximately 3 miles west of the city of Elizabeth and had a population of 13,021 in 1930. It is a suburban residential community for the industrial center of Elizabeth and Newark.

The old library occupied rented quarters in a nonfireproof building. The new library is carried out in brick with wood trim and provides a large reading room, a book stack room, and a librarian's office on the first floor; a mezzanine story for book stacks, and a basement containing a clubroom as well as the heating plant. The reading room has a vaulted ceiling of sand-finished plaster, walls entirely paneled in wood, and an asphalt tile floor.

The over-all dimensions of the building are 70 by 66 feet. It was completed in November 1937 at a construction cost of $41,918 and a project cost of $46,177.

## Noah Webster Memorial Library
### *West Hartford, Connecticut*

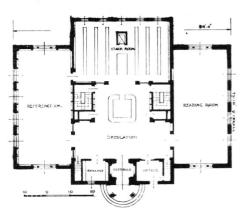

This building is next to a town hall and replaces a small and inadequate building.

The new building is on a lot 200 by 340 feet, and has a ground-floor area of 6,000 square feet. It has a volume of 201,000 cubic feet. It contains rooms for the D. A. R., a reference room, children's reading room, workroom, two administrative rooms, six stack rooms, kitchenette, and a repair room. Its over-all dimensions are 94 by 73 feet. Each side wing is 25 feet wide by 54 feet long.

It is fireproof, and the walls are red hand-made brick, with marble trim. Cornices and the entrance are wood. It was completed in November 1937 at a construction cost of $120,559 and a project cost of $130,944.

Topsfield Library, *Topsfield, Massachusetts*

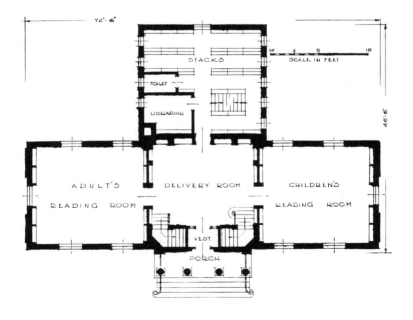

The town of Topsfield received a bequest for the purpose of building a public library. The P. W. A. aided in the enterprise with a loan and grant totaling $15,300 which represented about 40 percent of the project cost.

The building as constructed is T-shaped in plan and can accommodate the 17,000 volumes already owned with space for expansion. There are adult and children's reading rooms, delivery room, a librarian's office, and 2 stack rooms.

The construction is semifireproof. The foundation walls are concrete, the walls above grade are brick with some cast stone and some wood trim, and the roof is slate. It was completed in February 1935 at a construction cost of $36,593 and a project cost of $38,533.

## Lockport Public Library
### *Lockport, New York*

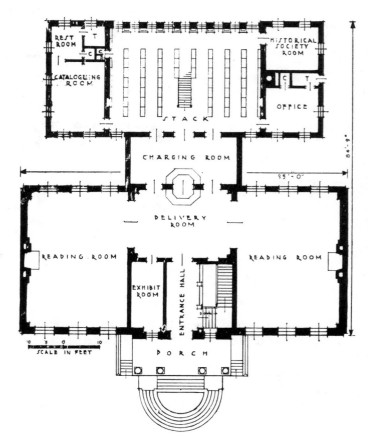

The Lockport Public Library project was begun as the result of two generous bequests from citizens of the town. It was carried out with the assistance of municipal and P. W. A. funds.

The building is H-shaped in plan and is set back from the street, which provides a small yard in front separated from the street by an iron fence. It contains an entrance hall, 2 reading rooms, exhibit room, stack room, an office for the librarian, cataloging room, and a director's room. In the basement are receiving and stack rooms, the children's room, and an auditorium seating 250.

The construction is fireproof. The entrance steps are granite, the main facade is limestone, the roof is slate, and the cupola is wood. The auditorium and the children's room each have separate entrances from the outside.

The project was completed in May 1937 at a construction cost of $131,980 and a project cost of $142,063.

Pennsylvania State College, *State College*, *Pennsylvania*

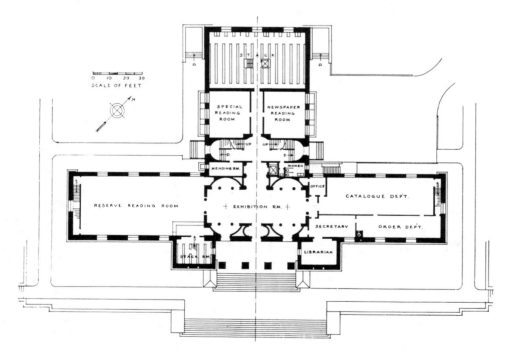

The Pennsylvania State College was founded in 1863. Its annual enrollment is approximately 4,800 men and 1,100 women. The college had lacked space for 1,000 students annually.

Other buildings were constructed for liberal arts, forestry, education, mineral industries, agricultural science, electrical engineering, chemistry and physics, agricultural engineering, and the poultry group, as well as a service building.

The library building has four stories in the middle tower portion and two stories in the three wings, with half basement throughout.

On the first floor there are an exhibition foyer, three reading rooms, five staff rooms, and a stack room. On the second floor are the main reading room, offices for staff, and stack room. On the mezzanine floor are a stack room and offices. On the third floor are special reading rooms, and on the fourth floor are offices and seminar rooms.

The structure is fireproof. The exterior walls are light-colored face brick. The estimated construction cost was $502,870 and project cost approximately $553,160.

Howard University, *Washington, D. C.*

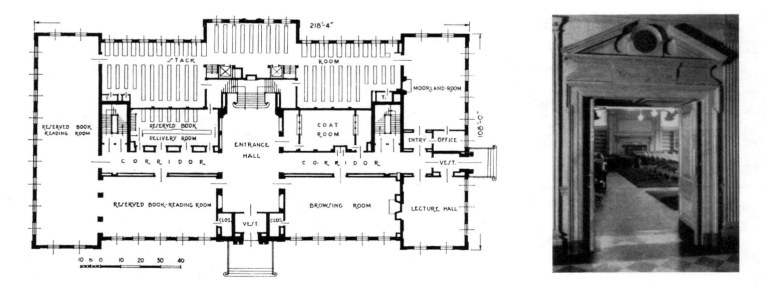

Howard University is an institution in Washington for 2,000 Negro students. This building is on the University quadrangle and is one of a number of buildings on the campus constructed by the Department of the Interior. It contains much additional space for future bookstacks. It is fitted for broadcasting chapel exercises over the campus. The building is air-conditioned.

It is of fireproof construction. The roof is covered with slate and the trim on the brick walls is limestone. The clock tower is 167 feet in height.

The building contains approximately 1,668,400 cubic feet. It was finished in November 1938 at a construction cost of $1,045,195 and a project cost of $1,090,566.

## Annex to the Library of Congress
### *Washington, D. C.*

The Library of Congress, completed in 1897, has a capacity of 5,000,000 volumes. The rapid increase of collections necessitated the annex, which has an available floor area of 20 acres and a capacity of 9,000,000 books. In addition to the catalog and reading rooms, there are 172 study rooms arranged on 2 levels, each with outside light. A tunnel connects the main building with the annex.

The building is faced on the exterior with white marble. It was completed by the Office of the Architect of the Capitol in 1938 at a total cost, including land and equipment, of $9,300,000. P. W. A. contributed $2,800,000.

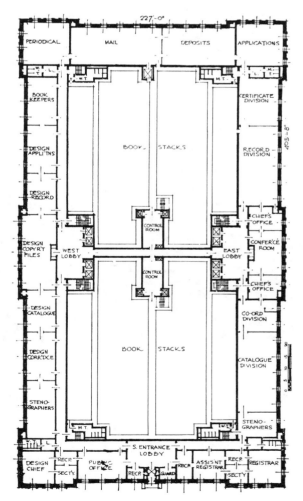

## Public Library

### *De Pere, Wisconsin*

This public library serves the city of De Pere and the rural area in the southern part of Brown County, Wisconsin.

The main unit is 24 by 80 feet. It has a large reading room, stack room, and reference room which has a fireplace. The children's department is in a wing 27 by 52 feet, and the librarian's office is adjacent to it. The rural library, about 20 feet square, serves primarily as a supply center of the traveling rural library.

The building is faced with local limestone in variegated colors.

It was finished in January 1937 at a construction cost of $27,406 and a project cost of $33,275.

## Main Public Library, *Massillon, Ohio*

The main public library is a joint undertaking of the city of Massillon and its school system. The project included the construction of the main library, the remodeling of the adjacent museum, and the erection of a branch library in another part of the city.

The main library was constructed as an addition to the city museum. It is irregular in plan and 120 by 87 feet in its over-all dimensions. On the first floor are the main reading room, reference room, librarian's room, and the stack room. The basement, due to sloping ground, is well lighted and contains the children's reading room, story-hour room, and a lecture room seating 200.

The red-brick exterior is trimmed with wood and stone and effective use is made of wrought iron. The project was completed in September 1937 at a construction cost of $177,009 and a project cost of $193,536.

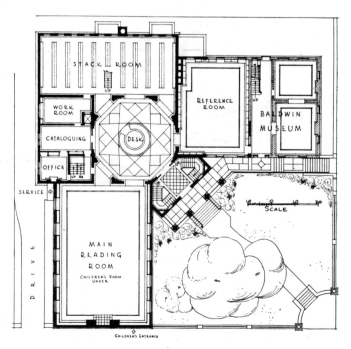

Public Library, *Elbow Lake, Minnesota*

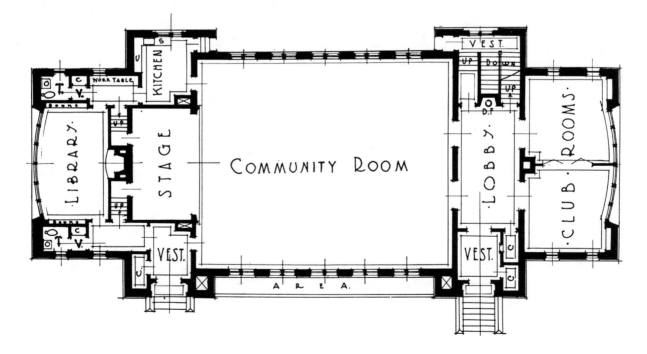

This building at Elbow Lake houses the public library and also serves as a community building. It is one story and a basement in height and contains the library with a separate entrance on one end, and a community room with a stage and a kitchen, and two clubrooms which are provided with an entrance and a lobby of their own. The clubrooms are separated by a folding partition so that they can be used as one room.

The structure is semifireproof with exterior walls of brick trimmed with stone. The project was completed in May 1934 at a construction cost of $33,670 and a project cost of $37,329.

## Public Library, *New Philadelphia, Ohio*

The circulation of library books in New Philadelphia doubled in a period of 6 years, reaching 133,000 in the first 6 months of 1935. The public library is also the library for the county schools.

The new building, which was badly needed, is 2 stories in height and 104 by 53 feet in over-all dimensions. It houses on the ground floor an auditorium seating 200 with a well-equipped stage and a research reading room, and on the first floor, adult and children's reading rooms, a control room between the two, and the stack room.

The structure is fireproof. The exterior walls are faced with red brick trimmed with limestone. It has a volume of 172,000 cubic feet and was completed in December 1936 at a construction cost of $54,195 and a project cost of $57,876.

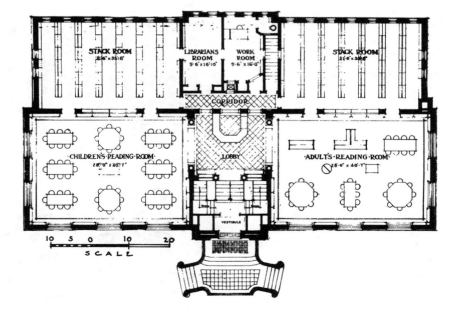

## Oak Park Public Library, *Oak Park, Illinois*

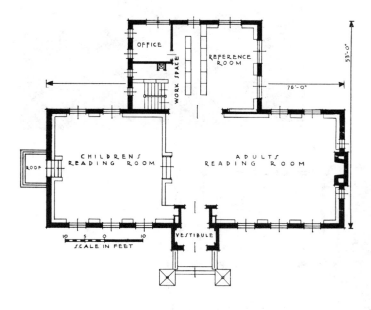

The first-floor construction is reinforced concrete with brick bearing walls. The roof is supported by exposed ornamental wooden trusses. The ceilings and walls have been covered with acoustical material.

The building was completed in October 1936 at a construction cost of $55,686 and the land cost approximately $10,000. The total project cost was $59,337.

The city of Oak Park is entirely surrounded by the city of Chicago. This building is located in the residential section.

It contains an assembly room for community use, seating about 100, located in the basement with a separate entrance. It has a room for children, located at the rear over the small auditorium. The shelves and stacks divide a book capacity of approximately 30,000 volumes.

## University of Virginia, *Charlottesville, Virginia*

The attendance at the University of Virginia had risen to 2,700 students and the accommodations for the library in the rotunda building had become entirely inadequate. The university, accordingly, secured a loan and grant from the P. W. A. and erected the new "Alderman Library" building.

Due to great differences of level on the site, the building is two stories high on the front and five stories in the rear. The basement contains a receiving room and general storage. On the first floor are offices, archives, and stack space. The second floor is occupied by reserve book rooms, rooms for public documents, and stack space. The third floor, which is the main entrance floor on the front, contains the memorial hall, a large general reading room, offices, and stack space. On

the fourth floor are seminar rooms and faculty study rooms.

The building is fireproof throughout. The exterior walls are red brick with stone and wood trim. Heat is supplied from the central heating plant of the university. The project was completed in June 1938 at a construction cost of $868,810 and a project cost of $944,923.

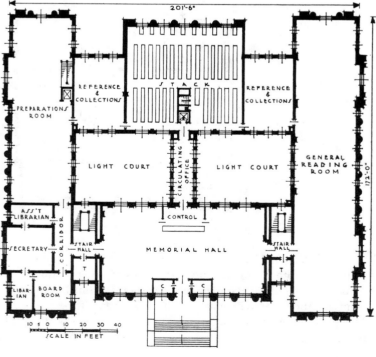

Library, State Teachers College, *Richmond*, *Kentucky*

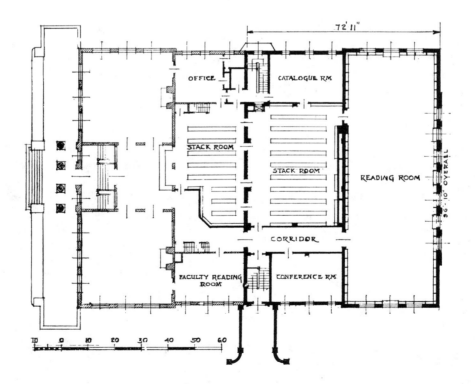

The State Teachers College has a student body of 2,200 and the library building has been outgrown entirely. At the time the library was built the student body was only a third of its present size and there were only 222 seats in the reading rooms.

This project consisted of a large addition to the rear of the existing building and was carried out in the same type of architecture and construction as the old building and greatly increased its facilities.

The addition is fireproof throughout, its exterior walls being brick trimmed with limestone. It was completed in January 1936 at a construction cost of $89,613 and a project cost of $96,075.

## Library, North Carolina State College
*Durham, North Carolina*

North Carolina State College was chartered and organized in 1925 as a coeducational college of liberal arts for Negroes. Its present student body is approximately 280.

A grant from the P. W. A. enabled the State to erect a library, an auditorium, and seven residences and a men's dormitory.

The library is a one-story-and-basement structure 97 feet by 71½ feet in over-all dimensions, which contains storage rooms and a heating plant in the basement and reference rooms, study rooms, and bookstacks on the first floor and on a mezzanine.

The construction is fireproof. The exterior walls are brick with cast-stone trim and a wood porch and cornice. The roof is slate-covered.

The entire project, including the library, was completed in December 1937 at a total cost of $281,467.

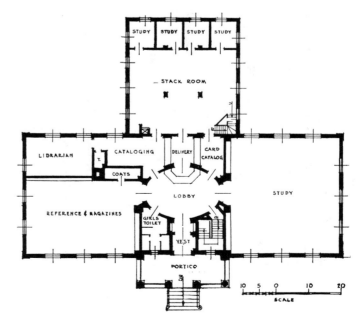

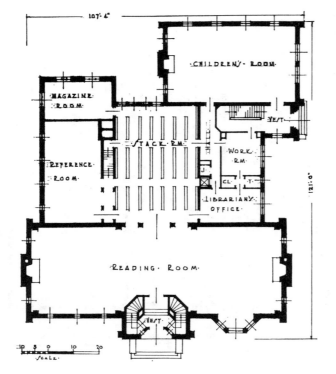

## Rochester Public Library
### *Rochester, Minnesota*

Rochester is in Olmsted County in the southeastern section of Minnesota. In 1930 it had a population of 20,621.

This library contains a distribution room, reading rooms for adults, and reference and stack rooms. It has a special feature in providing a children's room as a self-contained unit, with a separate entrance from a side street and small-size furniture for juvenile use.

The building is fireproof and is 121 by 107 feet over all. It was completed in July 1937 at a construction cost of $169,975 and a project cost of $178,548.

Public Library, *Fort Worth, Texas*

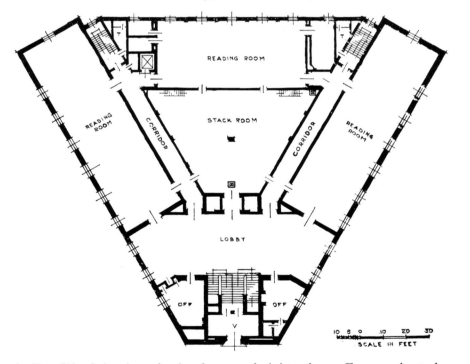

The new public library in Fort Worth is triangular in plan due to an irregular site. The main entrance is on the truncated point of one of the angles and leads into a spacious entrance hall. The stack room occupies the central portion of the building and is surrounded by the reading rooms, two of which are entered directly from the entrance hall and the third is approached through two corridors. Ample administrative offices and study rooms are provided.

The structure is fireproof. The frame is reinforced concrete and the exterior walls are faced with limestone. The principal rooms are paneled in wood and their ceilings are acoustically treated.

The project was completed in June 1939 at a construction cost of $370,688 and a project cost of $390,861.

## University of New Mexico, *Albuquerque, New Mexico*

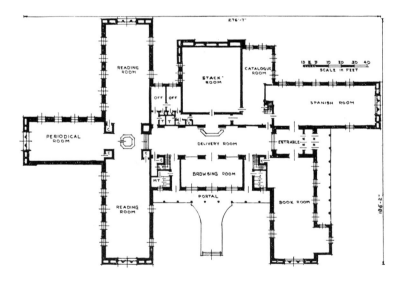

The University of New Mexico has undertaken quite an extensive building program with the assistance of the P. W. A. One unit is the university library, which has been designed in the traditional "Pueblo" or "Santa Fe" style, and is an adaptation of the native Indian architecture of the State and conforms in character to the other buildings on the campus.

The building consists of a 9-tier fireproof book stack with a capacity of approximately 230,000 volumes. Around the stack on the first floor are grouped reading rooms, reference rooms, and the distributing service, and on the second floor additional reading and reference rooms, seminar rooms, and study rooms. Five hundred and eighty students can be accommodated in these rooms, which is 40 percent of the student body of the university. The structure is so designed that future additions can be made to both the stack and reading rooms with great ease.

The entire project of which the library was a part was completed in April 1938 at a total project cost of $694,086. The construction cost of the library building was $328,834 and its project cost $364,164.

## Administration and Library Building
## University of Texas
### *Austin, Texas*

The dominating building of the university group is the administration and library building with its lofty tower and belfry containing a carillon of 16 bells. Ultimately it will be entirely devoted to the university library but at present is occupied by the administrative offices, classrooms, and seminar rooms, as well as the library.

Periodical and reserve reading rooms, offices, and the stenographic bureau are on the ground floor. The first floor is occupied by offices of the president, board of regents, dean, and comptroller, a post-office substation, and library offices. On the second floor are administrative offices, a large room for university functions, library reading room, and classrooms. A cast museum, research collections, and seminar rooms are on the third floor. The tower is designed for stack space but is being used at present for seminar rooms.

Construction is fireproof, of steel and reinforced concrete slabs. The exterior walls are faced with limestone with granite trim. The project was completed in August 1937 at a construction cost of $1,736,183 and a project cost of $1,864,385.

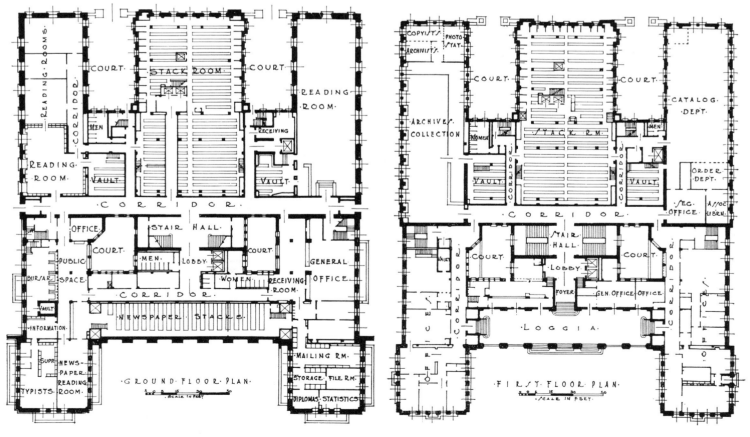

·GROUND·FLOOR·PLAN·

·FIRST·FLOOR·PLAN·

## Arkansas Polytechnic College

### *Russellville, Arkansas*

One of the new buildings recently erected at the Arkansas Polytechnic College was the library.

It has a stack room with a capacity of 53,000 volumes and there is additional shelving in the reading rooms. The delivery room is flanked by 2 reading rooms, each 36 by 47 feet, and there are in addition a conference room, faculty room, workroom, and office.

The structure is semifireproof. The exterior walls are red face brick with some stone trim and concrete base. The portico, cornices, cupola, and some of the trim are wood.

The project was completed in August 1936 at a construction cost of $55,234 and a project cost of $59,883.

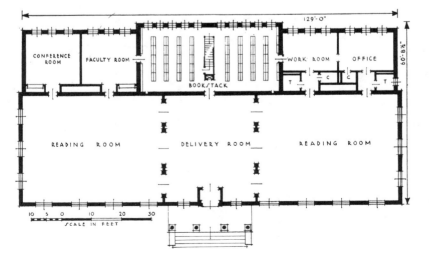

## University of Arkansas Library
### *Fayetteville, Arkansas*

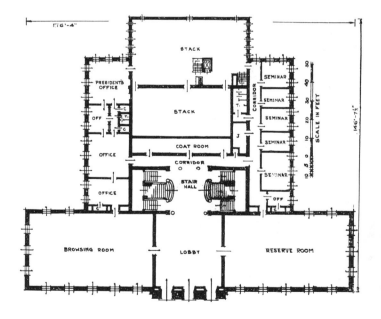

Before construction of this new building, the library of the University of Arkansas was housed in the nonfireproof administration building.

The new structure has a capacity of 265,000 volumes and furnishes study desks for approximately 600 students. In addition, there are cubicles in the stack room where research work can be carried on.

The basement has a museum across the entire front of the building, including work space, receiving, storage, and util-ity rooms. On the first floor are browsing and research rooms, offices, and seminar rooms. The main reading room extends the full length of the building on the second floor and there are also on this floor catalog and delivery rooms and offices.

The structure is fireproof, with exterior walls faced with stone. It was completed during 1935 at a construction cost of $434,590 and a project cost of $464,753.

## Ponca City Library, *Ponca City, Oklahoma*

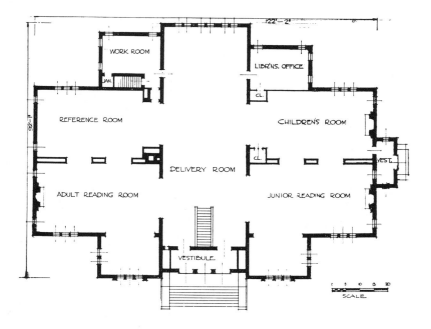

During the 2 decades from 1910 to 1930 the population of Ponca City increased from 2,500 to over 16,000 people. As a result of this, the small Carnegie library that the city owned had become totally inadequate.

The city erected the new building which is one and part two stories in height. It contains a reading room for adults, a junior reading room, children's room, reference room, delivery room, workroom, and a librarian's room, as well as the necessary stack space.

It is a semifireproof structure with light-colored brick walls elaborately trimmed with terra cotta. The foundation walls and floors are reinforced concrete.

The project was completed in December 1935 at a construction cost of $80,019 and a project cost of $100,644.

## Visalia Public Library, *Visalia, California*

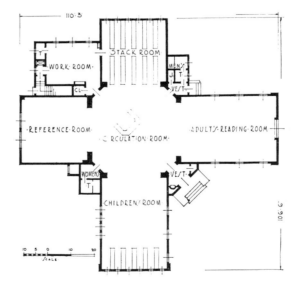

The old library at Visalia had become too small, was difficult to enlarge and was not in a suitable section of the city for centralized public use. The site selected for the new library is in a public park in the center of the city.

Its central portion, 36 feet square, extends two stories in height thus providing light and ventilation for the circulation room. There are four wings, one each for adults' read-ing room, children's room, reference room, and bookstacks.

The building is constructed of reinforced concrete with exposed hand-hewn wood roof trusses and is designed to resist seismic disturbances. The interior has been treated through-out with acoustical materials.

It was completed in June 1936 at a construction cost of $33,076 and a project cost of $35,394.

## Alameda Public Library, *Alameda, California*

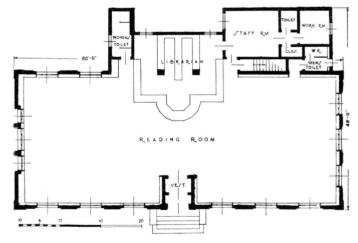

The city of Alameda is in the environs of Oakland, lying south of it. In 1930 it had a population of 35,033.

In preparing the design for the new library building, much attention was devoted to acoustics and to the material and artificial lighting of the main reading room. The results have been most satisfactory.

The building was constructed with rigid concrete framing, designed to withstand seismic disturbances. The roof is covered with Spanish tile.

The project was completed in July 1936 at a construction cost of $25,883 and a project cost of $32,826.

## Chaffey Junior College Library, *Ontario, California*

This library was built as a memorial to George and Benjamin Chaffey, brothers, who were early settlers in this city and developers of it.

It contains library facilities for both the high school and junior college pupils and is situated on the campus between the two schools. It contains 13,591 square feet of floor area. The stack room, 32 by 52 feet, has a capacity of 50,000 volumes in its two stories. The reading rooms and the memorial hall have been treated acoustically.

The entire school plant has an enrollment of about 2,200 pupils. The building will accommodate 250 persons. It is constructed of reinforced concrete and designed to withstand seismic disturbances.

The project was completed in October 1935 at a construction cost of $85,137 and a project cost of $92,021.

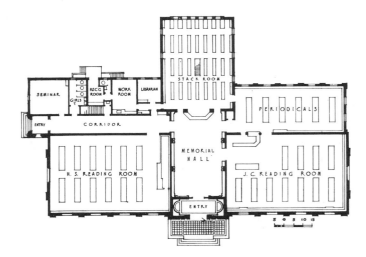

## Library, University of Utah

*Salt Lake City, Utah*

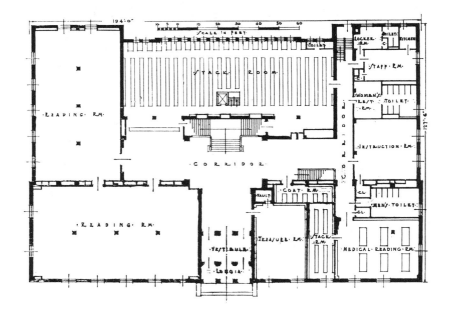

The new library building at the University of Utah replaced the old and inadequate quarters which were situated in the administration building. Its over-all dimensions are 194 by 127 feet and it provides 66,000 square feet of floor area.

On the ground floor there are two undergraduate reading rooms, a medical reading room, a treasure room, and rooms for instruction, for the staff, and for bookstacks. On the second floor is the general reading room, 47 by 192 feet in size, extending through 2 stories. It accommodates 350 students. On this floor are also a periodical room, 43 by 76 feet, accommodating 124 students, 3 librarians' rooms, a vault, a cataloging room, and the main bookstacks which cover an area 37 by 104 feet. The third floor contains 2 graduate reading rooms as well as seminar and study rooms.

The building has a concrete frame which is faced with stone and it is fireproof throughout. It was completed in October 1935 at a construction cost of $496,020 and a project cost of $524,301.

## Public Library

### *Glendale, Arizona*

The city of Glendale has replaced an old wornout structure with this little public library which, with its painted brick walls and Spanish tile roof, fits into its setting of palms and other semitropical trees and shrubs.

It is one story in height, without a basement, and contains reading rooms for adults and children, stack space, a workroom, and an office. A small room next to the office houses equipment to air-condition the entire building.

The building is semifireproof. Exterior walls are brick, the floors concrete, and the roof wood under the tile covering. It has a floor area of 2,000 square feet and was completed in March 1938 at a construction cost of $10,622 and a project cost of $11,626.

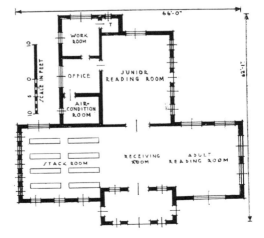

McMinnville Library, *McMinnville, Oregon*

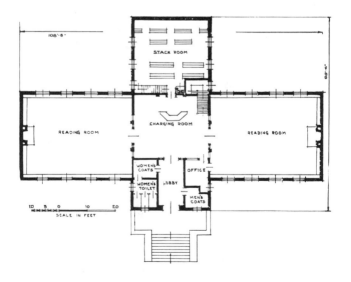

This library adjoins a small university and conforms to the campus plan. The basement contains book stacks and reading rooms. The first floor has two reading rooms, book stacks, and office rooms.

The floors and walls are reinforced concrete with brick veneer exterior. Finished floors are asphalt tile. The roofing is asbestos shingles.

The project was completed in November 1936 at a construction cost of $59,586 and a project cost of $65,437.

Oregon State Library, *Salem, Oregon*

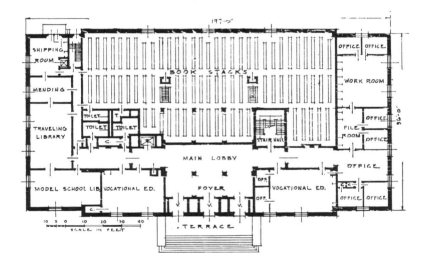

This structure is the first of the buildings which will ultimately compose the "Capitol Group" on the plaza which leads to the State capitol. It includes the stack space which occupies the entire central rear portion, the vaults and rooms connected with the library, and also 57,200 square feet of floor space for offices of various departments of the State government. The stack space is furnished with elevators and a book conveyor.

The construction is fireproof and the exterior walls are faced with marble. The building was 98 percent completed in June 1939, the estimated construction cost being $803,445 and the project cost $871,119.

## War Memorial Building, *Holyoke, Massachusetts*

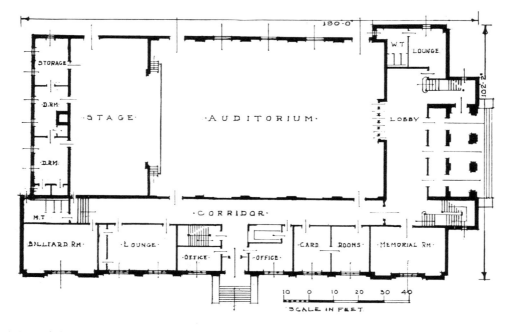

This War Memorial Building serves the city of Holyoke as a community center.

The ground floor contains a large room for dances and entertainments, a kitchen, and a men's lounge in addition to the various service rooms.

The first floor is entered through a portico and includes a lobby, an auditorium with a stage and dressing rooms, the memorial hall, a lounge, cardrooms, a billiard room,

women's lounge, and offices for the commission and custodian. The second floor has the auditorium balcony, the organization rooms, and two offices.

The construction is fireproof and the two street facades have a granite base and limestone walls. The rear walls are brick.

The project was completed in September 1937 at a construction cost of $204,785 and a project cost of $221,605.

## Restoration of Old Economy

### *Ambridge, Pennsylvania*

Economy is a small town 17 miles below Pittsburgh on the Ohio River and was founded in 1824, as part of a social and economic experiment, by the Harmony Society. The society became extinct because its members took a vow of celibacy shortly after its foundation and today there is only one person alive who was in any way connected with it.

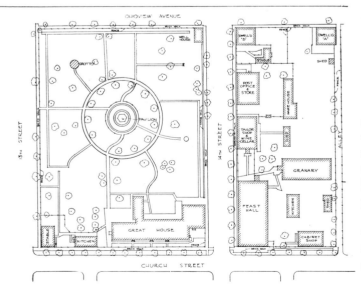

The industrial life of Economy included the making of cotton and woolen cloth, distilling of whisky, making of wine, and milling of flour, and buildings of many kinds were required. In addition, a meeting hall, hotel, church, shops, the Great House and the Feast Hall were built, and the last is illustrated above. The other illustration is a garden pavilion surrounded by a fishpond.

Careful research has been done and is continuing and the whole restoration is by no means complete. The part undertaken with P. W. A. aid was completed in July 1938 at a construction cost of $32,164 and a project cost of $37,175.

## Morristown National Historical Park, *Morristown, New Jersey*

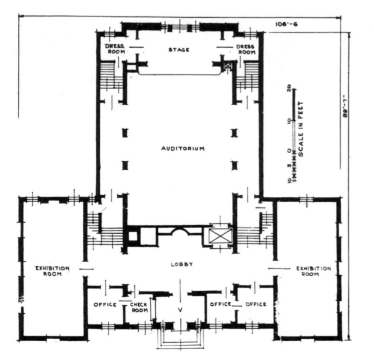

The American Army under General Washington occupied the site of the Morristown National Historical Park throughout the period of the War of the Revolution, both for a camp and for a hospital. General Washington spent two winters here.

At the time when the Government acquired the property, the buildings were in very poor condition and the projects carried out and financed under P. W. A. included the restoration of the Guerin house, the restoration of the Temp Wick house and its outbuildings, the construction of a replica of one of the log buildings such as were used for hospital purposes, and the construction of the museum and library building shown above.

The museum contains many relics of General Washington and of the period of the Revolutionary War, and the auditorium is frequently used for lectures on historical subjects.

The architectural character of the building is entirely in keeping with the colonial buildings of this part of New Jersey. The exterior walls are stucco with wood trim and the construction is entirely fireproof. The building was completed in February 1937 at a construction cost of $139,141.

This structure contains a large auditorium, exhibition and museum rooms, workshops, and offices, and it is the headquarters of all of the exhibitions and all phases of the work carried on in the park.

Pierce Mill Restoration, *Washington, D. C.*

One of the restorations carried out by the National Park Service was that of the old Pierce Mill in Rock Creek Park. The structure was built in 1810 of native split stone taken from a nearby quarry, and with its 10½-foot wheel and equipment for grinding meal is typical of the old mills of a bygone age.

The building is 50 feet long by 40 feet wide. One gable is stone and the other frame, and the small wood sash have heavy muntins and small panes of glass. The floors are wide oak plank and the roof is covered with wood shingles. The equipment has been faithfully reproduced.

The project was completed in March 1936 and the total P. W. A. allotment for the restoration was $26,614.12.

Museum of Art

*Richmond, Virginia*

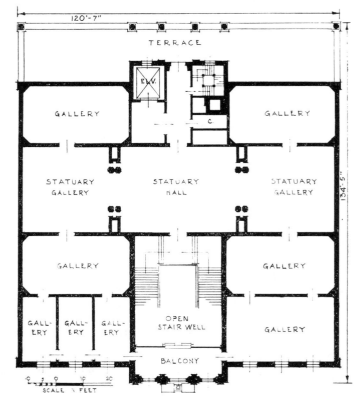

Before the erection of this art museum, the city of Richmond had no building suitable for the exhibition and storage of works of art. The structure is placed on the grounds of the soldiers' home and the area surrounding it has been landscaped with lawns and planting.

The building is fireproof and is approximately 120 by 134 feet in plan. It is constructed of steel and reinforced con-

crete and the exterior walls are faced with stone up to the second floor level and with a red Virginia brick trimmed with stone above that.

The project was completed in November 1936. Its total cost was $287,974, of which $76,523 was provided by the P. W. A. as a grant, the remainder being provided by the Virginia Art Commission.

## Passenger Building and Freight Shed

*Colonial National Historical Park, Virginia*

The Colonial National Historical Park, carried out by the National Park Service, embraces Yorktown, Jamestown, and Williamsburg. The passenger building, freight shed, and wharf at Yorktown were required to care for the traffic by water and have been designed in the style of similar buildings of the Colonial period. The passenger building is frame construction and the freight shed is brick. The wharf is concrete and was completed in January 1936 at a cost of $55,758.33.

## Headquarters Building, Swan Tavern

*Colonial National Historical Park, Virginia*

The headquarters building is a reconstruction of the Swan Tavern on its original foundations. The design conforms to all evidence that has been gathered regarding the original structure and provides a central hall with four rooms opening from it on both first and second floors. The basement contains workrooms and a fireproof record vault. The project includes a stable and smokehouse and was completed in December 1934 at a cost of $38,260.

## Restoration of Fort
### *Fort Pulaski National Monument, Georgia*

In the beginning of the P. W. A. practically every one of the national parks received financial assistance from it. Some of the parks and monuments were new and unimproved and others needed finishing. Among the many buildings were the Administrative Building and Museum near Hot Springs, Arkansas, the Administrative Building and Museum at Chickamauga, and the restoration of Fort Pulaski in Virginia.

This old fort was built in 1810. The project consisted of repairs and rehabilitation and provision of space for a museum.

The work was completed in July 1936 at a construction cost of $76,453.

## Soldiers' Memorial Building

### *St. Louis, Missouri*

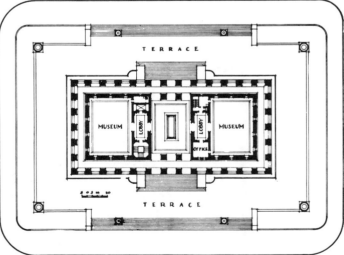

This building was erected as a memorial to soldiers who lost their lives in the World War. In the center hall on the first floor is a black granite cenotaph bearing the names of the soldiers. On each side is a museum containing World War relics, records, and other data. Surrounding the structure are 38 square columns, 5 by 5 feet, and 35 feet high.

The building is one unit of a well-planned civic center, the construction being of steel and reinforced concrete. The walls are faced with limestone. Marble and granite were used extensively. It is 190 by 89 feet, and 67 feet high.

It was completed in July 1939 at a construction cost of $715,684 and a total project cost of $760,973.

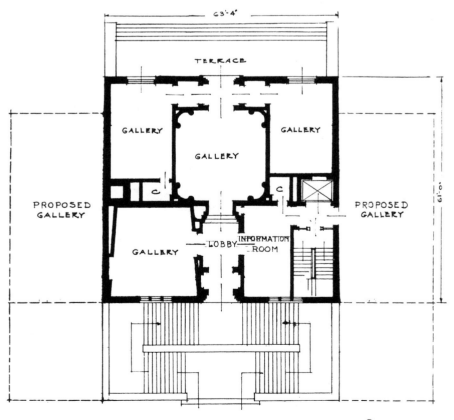

## Art Museum
### *Wichita, Kansas*

Wichita is in the southern central portion of the State. In 1930 its population was 111,110.

Under the will of a citizen, the income of a certain property was to be used to purchase an art collection. The will stipulated that a suitable building was to be provided for this collection by the city. The city constructed this first section of what is to be in the future a large museum. It also contains classrooms on the ground floor for the study of art.

The building is fireproof, is two stories high, and approximately 61 by 63 feet in plan.

This project was completed in July 1935 at a construction cost of $70,127 and a project cost of $78,197.

Dallas Museum of Natural History, *Dallas, Texas*

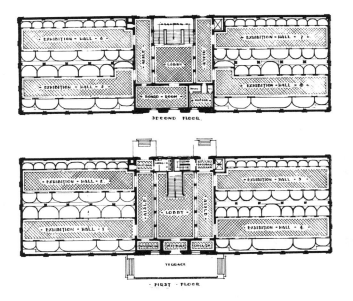

At the time of the Texas Centennial Exposition at Dallas in 1936 certain of the buildings constructed were made permanent, and one of these was the Museum of Natural History.

The structure is two stories in height and 71 by 224 feet in plan. The spacious entrance lobby connects with numerous exhibition halls containing cases in which are shown specimens of the plant and animal life of Texas.

The building is semifireproof. The frame is reinforced concrete and the exterior walls are stone. Texas shell stone is extensively used on the interior, with bases of marble and floors of rubber tile.

The project was completed in August 1936 at a construction cost of $248,387 and a project cost of $261,108.

San Jacinto
Battleground Memorial
*Houston, Texas*

Impressive celebrations were held throughout the State of Texas in 1936 to commemorate the centennial of its secession from the Republic of Mexico. One of the most important events leading to this act was the decisive Battle of San Jacinto fought on April 21, 1836, in which the Texans were completely victorious. It was therefore decided to erect a memorial on the battlefield honoring the heroes who fought so well.

The monument rests on two terraces which rise 15 feet above the natural grade and consists of a base 36 feet high from which the shaft extends to a total height of 564 feet. The shaft is 50 feet square at the base and diminishes to 30 feet square at the top and is surmounted by an enormous star, 45 feet high and 30 feet wide, which symbolizes the "Lone Star State." On the extreme tip of the star is a beacon light that serves as a protection to air traffic.

Within the base are an historical museum, a meeting hall, and an art gallery, as well as the lobby leading to the stairs and elevator.

The base and shaft are faced with limestone and are decorated in certain places with bas-relief sculpture and inscriptions which depict and describe outstanding events in the early history of Texas.

The project was completed in July 1938 at a construction cost of $800,172 and a project cost of $843,059.

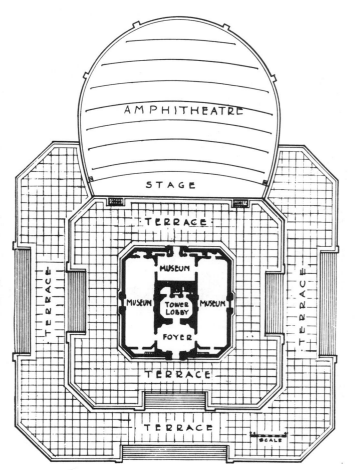

State Museum Building, University of Arizona, *Tucson, Arizona*

These illustrations are of the new museum building on the campus of the University of Arizona. It is 76 by 140 feet with a museum room on the first floor 87 by 70 feet, two small rooms each 31 by 23 feet, and offices for the curator and staff. A mezzanine exhibition gallery extends around the building. Construction is semifireproof with exterior walls of brick trimmed with stone. The project was completed in March 1937. The project cost of $1,043,174 included 16 buildings for the university.

## Museum, Tumacacori National Monument, *Southern Arizona*

The Tumacacori National Monument is 49 miles south of Tucson. It was acquired by the National Park Service in 1908 and includes the Mission of San Jose de Tumacacori, the buildings of which had fallen into a ruined condition. The mission church and its dependencies were carefully restored and the museum building was constructed in the same style of architecture as the mission.

It contains rooms for the display of objects related to the

Franciscan monks and the work of the mission with the Indians. It contains also quarters for the custodian and a ranger.

The construction is semifireproof. The masonry walls are covered with stucco and the interiors have wood beam ceilings, such as were used by the Spaniards.

The project was completed in December 1937 at a construction cost of $28,890 and a project cost of $32,000.

Eliot School, *Natick, Massachusetts*

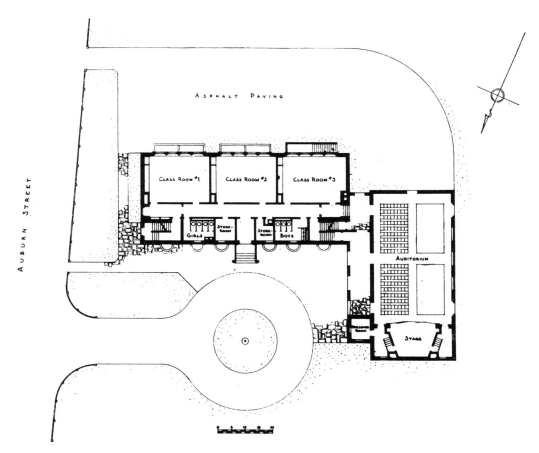

This new school building replaces a structure which was over 100 years old and which was heated by a boiler 42 years old, was devoid of modern plumbing and ventilation, and was in addition located on a curved street carrying heavy traffic.

The new structure is 2 stories and a basement in height and L-shaped in plan. It contains 6 classrooms, a teacher's room, playroom, kitchen, and an auditorium seating 288 and provided with a stage.

It is simply and beautifully designed in red brick with wood trim and a slate roof. The project was completed in October 1938 at a construction cost of $105,434 and a project cost of $125,970.

East School, *Stoneham, Massachusetts*

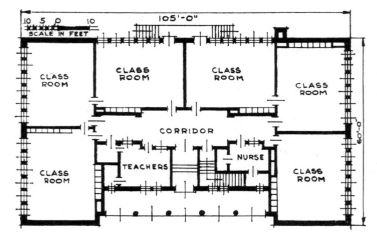

Stoneham, a residential suburb of Boston, had a population of 10,060 in 1930.

This project consisted of two school buildings, which replaced three wooden ones 75 years old. The East School, which is illustrated, contains six classrooms, playrooms, and offices.

It is semifireproof and has complete mechanical ventilation. It was completed in August 1938 at a construction cost of $136,027 and a project cost of $160,259.

## Harmony and Chepachet Schools

*Glocester, Rhode Island*

The larger illustration is of the Harmony School and the smaller is of the Chepachet School. Both were constructed by the town of Glocester to replace old frame buildings, and the plans of the two are the same.

Both are one story and part basement in height and provide four classrooms, a lunchroom, and rooms for the principal and teachers. The Harmony School is 156 by 63 feet and the Chepachet School is 169 by 63 feet.

The construction is semifireproof. The exterior walls are red brick trimmed with stone and wood and the roofs are slate.

The two buildings were completed in January 1935 at a construction cost of $93,398 and a project cost of $105,788.

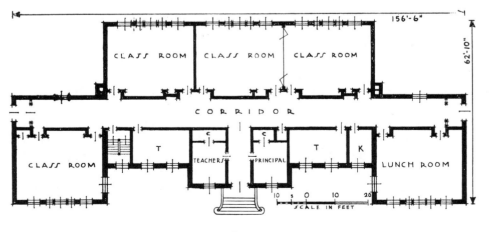

## School and Town Office Building

### *Clarksburg, Massachusetts*

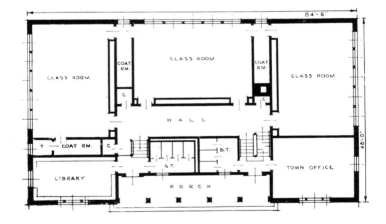

The town of Clarksburg is in the northwestern part of Massachusetts near North Adams and the Vermont State line. The principal industries are farming, dairying, and the manufacture of woolen cloth. In 1930 the population was 1,296. It is increased considerably during the summer vacation season.

The former school building was destroyed by fire in December 1936 and the pupils were temporarily housed in a chapel and in a wooden building formerly used as a dance hall.

The new building houses accommodations both for the old school and for the town offices. It has three classrooms, the town library, town office, and toilets on the first floor. In the basement are a meeting room, vault, room for the sealer of weights and measures, rooms for manual training and domestic science, boiler room, and storage rooms.

The walls are colonial texture red brick. The columns and trim are white pine and the roof is covered with slate. The floors are wood and the walls and ceilings are plaster on metal lath. The walls are decorated in pastel shades. The corridor has a wainscot of knotty pine and the town office has one of painted wood. The toilets have metal partitions and terrazzo floors.

The building was completed in August 1938. The construction cost was $39,721 and the project cost was $43,471.

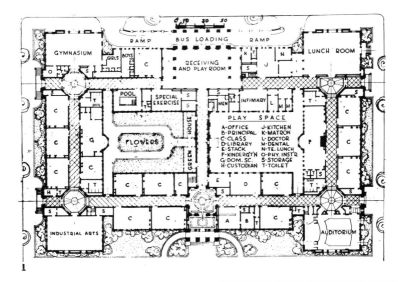

## Willis and Elizabeth Martin
## Orthopedic School
### *Philadelphia, Pennsylvania*

The Willis and Elizabeth Martin Orthopedic School is a one-story structure approximately 230 by 330 feet in plan, built around two interior courts, one of which is a playground and the other a garden for cultivation by the pupils. It provides 15 classrooms, a library, rooms for domestic science, industrial arts, and special exercise, an infirmary, a kindergarten, a lunchroom, a gymnasium, an auditorium seating 150, offices for administration, a playroom, and a greenhouse connected with the garden.

It is of fireproof construction, the roof being of structural steel supporting lightweight concrete slabs and the exterior walls red brick trimmed with limestone. The roof is covered with slate.

The project was completed in August 1937 at a construction cost of $541,040 and a project cost of $577,640.

## Township of Manor School
### *Hambright, Pennsylvania*

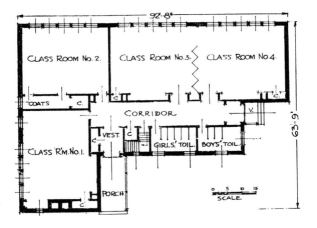

This little building provides elementary school facilities for the township of Manor, which is an agricultural district lying along the Susquehanna River.

It is one story in height with a partial basement and provides four classrooms. The project included the construction of an approach drive and the landscaping of the site.

The building is nonfireproof. The exterior walls are red brick, the trim, porches, shutters, cupola, and gable sheathing are wood, and the roof is slate. The floors of all rooms are maple and those of the corridors are asphalt tile.

The project was completed in September 1936 at a construction cost of $23,879 and a project cost of $28,533.

## Burgwin School, *Pittsburgh, Pennsylvania*

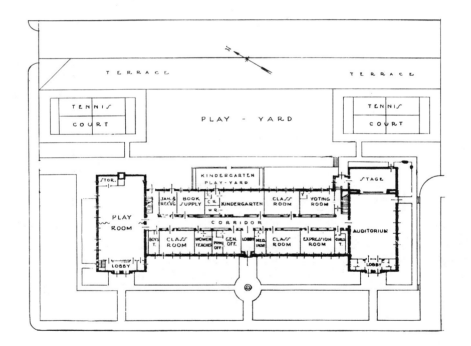

The construction of the Burgwin School, in a residential district adjacent to a mill and commercial district, made possible the elimination of the old Hazelwood School built in 1875, and of the Glenwood School built in 1882, both of which were obsolete.

The building is 3 stories in height and H-shaped in plan with over-all dimensions 96 by 279 feet. It accommodates 920 pupils in 22 classrooms and a kindergarten. In addition, it has 2 nature-study rooms, rooms for the study of art and music, a library, 2 playrooms separated by folding doors

which can be folded back to form a large gymnasium, an auditorium with a seating capacity of 325, a general clinic, medical inspector's office, administration offices, and supply and storage rooms. In the rear of the school is a playground surfaced in fine red clay and 2 tennis courts with cork asphalt surfaces.

The building is fireproof throughout. The exterior walls are light-colored brick with limestone trim. It was completed in August 1937 at a construction cost of $363,004 and a project cost of $389,751.

Woodrow Wilson School, *Westfield, New Jersey*

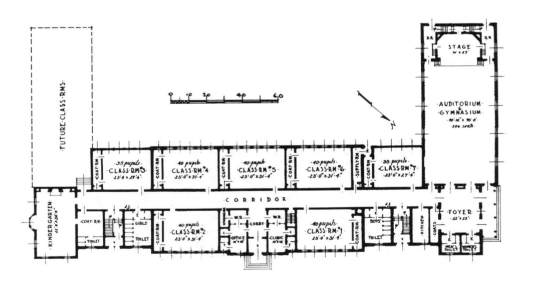

This school made possible the abandonment of four dilapidated portable buildings which were being used for classes due to the extreme overcrowding of the two existing elementary schools.

The project and its equipment are planned for a future addition which will increase the present capacity of 510 students by more than 30 percent. The building as built is 2 stories high in the central part and has a 1-story wing at each end. It contains 13 classrooms, a kindergarten, offices, service rooms, teachers' room with a kitchen attached, a clinic, and a combined auditorium-gymnasium for use by the pupils and by the community.

The construction is fireproof. Exterior walls are red brick with white marble and wood trim and the roof is grey tile. The reinforced concrete floor slabs are in general covered with linoleum. The boilers are of sufficient capacity to care for the future increase of the building. There is a unit system of ventilation with thermostatic control, an electric time system, and wiring for radio. The structure has a ground floor area of 10,518 square feet, a volume of 642,192 cubic feet, and was completed in August 1935 at a construction cost of $252,780 and a project cost of $275,464.

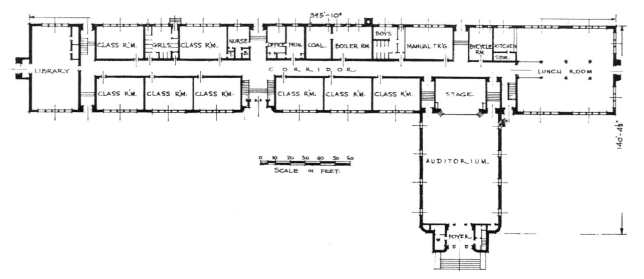

## Ocean View School, *Norfolk, Virginia*

The original application for a grant from the P. W. A. of $45,900 contemplated an annex to the existing school at an estimated cost of $102,000. Investigation disclosed that the old building was a fire hazard, so the city demolished it and without an additional grant constructed a new building which contains 24 classrooms and an auditorium. The construction is reinforced concrete throughout, the exterior walls being stuccoed. The project was completed in March 1939 at a construction cost of $246,754 and a project cost of $264,059.

Magnolia School, *Magnolia, Delaware*

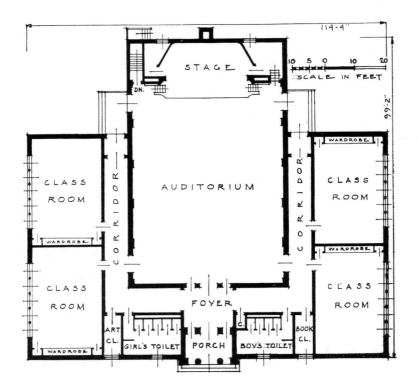

The new Magnolia School replaces a four-room frame structure which had served the school district for 50 years and which was heated by stoves and lacked proper sanitary accommodations.

The new building is one story in height, with provision in the basement for the heating plant, and provides four classrooms and an auditorium with a stage.

The construction is semifireproof. The exterior walls are red brick backed up with hollow tile and trimmed with wood and limestone. The first floor is a concrete slab and the roof construction is wood covered with slate.

The project was completed in June 1935 at a construction cost of $73,536 and a project cost of $80,445.

## Washington Elementary School

### *Evansville, Indiana*

This new elementary school is the first school building that had been erected in Evansville for 5 years, during which period the city population had increased by 10 percent.

The building is 2 stories in height and 390 by 335 feet in over-all dimensions. It provides 19 standard classrooms, a kindergarten, an industrial-arts room, a general science room; rooms for art, music, and science; an ungraded room, an auditorium seating 600, a gymnasium seating 200 in a balcony, and the necessary administrative offices.

The construction is fireproof with steel frame and concrete floors and roof. The exterior walls are red brick with stone and wood trim. Extensive use is made of radio in the classrooms.

The project was completed in June 1937 at a construction cost of $427,875 and a project cost of $451,973.

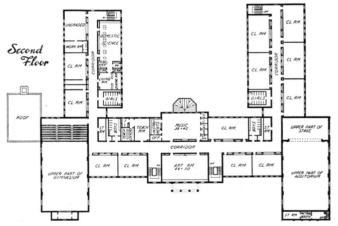

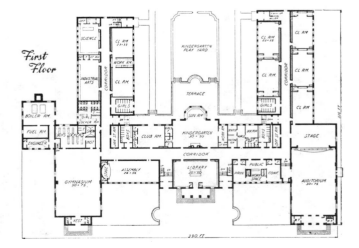

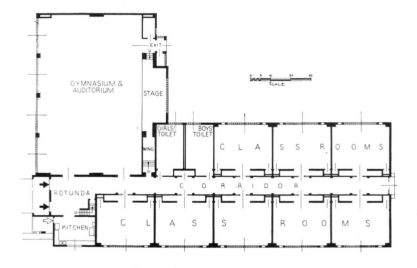

## Coolspring School

### *Coolspring Township, Indiana*

This building replaces five rural one-room schools and one village two-room school. It is placed on an ample semirural site suitable for the development of playgrounds.

It provides eight modern classrooms, a vocational and domestic science room, teachers' and principal's rooms, and a combined auditorium-gymnasium with a stage.

The design and construction is of interest. It is modern in character and consists of exterior walls of glazed load-bearing tile which are interchangeable in size with the glass blocks used in large panels to light the rooms. The tile are glazed on both sides so that they form a finished wall inside and out, thus eliminating plastering on the interior walls. Minor windows on the sides of the glass-block panels allow a direct ventilation in the classrooms.

The building is 120 by 185 feet in plan and has a volume of 282,000 cubic feet. It was completed in August 1938 at a construction cost of $78,036 and a project cost of $85,596.

## Northville Grade School, *Northville, Michigan*

The enrollment in the Northville school district increased from a student body of 500 in 1920 to 719 in 1935. As a result, the 30-year-old nonfireproof elementary school was crowded, and overflow classes were being held in an old residence. The new building is 2 stories and a basement in height and provides 12 classrooms, a kindergarten, a library, a playroom, teachers' rooms, and administrative offices. It is of fireproof construction with reinforced concrete foundations, walls, and floors. The exterior walls are faced with brick and the parapet walls are capped with stone. The building was selected by the American Institute of Architects to be illustrated in the United States pavilion at the Paris Exposition in 1937. It was completed in February 1937 at a construction cost of $92,583 and a project cost of $99,634.

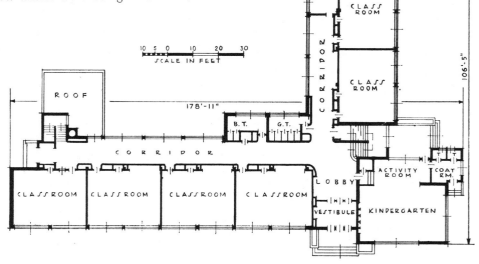

## Carl L. Bailey School
*Hillsdale, Michigan*

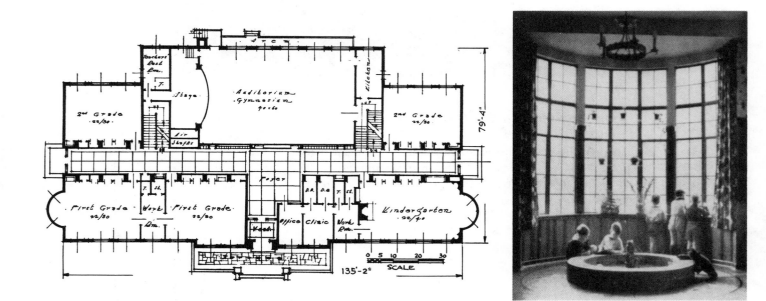

The old school that occupied the site on which this school was built was in such poor condition that portions of it had been closed by the State fire marshal.

The new school is 2 stories in height and approximately 135 by 79 feet in plan. It provides 13 standard classrooms for 385 pupils, a kindergarten, an auditorium-gymnasium with a stage, and the necessary administrative offices.

The floors and stairways are of fireproof construction and the exterior walls are red brick trimmed with wood. The building was completed in December 1936 at a construction cost of $106,686 and a project cost of $116,000.

West Side Elementary School for Colored, *Chattanooga*, *Tennessee*

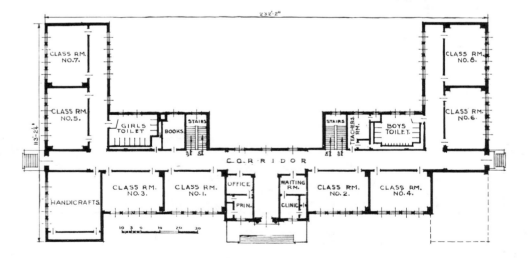

This project consisted of the construction, alteration, addition, or repair of 13 school buildings. The West Side School for Colored Children is a two-story structure containing administrative offices, classrooms, and a library. It is semifireproof, with concrete frame and floors, exterior walls of brick trimmed with limestone, and a roof of wood covered with slate. It has a volume of 546,235 cubic feet. Heat is provided from a boiler room in a small basement. It was completed in March 1937 at a construction cost of $109,725 and a project cost of $118,503.

## Old Orchard School, *Toledo, Ohio*

This school is 1 unit of a P. W. A. docket which included 18 new school buildings and repairs to 35 others. Its site is large and provides ample playground space.

The building accommodates 480 pupils. It has a central auditorium-gymnasium flanked by 2 wings containing 8 standard classrooms, a kindergarten, a library, domestic science room, and shop.

The traditional design is carried out in red brick with stone trim. It was completed in February 1937 at a construction cost of $228,275 and a project cost of $251,092.

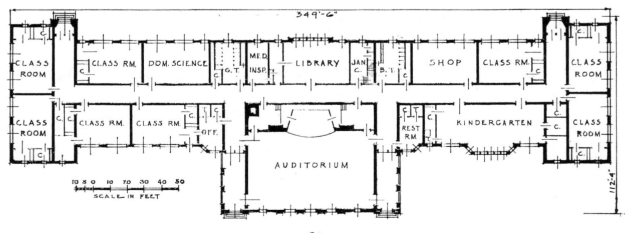

## North and South Miami Beach Elementary Schools, *Miami Beach, Florida*

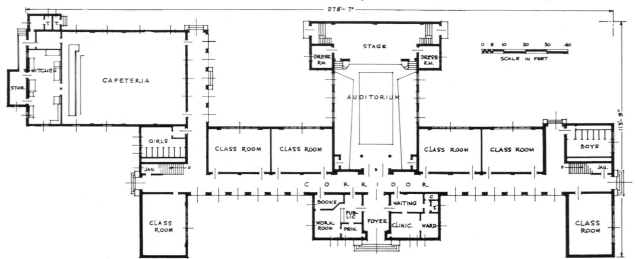

These two elementary schools were part of a program which included also a high school illustrated elsewhere in this volume. The North Beach School, illustrated above, is 2 stories in height and contains 12 classrooms, a clinic, 2 offices, 4 restrooms, a cafeteria, and a physical education room. The South Beach School, illustrated below and by the plan, also 2 stories in height, contains 11 classrooms, an auditorium, a cafeteria, offices, a clinic, 4 restrooms, and a physical-education room. Completed in September 1937, the construction costs were $127,176 for the North Beach School and $138,465 for the South Beach School, and the project costs were $139,486 and $150,190, respectively.

## Frankfort Elementary School

*Frankfort, Kentucky*

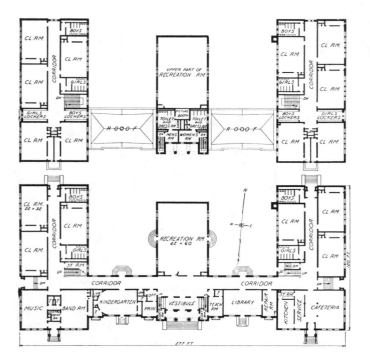

This elementary school replaced an old building which for a number of years had been considered unfit for school purposes by the board of education.

The plan of the structure is E shaped, the central portion and 2 wings being 2 stories in height and the rest being 1 story. The first floor provides 8 classrooms, a kindergarten, library, cafeteria, and recreation room. On the second floor are 10 classrooms.

The foundation walls are local quarry stone, the footings and framing are concrete, and the exterior walls are red brick with stone trim.

The project was completed in April 1937 at a construction cost of $221,325 and a project cost of $232,629.

## Hyde Park School, *Memphis*, *Tennessee*

This is a grade school for colored children constructed by the board of education of the city of Memphis.

The building is one story high with two inner courts. The outside dimensions are approximately 214 by 284 feet. Each courtyard is 60 feet square. There are 24 classrooms, 4 offices, and an auditorium 43 feet wide by 81 feet long, with a stage at the end 15 feet deep.

The exterior walls are brick and the interior partitions are hollow clay tile. The floor slabs are reinforced concrete. The roof is frame construction supported by steel trusses. The building is semifireproof.

The project was completed in September 1936. The cost of construction was $157,627 and the cost of the project was $175,692.

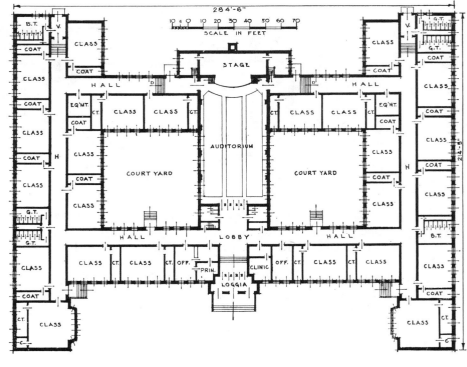

Jefferson School, *Creston, Iowa*

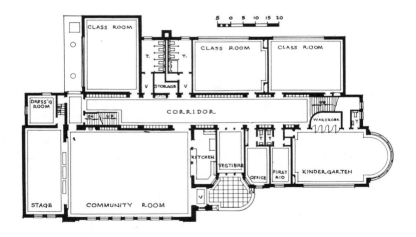

Creston is located in the southwestern part of the State, at the headwaters of the Platte River. In 1930 its population was 8,615.

This grade school contains 6 classrooms, a principal's office, a kindergarten, and a community room seating 350, with a stage. The community room has a separate entrance at the main entrance of the building. It provides space for local community meetings.

The construction is fire resistive. The floors are covered with asphalt tile. The exterior walls are of light colored brick with limestone trim. Photoelectric cells automatically control lighting in the classrooms.

The building was completed in October 1937 at a construction cost of $74,629 and a project cost of $81,662.

## Holmes Elementary School, *Lincoln, Nebraska*

The Holmes School occupies a 10-acre plot, thus providing ample space for playgrounds. It accommodates 160 pupils.

The building is one story and a basement in height, and is T-shaped in plan. It contains three classrooms, a combination library and museum, a playroom, a storage room for bicycles, and a community room which has a stage and a kitchen.

The construction is semifireproof. Exterior walls are brick trimmed with wood, the floor is reinforced concrete, and the roof is wood covered with slate. It was completed in August 1937 at a construction cost of $58,401 and a project cost of $61,030.

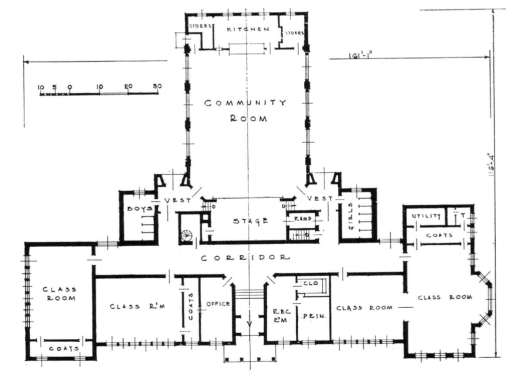

Grade School

*Parco, Wyoming*

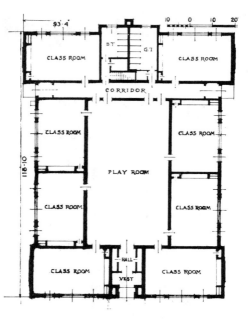

The town of Parco is in Carbon County, Wyoming, located 7 miles east of Rawlins, which is the county seat and a division point on the Union Pacific Railroad. Carbon County is the largest agricultural county in the State. The new building replaced a leased 4-room dilapidated wooden structure and two apartments rented for classrooms in an apartment building.

It provides eight classrooms and a centrally located combination playroom-auditorium with clerestory windows.

The construction is semifireproof, the walls being brick and the roof wood covered with Spanish tile. The exterior walls are faced with two colors of brick, the darker shade being used for a base and trim around the entrance and certain windows.

It was completed in December 1936 at a construction cost of $46,722 and a project cost of $50,913.

Lily B. Clayton School Addition, *Fort Worth, Texas*

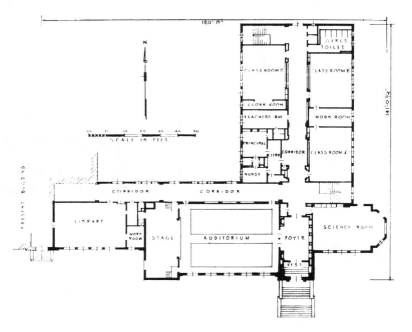

This structure is one unit of a large rehabilitation and building program begun by the Fort Worth Independent School District in 1934. The addition provides six classrooms, a library, a kindergarten, a cafeteria, and an auditorium seating 400. The construction is reinforced concrete with wood roof framing. Exterior walls are faced with buff brick and trimmed with artificial stone of a similar color. With the addition, the school will accommodate 480 pupils. It was completed in February 1938 at a construction cost of $110,313 and a project cost of $115,644.

## Day School and Community Center, *Moenave, Arizona*

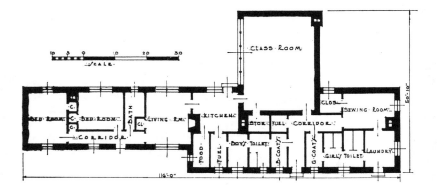

The day school and community center shown in the upper photograph is located in the Western Navajo District at Moenave, Ariz. It is one of five buildings of similar character constructed by the Office of Indian Affairs, Department of the Interior.

It houses the teachers' living quarters, a classroom, and space for community activities. The section for the school and the community activities is 65 by 26 feet, exclusive of the classroom wing. The section containing the living quarters is 51 by 20 feet and has two bedrooms, a living room, bath, and a kitchen. The classroom is constructed so that another room may be added. Other facilities in the building include a sewing room, laundry, storage rooms, cloak rooms, and showers.

Local materials were employed almost exclusively. The exterior walls are adobe blocks and the roofs are covered with adobe.

The smaller photograph shows a group of the hogan-type school and community structures connected by a communicating passage. Each hogan houses a classroom or community activity. The dome roofs are covered with adobe.

The five buildings were completed at a project cost of $143,565.

## Eugene Ware Public School
### *Fort Scott, Kansas*

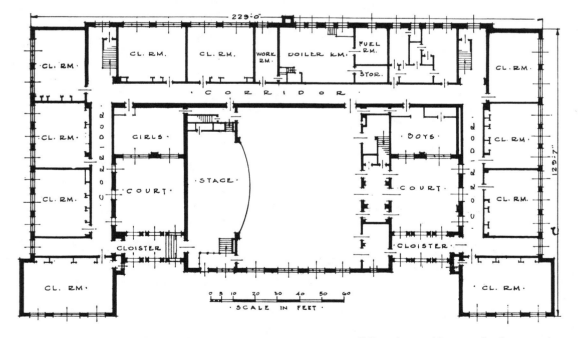

This new school replaces two obsolete buildings approximately 50 years old. It is part one and part two stories in height and provides eight standard classrooms, two primary classrooms, a principal's office, a teachers' room, a workroom, and the auditorium which has a well-equipped stage and a kitchen.

The building is semifireproof. Its exterior walls are red face brick trimmed with stone and the cupola is wood.

It was completed in June 1935 at a construction cost of $157,116 and a project cost of $190,640.

## Vernon School, *Wyandotte, Kansas*

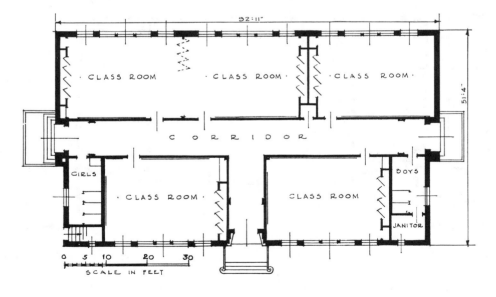

This small school was erected in the Wyandotte school district No. 17 to relieve serious overcrowding in the existing buildings. It is a one-story, semifireproof structure with exterior brick walls and a stone entrance. It provides five classrooms and was completed in July 1936 at a construction cost of $21,030 and a project cost of $22,400.

New York Street Grade School, *Lawrence, Kansas*

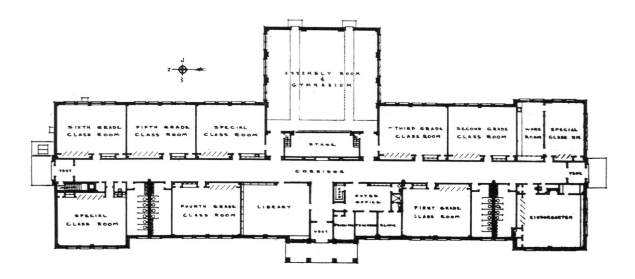

This school provides 6 standard classrooms, 3 special classrooms, a kindergarten, a library, administrative offices, and a combination assembly hall and gymnasium with a stage. All of the classrooms are equipped for 38 students except one of the special classrooms, which is equipped for 20.

The building is constructed with a reinforced concrete foundation, frame, floor slab, and ceiling slab. The exterior walls are red brick backed with concrete blocks, which form the finished wall on the inside. The pitched roof is frame construction and is covered with asbestos shingles.

The volume of the structure is 380,000 cubic feet, and it was completed in November 1934 at a construction cost of $99,961 and a project cost of $125,819.

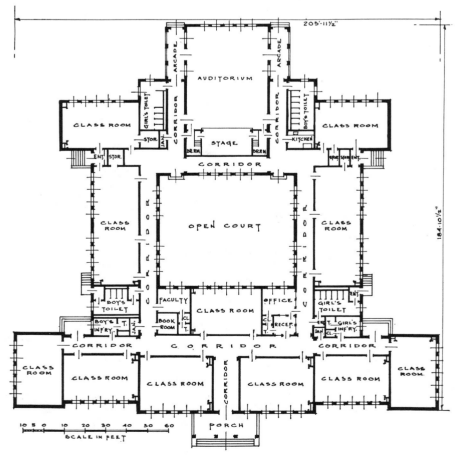

## North Crowley School

*Acadia Parish*

*Louisiana*

The school board of Acadia Parish undertook a large program in 1937–38 that involved the erection, enlargement, or reconditioning of 15 buildings, as well as modernization and furnishing of equipment throughout the school district. The North Crowley School is one of the new buildings. It is built around an interior court, is a one-story structure providing nine standard classrooms and two large classrooms, an auditorium with a stage, small kitchen, an office, a teachers' room, and small infirmaries for boys and girls. It is semifireproof with exterior brick walls and a tile-covered roof. It was completed in March 1938 at a construction cost of $206,851 and a project cost of $219,493.

Rogers School, *Rogers, Arkansas*

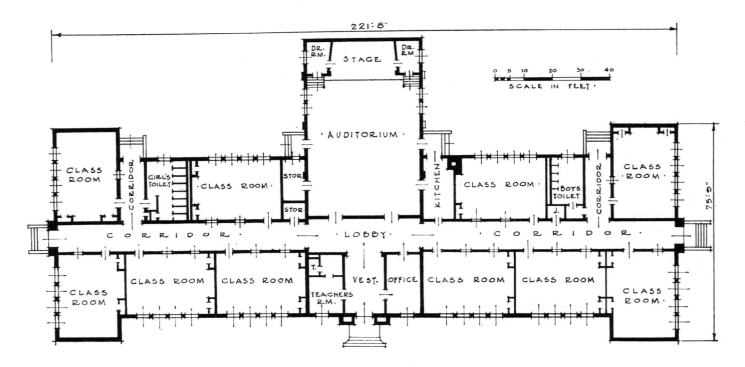

This school building replaces two worn-out structures which were demolished and some of the materials salvaged were re-used in the new building. It is 1 story in height and contains 10 classrooms, an office, a small kitchen, and an auditorium with a stage and dressing rooms. A small basement below the stage houses the heating plant. The construction is non-fireproof. Exterior walls are brick trimmed with wood and the floors and roof are wood. The project was completed in October 1936 at a construction cost of $50,321 and a project cost of $54,422.

Earthquake Damage—Corrective Measures, School Buildings, *State of California*

These six illustrations show typical examples of the damage to the school buildings of southern California by the major earthquake which occurred on March 10, 1933. Before this, seismic disturbances had not been given consideration in the design of school buildings. After the 1933 earthquake, the State Legislature enacted a law known as the Field Bill, requiring the State Division of Architecture to regulate, inspect, and supervise the construction, reconstruction, alteration, or addition to all public buildings in California, which, of course, included schools. Every structure is now required to withstand horizontal forces equal to one-tenth of its gravity factor and all the new schools constructed with P. W. A. aid conform to this wise regulation.

## Huntington Park Elementary School, *San Marino, California*

San Marino is a residential community 10 miles south of the city of Los Angeles. It had a population of 3,730 in 1930. Its new school plant consists of several buildings with a total floor area of 17,600 square feet and are typical of the architecture being produced in California at the present time. The illustration is of the sunlit court at one end of the classroom building.

The structure is one story in height and provides five classrooms, a children's rest room, a teachers' room, and a kindergarten to which are attached two workrooms. In addition to this, in the group, are buildings which provide administrative offices, an auditorium, gymnasium, shops, and rooms for domestic science and the arts.

The construction is a combination of concrete and wood frame, the exterior walls being finished in stucco and roof covered with mission tile. The project was completed in June 1938 at a construction cost of $95,251 and a project cost of $103,425.

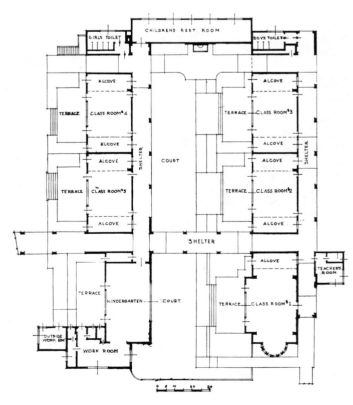

## Lugonia Kindergarten, *Redlands, California*

The Lugonia Kindergarten is entirely detached from other buildings on the school site.

It is a one story and basement structure which contains one classroom, a group room, a library, and workroom and a covered arcade or cloister. To break the monotony of the concrete surfaces of the ceiling, cork panels have been inserted in the roof slab and on the sides of the arched ceiling beams, which not only are decorative but are of acoustical value. The low tile wainscot has inserts of colored tile illustrating Mother Goose and other characters of fairy tales and fables.

The construction is designed to resist earthquake disturbances and consists of reinforced-concrete footings, walls, floor, and roof. The roof is covered with Spanish tile.

The project was completed in September 1937 at a construction cost of $38,562 and a project cost of $43,238.

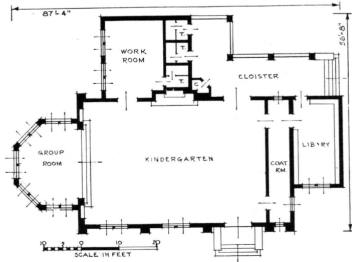

Sunshine School, *San Francisco, California*

The school for crippled and undernourished children in San Francisco, which is commonly known as the "Sunshine School," is specially designed to care for the education of the physically handicapped children of the city.

The building is two stories in height. The first floor is entirely devoted to crippled children and provides every facility for their education and care. The patio provides an ideal play area in which they can move about freely in their wheel chairs or can engage in any type of athletics or sports that their condition permits. The second floor is devoted to the undernourished and cardiac-case children. It should be specially noted that each classroom on this floor is provided with a rest room which has a glass roof to admit the sunlight and which is provided with cots for use during the rest periods.

One of the most interesting features of the equipment is the therapeutic bathing pool, which is raised about 3 feet above the floor to facilitate the handling of the physically handicapped children.

The illustration on this page shows the street facade of the school and the main entrance.

*Continued on following page.*

major and minor earthquake disturbances. A considerable use is made of decorative tile which greatly adds to the color and reflection of light. Everything possible has been done to create the most cheerful possible atmosphere in order to encourage the children to forget as far as possible their disabilities. Each dining room is provided with a small stage on the side opposite the doors opening onto the patio. There is a corrective gymnasium on each floor and, in addition to the classrooms on the first floor, there are rooms for manual training, art, music, and domestic science, and a small library.

*Continued on following page*

## Sunshine School
### *San Francisco, California*

*Continued from preceding page*

The illustrations on this page show two views of the patio playground with its paved areas surrounded by the arcades of the building. The two plans show the arrangement of rooms on both floors.

The entire building is constructed of reinforced concrete, is fireproof throughout, and is designed to resist both

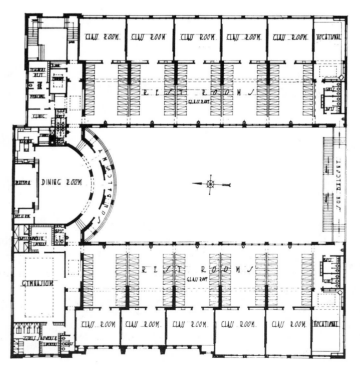

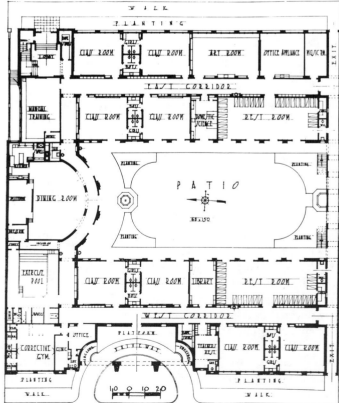

## Sunshine School, *San Francisco, California*

*Continued from preceding page*

The illustrations on this page show the main entrance, one of the dining rooms, a rest room on the second floor, and the therapeutic bathing pool.

The whole building has been well and thoughtfully designed and carried out. Where special purpose structures are required, this may well serve as a model in planning and general arrangement.

The project was completed in September 1937 at a construction cost of $268,987 and a project cost of $287,713.

## Las Vegas Grammar School, *Las Vegas, Nevada*

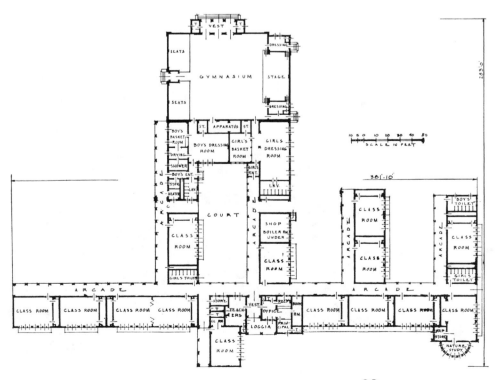

The old Las Vegas grammar school was destroyed by fire in 1934 and tents had to be used for classes until this new building could be completed.

It includes six separate classroom buildings all connected by arcades. The accommodations consist of 14 classrooms, a shop, teachers' and principal's offices, and a gymnasium with a stage, dressing rooms, and some seating.

The construction is entirely reinforced concrete except for the roof, which is wood covered with tile.

The floor area is 35,000 square feet and the project was completed in October 1936 at a construction cost of $184,923 and a project cost of $217, 093.

Wellesley Senior High School, *Wellesley, Massachusetts*

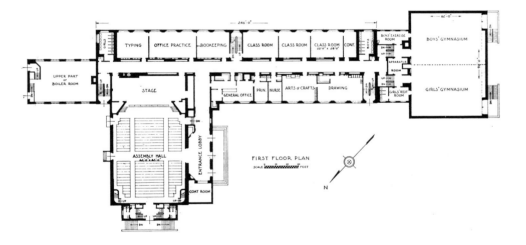

FIRST FLOOR PLAN

Wellesley is a residential suburb of the Boston area. Due to the rapid increase in population, there has been need for a large senior high school for many years.

This new building has 70 rooms, accommodating 750 students. There are 17 standard classrooms, 4 conference rooms, 6 laboratories, and an industrial-art shop. Besides these, the special rooms are a library, music room, auditorium with balcony and stage, cafeteria also used as a study hall, 3 conference rooms; a gymnasium for boys and another for girls, which, by means of a sliding partition, can be made into one large room; library convertible into a study hall, apparatus room, special exercise room, girls' rest room, lockers, and shower rooms. The miscellaneous service rooms are 2 rooms for teachers, 5 for officers, rooms for bicycles and science apparatus, laundry, kitchen, serving room, 4 storerooms, janitor's rooms, and 2 clothes-drying rooms.

The building is carried on steel-jacket concrete piles from 40 to 50 feet long. The framing is reinforced concrete, except steel framing in the auditorium and gymnasium. The floor slabs are reinforced concrete. The building was completed in August 1938 at a construction cost of $690,072 and a project cost of $755,182.

## Fitchburg High School
*Fitchburg, Massachusetts*

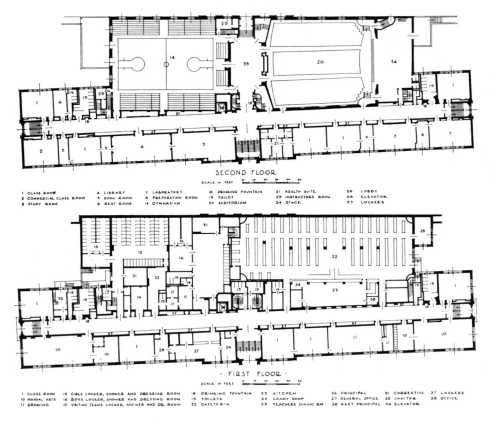

SECOND FLOOR

SCALE IN FEET

1 CLASS ROOM          4 LIBRARY          7 LABORATORY          18 DRINKING FOUNTAIN     21 HEALTH SUITE        35 LOBBY
2 COMMERCIAL CLASS ROOM    5 BOOK ROOM         8 PREPARATION ROOM     19 TOILET               25 INSTRUCTORS ROOM     36 ELEVATOR
3 STUDY ROOM           6 REST ROOM         14 GYMNASIUM            20 AUDITORIUM           34 STAGE               37 LOCKERS

· FIRST FLOOR ·

SCALE IN FEET

1 CLASS ROOM     15 GIRLS LOCKER, SHOWER AND DRESSING ROOM    18 DRINKING FOUNTAIN    23 KITCHEN           26 PRINCIPAL        31 CORRECTIVE     37 LOCKERS
10 MANUAL ARTS    16 BOYS LOCKER, SHOWER AND DRESSING ROOM     19 TOILETS              24 CANDY SHOP        27 GENERAL OFFICE    33 JANITOR        38 OFFICE
11 DRAWING       17 VISITING TEAMS LOCKER, SHOWER AND DR. ROOM  22 CAFETERIA            25 TEACHERS DINING RM  28 ASS'T PRINCIPAL   36 ELEVATOR

One of the Fitchburg high schools was destroyed by fire and the resulting crowding of students into other buildings necessitated the erection of this new four-story structure.

The first floor contains administrative offices, 5 classrooms, a printing shop, mechanical drawing and manual training rooms, a cafeteria seating 700, and locker rooms. The second floor has 5 classrooms, 2 biology laboratories, a health suite, a study, library, bookkeeping room, and an auditorium seating 1,508, with a stage. There is also a gymnasium with bleacher seats for 958 and a folding partition to divide it for boys and girls. The third floor contains 4 classrooms, 3 typewriting rooms, 2 bookkeeping rooms, a physics laboratory and chemistry laboratory with connecting lecture room, and the auditorium balcony. On the fourth floor are 10 classrooms, a bookkeeping room, food laboratory, sewing room, demonstration and storage rooms, a study, 2 biology laboratories, an oral English and music room with stage, and a freehand drawing room.

The project was completed in November 1937 at a construction cost of $1,123,709 and a project cost of $1,228,618.

## Hope Street Senior High School, *Providence, Rhode Island*

Enrollment of 3,050 students in 1923 in the three senior high schools in Providence increased 130 percent in 10 years to a total of 7,010. To meet this increase, the Hope Street Senior High School replaced a former building and the Mount Pleasant High School is a new unit.

The Hope Street High School is one of the largest high schools in America, accommodating 2,200 pupils. It is in the vicinity of Brown University. It has 60 classrooms, an auditorium seating 1,285, a large stage and sound-moving-picture equipment, a library, study hall, cafeteria which

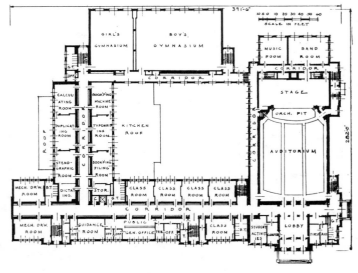

accommodates 700 at one sitting, modern kitchen facilities, boys' gymnasium, and a girls' gymnasium with 105 individual shower stalls. There are special rooms for woodworking, art metal, machine-shop work, music rooms, and music library.

It is fireproof. The main entrance doors are bronze, the library, study room, and main offices are paneled in white oak. The building is 391 by 282 feet and has a volume of 4,438,960 cubic feet.

It was completed in June 1936 at a construction cost of $1,979,068 and a project cost of $1,995,748.

## Ansonia High School

### *Ansonia, Connecticut*

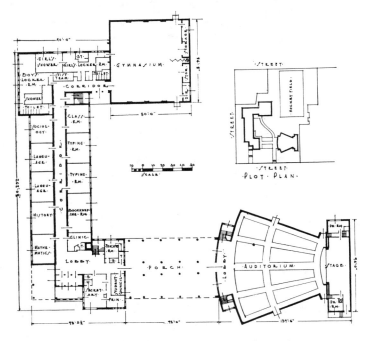

The plan of this building is a departure from the customary school plan. The auditorium is separated from the classroom wing by an open porch, above which are classrooms. The building contains 24 classrooms, administrative offices, a small clinic, a gymnasium, and an auditorium seating 752 students and having a well-equipped stage. The shape of the structure allows extensive playing fields on the property.

The construction consists of salmon-colored brick backed with tile for exterior walls, concrete floor slabs supported by Lally columns, structural steel girders, and beams.

The volume of the building is 1,200,000 cubic feet. It was completed in October 1937 at a construction cost of $412,251 and a project cost of $459,391.

Jonathan Dayton Regional High School, *Springfield, New Jersey*

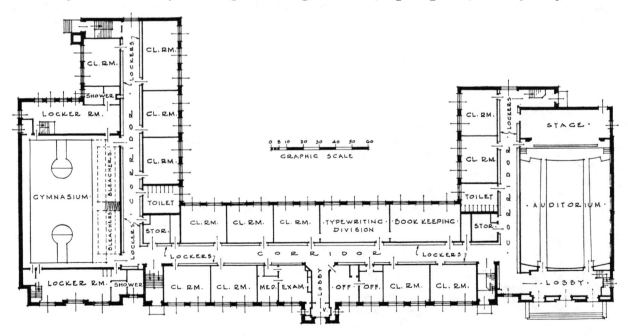

This high school in Union County accommodates the students of 7 communities which formerly had no high-school facilities within their boundaries. Its site has an area of 16½ acres and has been graded and landscaped and provided with playing and athletic fields. The building is 2 stories and a part basement in height and contains in the basement a cafeteria, kitchen, print shop, general shop, and storage rooms. On the first floor is an auditorium, gymnasium, 13 classrooms, administration offices, and rooms for bookkeeping and typewriting. On the second floor are 7 classrooms, a library, teachers' rooms, locker rooms, and rooms for physics, chemistry, general science, biology, art, and domestic science. The construction is steel and concrete with exterior walls of brick trimmed with limestone and wood, and the roof is wood, slate-covered. The project was completed in July 1937 at a construction cost of $475,618 and a project cost of $542,039.

## Norwalk High School, *Norwalk, Connecticut*

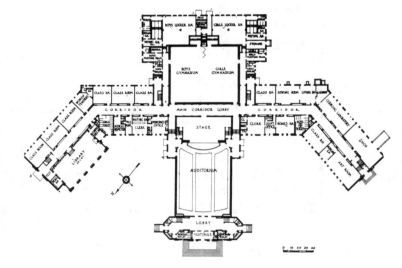

This structure replaces an old high-school building which had become inadequate to care for the student body of 1,200.

The building contains 32 classrooms, an auditorium, boys' and girls' gymnasiums, administrative offices, a library, domestic science rooms, shops, a study hall, a cafeteria, and rooms for music.

The construction consists of a steel frame, exterior brick bearing walls trimmed with cast stone and reinforced concrete floor slabs on metal lumber.

The structure is three stories and a basement in height and its dominating feature is the tower at the auditorium entrance. It was completed in December 1937 at a construction cost of $789,379 and a project cost of $909,689.

## Manhasset High School
### *Manhasset, New York*

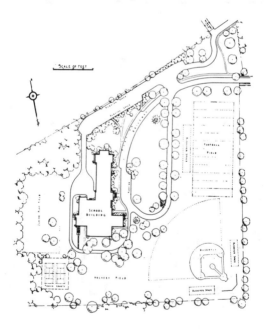

Manhasset is a suburb of New York City located on the northern shore of Long Island. This school is situated on a 22-acre lot, rolling in character, and overlooks Manhasset Bay. The grounds are arranged for football and baseball fields, archery, junior playgrounds, tennis courts, and landscaped areas.

The building is not symmetrical in plan. It contains seven classrooms of the types used in the best modern schools and also a large greenhouse where flowers are grown and transplanted into the school gardens by the pupils.

It is of fire-resistant construction with special interior finish. The exterior walls are brick, trimmed with stone.

Its over-all dimensions are 312 by 144 feet. It was completed in December 1936 at a construction cost of $467,945 and a project cost of $516,736.

Franklin K. Lane High School, *Brooklyn, New York*

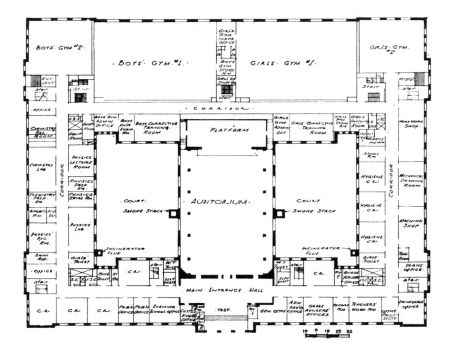

This is one of the largest and most modern schools in New York City and has been highly rated by the Municipal Art Commission. It is in a residential district.

It contains the usual administrative offices, service rooms, 84 classrooms, library, commercial museum, 4 gymnasiums, rooms for social activity, homemaking, artcraft, 8 drawing rooms, a swimming pool, and an auditorium. The student capacity is 1,700. The construction is fireproof. Marble and Caen stone are used in the lobby and auditorium.

The building is 362 feet long by 284 feet wide, with a basement, four stories and penthouse, and is 82 feet high. It was completed in March 1938 at a construction cost of $3,274,867 and a project cost of $3,421,830.

## South Junior High School
### *Newburgh, New York*

The South Junior High School at Newburgh is one of 2 schools which comprised this project. It is on the highest point of a 12-acre site and commands a superb view of the Highlands of the Hudson. It serves 19 percent of the area of the city and 39 percent of its population. The building is 2 stories in height with a small third story devoted to a band practice room, a choral room, and a room for public speaking. On the first floor is an auditorium seating 500, a gymnasium, 6 classrooms, rooms for special subjects, a lunch room, study hall, library, a small clinic, and administration offices. The second floor contains the domestic-science department, 4 classrooms, 2 art rooms, teachers' rooms, 2 science rooms, and a storeroom. The exterior walls are red brick on a granite base and are trimmed with limestone. The roofs are covered with slate. The project was completed in November 1937. The estimated construction cost of the South Junior High School is $536,905 and the project cost $640,971. The construction cost of both schools was $1,165,110 and their project cost $1,391,341.

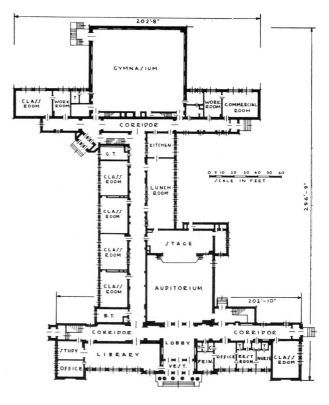

## Chancellor Livingston High School, *Hudson, New York*

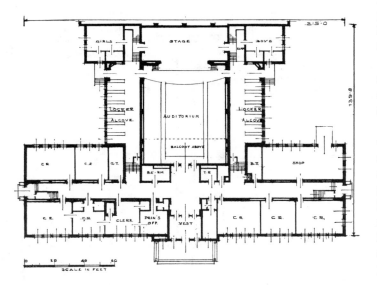

Hudson, New York, is located on the east side of the Hudson River, about 40 miles south of Albany. In 1930 it had a population of 12,337. The former high school, which is now being used as a junior high school, became seriously overcrowded.

The new building contains special rooms for a shop, library, music, art, homemaking, science, and a cafeteria, as well as an adequate number of classrooms. It has a gymnasium and an auditorium.

The construction is fire resistive, with brick exterior bearing walls and interior steel columns and steel joists. The exterior trim is limestone and the roof is covered with slate. The cornices, railings, and the cupola are wood. The classrooms and auditorium have mastic tile floors and the gymnasium has a wood floor with a cork wainscot. All of the principal rooms have acoustic ceilings. The entrance vestibule and lobby have wainscots of marble and the corridors of terra cotta. The over-all dimensions of the building are 215 by 140 feet. It has a basement, three stories, and a storage attic.

It was completed in November 1937 at a construction cost of $456,169 and a project cost of $508,674.

Pierre S. Dupont High School, *Wilmington*, *Delaware*

This new high school stands on a 25-acre site which is provided with an athletic field, bleachers, tennis courts, basketball field, and a practice field.   The building replaced an old structure which was much smaller and in which a half-time program was necessary.

The plan is somewhat irregular with over-all dimensions of approximately 489 by 303 feet.  It contains 33 standard classrooms, 46 special rooms, a gymnasium for girls, one for boys, a corrective gymnasium, a cafeteria, auditorium, library, library classrooms, rooms for public speaking, general science rooms, a room for mechanical drawing, laboratories for biology, chemistry, and physics, and rooms for typewriting, bookkeeping, office practice, commercial practice, art, music, and domestic science.

The building is three stories high with a partial basement and is constructed with a skeleton steel frame, brick bearing walls, and floors of reinforced concrete.  The exterior walls are faced with red brick and trimmed with stone and terra cotta.  The project was completed in September 1935 at a construction cost of $1,619,575 and a project cost of $1,885,444.

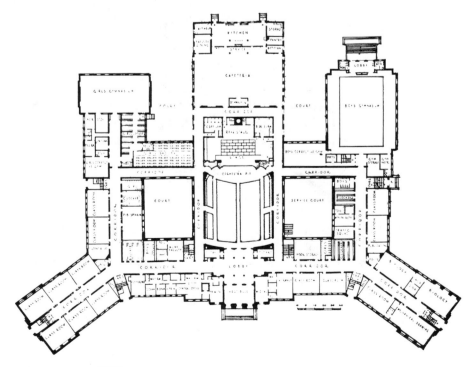

## Junior and Senior High School, *Glen Cove, New York*

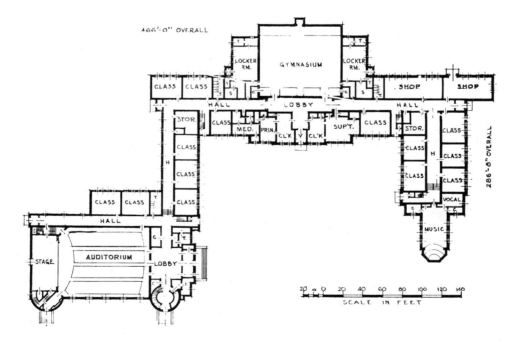

The city of Glen Cove is on the north shore of Long Island and is surrounded by one of the fashionable residential areas of the district. In 1930 the population of the city was 11,430. This building replaces an old frame high school built in 1893.

Among the rooms on the first floor are 14 classrooms, a gymnasium, auditorium, offices, music room, and wood and metal workrooms. The second floor has two art rooms, two men teachers' rooms, seven classrooms, a study, lunch room,

kitchen, workroom, library, study hall, student activity room, laboratories, and domestic science room.

The building is fireproof. The interior walls are cinder concrete block. The roof framing is of bar joists, covered with 4-inch gypsum plank.

The project was completed in June 1939 at a construction cost of $716,131 and a project cost of $823,342.

High School Annex, *Punxsutawney, Pennsylvania*

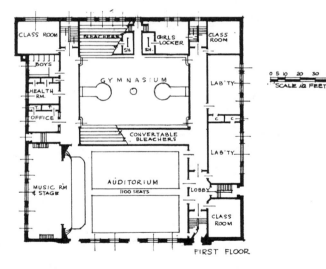

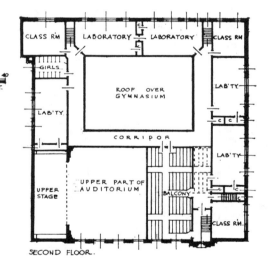

The existing high school at Punxsutawney is on the opposite side of the street from this new annex and could not be expanded due to the fact that permanent structures were on each side of it.

This annex is 2 stories and a basement in height with over-all dimensions approximately 150 by 150 feet in plan and provides 6 classrooms, an auditorium seating 1,100, a gymnasium with accommodations for 1,000 spectators, medical and administrative offices, and 7 laboratories.

The construction is fire resistant. It is of the wall-bearing type, with steel studs in interior partitions. The gymnasium floor is carried on wood joists. The auditorium floor is a concrete slab laid on earth. All other floor construction is carried on steel joists. The gymnasium and auditorium roofs are carried on clear span trusses. Other roof sections are on steel joists.

The exterior walls are salmon-colored sand-finished brick with Kasota stone for the base, coping caps and part of the door trim. Some Virginia serpentine is also used for the door trim. Glass block panels, which are surrounded with black brick, are used instead of windows on the street front. The spandrels above these panels are black brick with slate caps. The auditorium is mechanically ventilated. The entrance doors are heavy paneled oak, decorated in color and gold leaf. The floors are linoleum in the classrooms, maple in the laboratories, and colored cement in the corridors.

The project was completed in July 1937 at a construction cost of $198,083 and a project cost of $240,768.

## John Piersol McCaskey High School, *Lancaster, Pennsylvania*

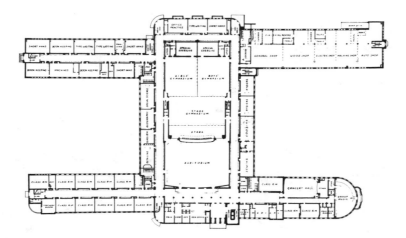

This high school occupies a site of 35 acres. Large play areas, 7 fields for games, 6 tennis courts, and 12 handball courts, as well as a stadium seating 2,626 and bleachers seating 1,000, are part of the plant.

The building accommodates 2,500 pupils. The academic, commercial, and science departments are in the wings on the left; and the shops, domestic science, and art departments on the right, with the auditorium and gymnasium between them. There are 52 standard and 30 special classrooms, a library seating 250, and a cafeteria with a capacity of 625.

The construction is fireproof. Exterior walls are red brick with limestone trim and lead-coated copper spandrels between windows. It was completed in February 1938 at a construction cost of $1,166,121 and a project cost of $1,383,020.

## Senior High School

*Norristown, Pennsylvania*

Norristown is near Philadelphia, to the northwest, on the Schuylkill River. In 1930 the population was 35,853.

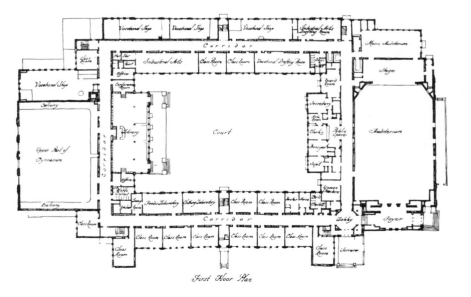

*First Floor Plan*

The building contains 65 rooms, including shops, laboratories, music rooms, an auditorium seating 2,011 people, a cafeteria for 600, a library for 120, and 2 gymnasiums which when thrown together make a room 88 by 112 feet. There is an outdoor theater and stage, with sloping, sodded seats of 3,300 capacity. The building is fireproof. The exterior walls are brick with limestone trim.

It was completed in April 1938 at a construction cost of $1,012,928 and a total project cost of $1,114,009.

# Central High School

## *Philadelphia, Pennsylvania*

The first Central High School in Philadelphia was built in 1838 and was the oldest high school in the United States outside of New England. It was replaced in 1844 and in 1900. This project replaces that erected in 1900.

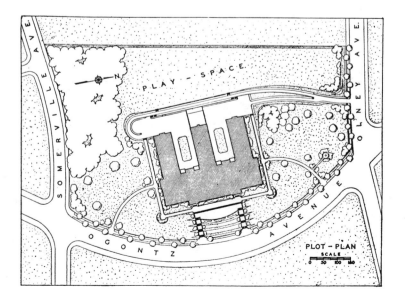

The building provides an extensive administration suite including a doctor's office, an infirmary, 28 classrooms, a lunch room for 1,000, a faculty lunch room for 60, a gymnasium, an auditorium with a capacity of 1,500, a library, and many art and science rooms and laboratories.

The front portion of the building is of structural steel with reinforced concrete floor slabs. The framing of the rear wings is of reinforced concrete construction. The library is finished in American walnut with an ornamental ceiling. The corridors have wainscots of marble or of tile.

The over-all dimensions are 369 by 262 feet. It was completed in September 1938 at a construction cost of $2,072,825 and a project cost of $2,461,444.

Knoebel School, *Knoebel, Maryland*

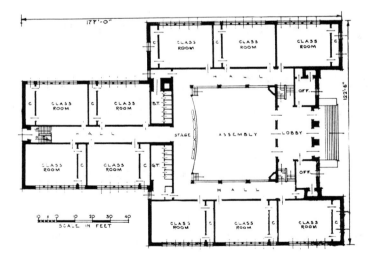

The Knoebel School was erected on a site of 10¾ acres and the project included a road to the school building from the county highway, an artesian well, and a septic tank. The nearest farm house is a half mile distant. The school consolidates and replaces six small schools of the one- or two-teacher type.

The building contains 10 standard classrooms, also rooms for home economics and industrial art and administration offices.

The construction is fire resistant. Exterior walls are a random rustic ashlar of local stone and trim. Windows and doors are wood.

The structure has an area of approximately 16,950 square feet. It was completed in September 1935 at a construction cost of $107,186 and a project cost of $115,629.

## Montgomery Blair High School, *Silver Spring, Maryland*

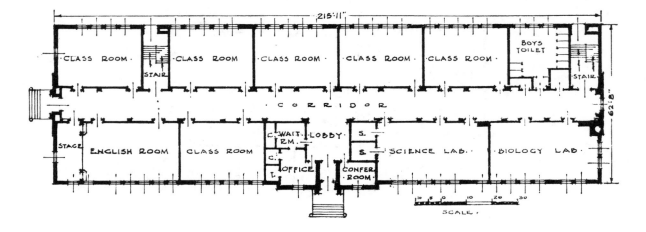

Silver Spring is a residential suburb of Washington, D. C., and two sides of the property on which the school has been erected adjoin a section of the National Capital park system in which are large playing fields and tennis courts.

The building contains 13 classrooms, a special English classroom with a stage, administrative offices, a conference room, laboratories for science and biology, a library, rooms for music and domestic science, and a cafeteria for the students. The school was named for the Postmaster General of President Lincoln's Cabinet.

The construction is steel frame with reinforced-concrete floor slabs, exterior walls of red brick trimmed with limestone and wood, and a roof covered with slate. Acoustical plaster is generally used for the ceilings.

The project was completed in September 1935 at a construction cost of $209,234 and a project cost of $275,013.

Bethesda-Chevy Chase Senior High School, *Bethesda, Maryland*

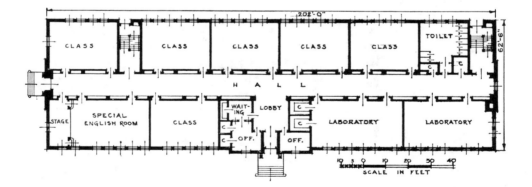

This senior high school has been built on a plot of ground not only large enough for athletic fields and tennis courts but of sufficient size to allow for future buildings when the school needs to expand. The main building contains 13 classrooms, English classrooms with stages, laboratories for science and biology, rooms for music and domestic science, a library, and a cafeteria. The construction is steel and concrete, with exterior walls of brick trimmed with stone and wood. It was completed in September 1935 at a construction cost of $218,440 and a project cost of $287,419.

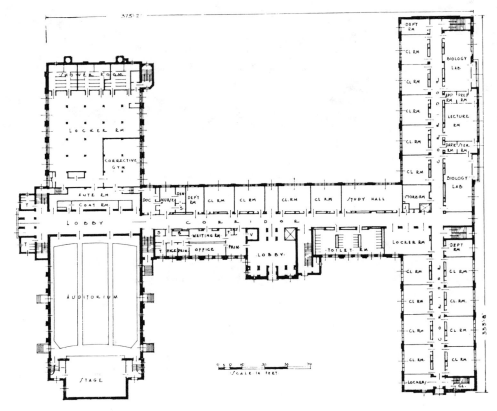

## Eastern High School for Girls

### *Baltimore, Maryland*

This high school, which has a student body of 2,520 girls, occupies a site of 24 acres in Venable Park, which is developed into an athletic field, a quarter-mile running track, fields for archery, handball, tennis, and badminton courts.

Of the 75 classrooms, 25 are equipped for special instruc-tion. There are also a lunchroom, an auditorium seating 2,200, and a gymnasium 80 by 129 feet with folding partition and folding bleachers seating 800.

The building is fireproof of the wall-bearing type. Columns and floor slabs are reinforced concrete and the auditorium and gymnasium roofs are concrete supported on steel trusses. Exterior walls are brick trimmed with limestone. The project was completed in July 1938 at a construction cost of $1,473,981 and a project cost of $1,532,717.

## Western High School, *Detroit, Michigan*

The new Western High School replaced, on a greatly enlarged scale, a high-school building that was destroyed by fire in the winter of 1935. It occupies the same site as this former building.

The building is three stories and a partial basement in height and is approximately 300 feet square. The auditorium, which is 96 by 110 feet, occupies the core of the structure and is entirely surrounded by corridors from which open the classrooms and laboratories.

The auditorium is on the first floor. It seats 1,300 on this floor, and its balcony, which is entered from the second and third floor corridors, accommodates 700 more. The stage is very well equipped. On the first floor are administrative offices, 2 large study halls, a music department, biology department, shop 36 by 110 feet, a large cafeteria, and a garage and repair shop. The second floor is occupied by the library, study halls, laboratories, classrooms, and the gymnasium. The third floor accommodates classes in typewriting, bookkeeping, the arts, mechanical drawing, and the physics laboratory.

The building is fireproof throughout. The exterior walls are red face brick with stone and wood trim.

The project was completed in August 1937. It has a volume of 3,500,000 cubic feet. The construction cost was $1,082,058 and the project cost $1,136,309.

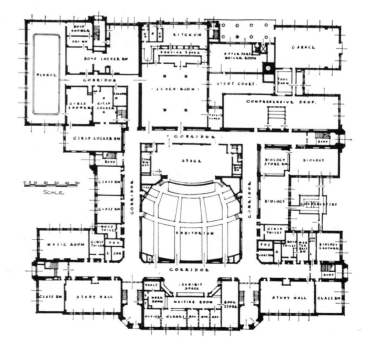

Junior High School, *Sheboygan, Wisconsin*

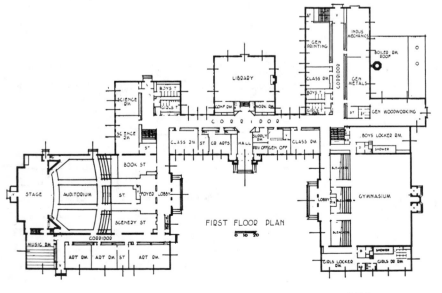

FIRST FLOOR PLAN

This building is approximately 256 by 388 feet. It contains administrative offices, library, auditorium seating 1,000, double gymnasium, and classrooms for art, music, biology, general science, mechanical drawing, printing, woodworking, and metal working, a study hall seating 200, 25 classrooms, and a cafeteria. The building has a volume of 1,900,000 cubic feet. The entire construction is fireproof.

The project was completed in June 1938 at a construction cost of $583,312 and a project cost of $654,468, including about $33,000 for land.

## Mariemont High School
### *Mariemont, Ohio*

Mariemont is located on the outskirts of Cincinnati, to the northeast. It was laid out in 1928 as a housing development. About 25 architects were selected from all over the country to participate in the building of the town.

This new combined junior and senior high school serves this town and the adjoining village of Plainville. It has 12 classrooms, a combined auditorium and gymnasium, cafeteria, a manual training department, domestic science room, library, laboratories, and the usual other facilities.

It is fireproof, faced with mottled colored brick, and contains 772,000 cubic feet.

It was completed in July 1939, at a construction cost of $249,196 and a project cost of approximately $292,000.

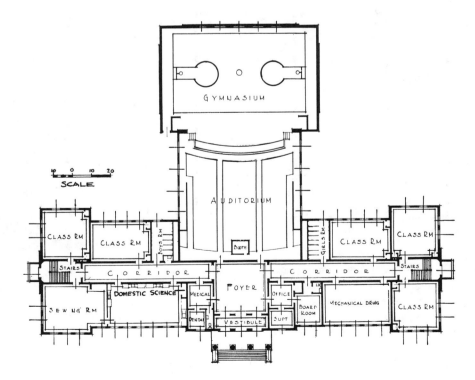

211

## Macomber Vocational High School, *Toledo*, *Ohio*

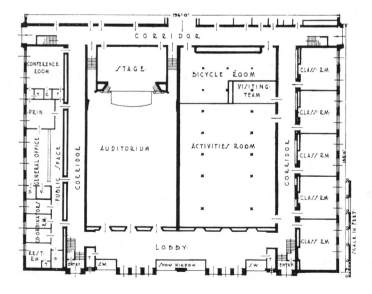

by dismantling and assembling standard equipment and in which the essentials of many trades are taught.

The building is fireproof, of structural steel and reinforced concrete. The exterior walls are faced with brick and trimmed with stone. Its volume is 4,270,000 cubic feet and it was completed in July 1939 at a construction cost of $1,545,948 and a project cost of $1,716,838.

This new vocational high school is part of an extensive school-construction program in Toledo which involved 19 new school buildings and repair work on many others. It is a unit for boys in the upper 3 years of high school, is 3 stories in height and contains an auditorium with a stage, a library, gymnasium, 17 classrooms, 12 laboratories, and 18 shops where students can learn the fundamentals of engineering mechanics

Columbia High School, *Columbia, Mississippi*

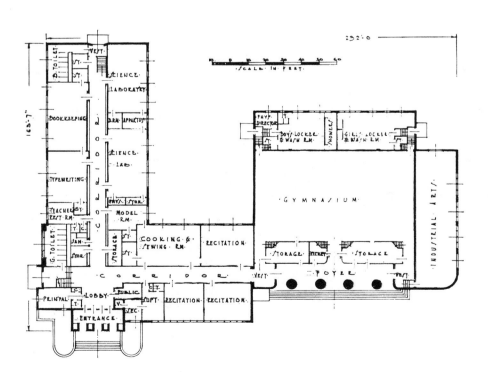

Columbia is the county seat of Marion County, in the southern central part of Mississippi. It has had a rapid development. It is the chief trading point of the surrounding section and also a manufacturing center.

The former school facilities consisted of 3 schools for white children and 1 for Negroes, with a total enrollment of 1,330, representing a material increase in recent years. This increase has caused great overcrowding of the high school and other school buildings.

This new building has 9 classrooms, a gymnasium, showers and lockers for the boys and girls, and an industrial shop on the ground floor. On the second floor are a library, eight classrooms, and a study hall.

The construction is of monolithic concrete, fireproof throughout. Glass blocks between piers and running from floor to ceiling are in some of the walls. The finished floors are wood. The ceilings are covered with soundproofing material.

The building was completed in November 1937 at a construction cost of $122,911 and a total project cost of $137,124.

Bailey Junior High School, *Jackson*, *Mississippi*

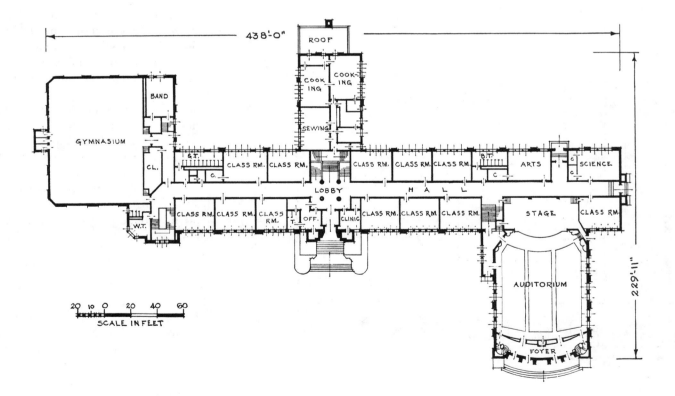

This school is part of a program carried out by the district which included the construction, repair, or alteration of 15 school buildings.

The building is two stories and a basement in height and, due to sloping site, part of the basement is entirely above grade.

*Continued on following page*

## Bailey Junior High School
### *Jackson, Mississippi*

*Continued from preceding page*

The basement contains locker and shower rooms, a cafeteria, kitchen, club rooms, assembly room, industrial-arts rooms, shops, workrooms, and laboratories. On the first floor are the gymnasium, band room; domestic-science department including an apartment, a sewing room, and a cooking room; also 12 classrooms, rooms for the fine arts and natural sciences, the auditorium with its stage, a clinic, and administrative offices. The second floor contains the bleachers for the gymnasium, 10 classrooms, a science laboratory; and rooms for fine arts, natural science, and music.

Construction is reinforced concrete throughout with structural-steel trusses over the auditorium and gymnasium. Roofs are composition. The project was completed in November 1937 at an estimated construction cost of $317,040 and a project cost of $388,641.

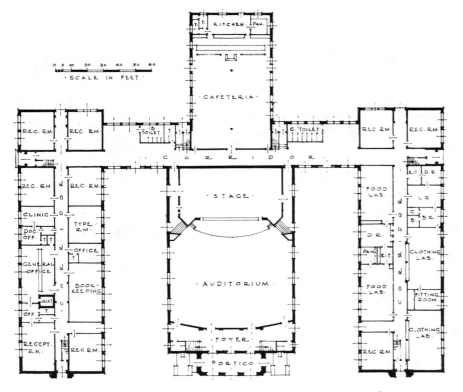

## Meridian High School
### *Meridian, Mississippi*

The Meridian Separate School District includes the city of Meridian and 65 square miles of surrounding territory. The school facilities had become entirely inadequate and to remedy the condition, 12 separate buildings were either remodeled or built, one of which was this new high school. It is a 2-story structure and contains on the first floor an auditorium, a cafeteria, 4 laboratories, a model apartment, and 10 classrooms. On the second floor are 2 laboratories, 14 classrooms, a study hall, art room, and a little theater with stage. The gymnasium is a separate building 2 stories in height with bleacher seats on 2 sides. The construction of both buildings is frame except for the exterior walls which are brick trimmed with limestone. The entire project was completed in November 1937 at a construction cost of $591,489 and a project cost of $688,195.

## Kenton County High School

*Independence, Kentucky*

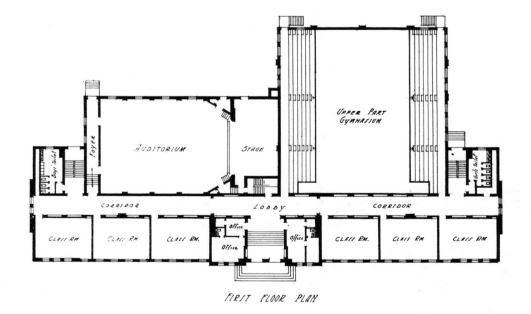

FIRST FLOOR PLAN

A careful study by the school officials of the inadequate school facilities of Kenton County resulted in the construction of two identical high-school buildings, one of which is considered on this page.

The Independence High School is 2 stories and a basement in height and includes 15 classrooms, a gymnasium, an auditorium, a cafeteria, study hall, library, and the necessary administrative offices.

The building has a frontage of 243 feet and is of fireproof construction. The exterior walls are brick with limestone trim.

The project was completed in December 1937 at a construction cost of $418,153 and a project cost of $456,978.

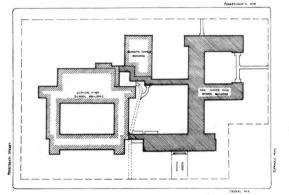

## Miami Beach Senior High School,
### *Miami Beach, Florida*

Miami Beach, with a normal population of 40,000, did not have adequate school accommodations for the children and, with the influx of the winter population, conditions had become so crowded that tent classrooms had to be used. This large extension to the high school and the erection of two elementary schools have relieved this situation. The plans and elevations on this page and the next are of the high school which is a fireproof structure finished in stucco with some brick trim and a tile roof. It was completed in September 1937 at a construction cost of $285,365 and a project cost of $308,229.

*Continued on following page*

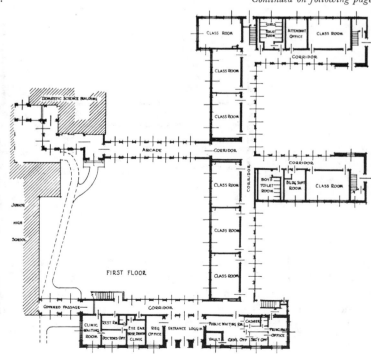

## Miami Beach Senior High School, *Miami Beach*, *Florida*

*Continued from preceding page*

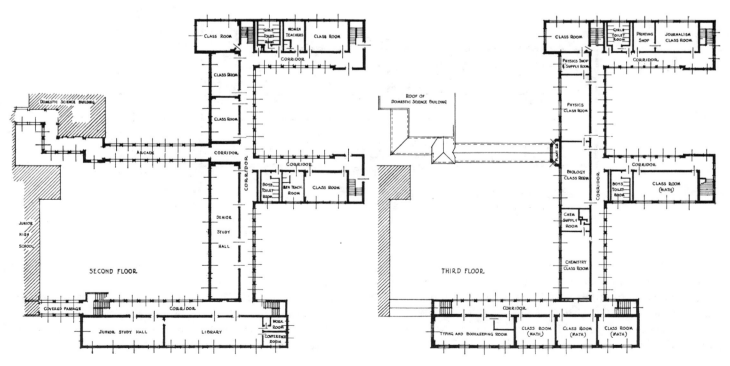

Chapel Hill High School, *Chapel Hill, North Carolina*

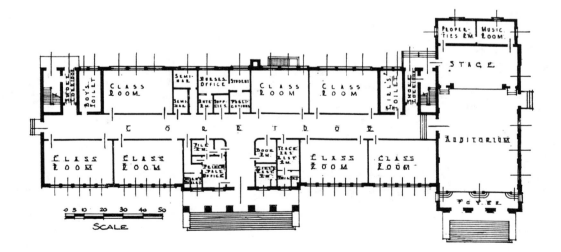

Orange County is located in the central part of the State, and is chiefly an agricultural community. It has had a rapid growth and the schools became inadequate for the population of 22,500 (1930). Four new schools were erected.

This school at Chapel Hill contains seven classrooms and an auditorium on the first floor. On the second floor are three classrooms and rooms for home economics, physics, biology, and chemistry. It is 240 by 60 feet in size.

It is of fireproof construction. The exterior walls are brick with stone trim. The portico and cornices are wood.

It was completed in March 1937 at a construction cost of $109,626 and a project cost of $114,189.

Douglasville High School, *Douglasville, Georgia*

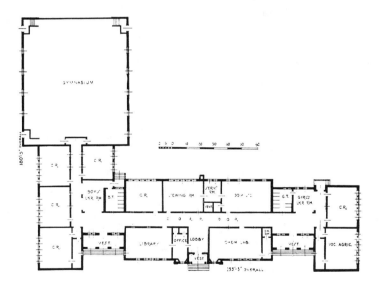

Douglasville, the county seat of Douglas County, is situated about 17 miles west of Atlanta and about 25 miles from the Alabama State line. In 1930 its population was 2,316. The old school building was inadequate and a fire hazard, necessitating the construction of a new one. It is the only high school available for the school district.

It contains 10 classrooms, an auditorium, a library, and other facilities.

The building is not fireproof. The outer walls are cinder block, covered with brick veneer. The interior and roof framing are wood. The auditorium roof is carried on steel trusses supported by steel columns. The upper part of the auditorium is constructed of wood, covered with wood siding.

The project was completed in December 1936. The total cost of construction, including equipment, was $52,038 and the cost of the project was $58,492.

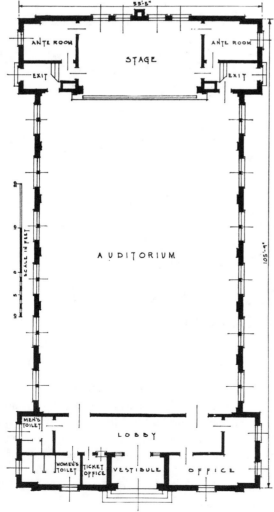

## School Auditorium

### *Hartsville*

### *South Carolina*

The city of Hartsville, 70 miles northeast of Columbia in Darlington County, had inadequate school facilities with no means of giving courses in manual training or domestic science and no auditorium. The school authorities secured a grant from the P. W. A. and together with local funds carried out this project which included the addition of two 3-story wings to the existing high school, containing classrooms, a library, and a study hall; a 1-story building for manual training; and an auditorium which has a seating capacity of 500. The auditorium is shown in the illustration with the manual-training building in the background. All the buildings are frame construction but have exterior walls of brick and roofs covered with composition shingles. The auditorium was completed in November 1938 at a construction cost of $22,702 and a project cost of $24,951. The total cost of the entire project was $94,594.

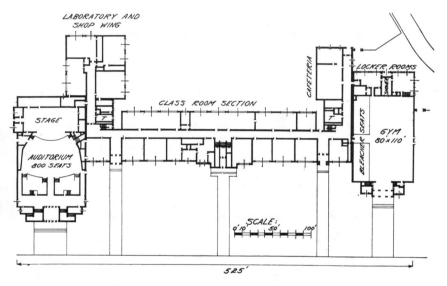

LABORATORY AND
SHOP WING

CLASS ROOM SECTION

CAFETERIA

LOCKER ROOMS

STAGE

AUDITORIUM
800 SEATS

BLEACHER SEATS

GYM
80 × 110'

SCALE:
0' 10'   50'   100'

525'

## High School, *Helena*, *Montana*

In 1935 an earthquake destroyed an elementary school and severely damaged a grade school and this high school.

The high school was rehabilitated and designed to resist earthquakes. The brick walls were removed, and reinforced concrete substituted with special column and beam reinforcing. The building was divided into individual units separated by 4-inch spaces.

The project was completed in January 1938 at an estimated construction cost of $146,476 and a project cost of $157,504.

## Taos High School

### *United Pueblo, New Mexico*

This is one of the many schools erected by the Office of Indian Affairs. It is built of adobe brick, plastered inside and outside. The roofs are also adobe supported on vegas with the construction showing.

It provides five classrooms, a general science room, shop, home economics room, arts and crafts room, and an auditorium 71 by 30 feet. It has a heating plant.

It was completed in November 1935 at a construction cost of $71,377 and a project cost of $76,353.

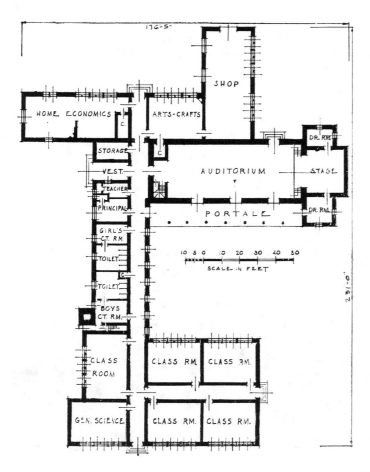

## Bayless High School, *St. Louis County, Missouri*

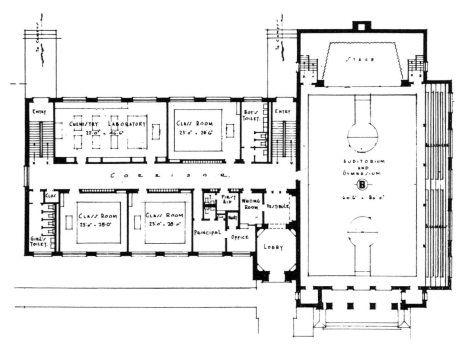

This high school is planned so that when the need arises additions may be made. The present building is T-shaped in plan and two stories in height. It provides seven classrooms, teachers' rooms, a principal's office, a chemical laboratory, a library, and a combination auditorium-gymnasium with a stage and bleachers. The auditorium-gymnasium is so arranged that it may be used by the community as well as by the school.

The construction is fireproof throughout. The exterior walls are red face brick with wood trim. The columns at the entrance of the auditorium are limestone.

The volume of the building is 573,780 cubic feet. It was completed in October 1935 at a construction cost of $133,818 and a project cost of $144,915.

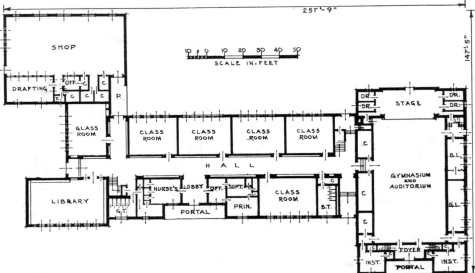

## Junior High School, *Santa Fe, New Mexico*

Between 1929 and 1936 the school population of Santa Fe increased from 15 to 18 percent each year. To remedy the overcrowding that resulted, the Leah Harvey Junior High School was built to accommodate 375 pupils.

It provides 10 standard classrooms, a library, rooms for the sciences, a shop, administrative offices, and a combination auditorium-gymnasium. The construction is fireproof, exterior walls being of hollow tile stuccoed. The project was completed in January 1938 at a construction cost of $132,874 and a project cost of $159,445.

226

## Junior High School, *Clovis, New Mexico*

The need for a new junior high school at Clovis was due to a considerable increase in population between 1920 and 1930. The building is 1 story in height and contains 13 classrooms, administrative offices, a study hall, and rooms for general science, art, and music.

The construction is fireproof. Exterior walls are brick trimmed with tile, stone, and terra cotta, floors are concrete, and roofs are concrete slabs on steel. Some tile is used for roof covering. The project was completed in September 1936 at a construction cost of $117,240 and a project cost of $123,102.

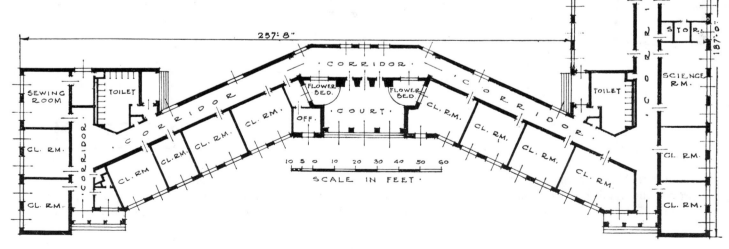

Southwest High School, *Houston, Texas*

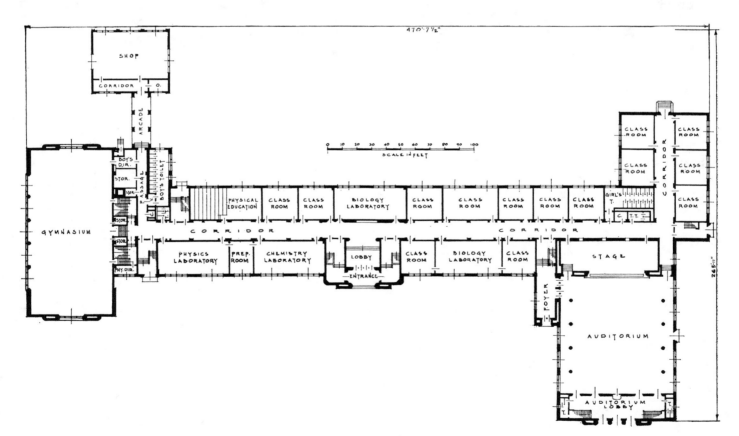

The Southwest High School is a unit of the large school-building program undertaken by Houston. It is a 3-story building containing 45 classrooms; chemistry, physics, and biology laboratories; library, lunch room, rooms for special courses, a gymnasium, and an auditorium. It is fireproof, with exterior walls of brick trimmed with stone. It was completed in December 1937 at a construction cost of $686,278 and a project cost of $780,507.

## Field House, *Port Arthur, Texas*

Owing to the growth of Port Arthur from a small town of 900 in 1900 to a city of over 50,000 in 1930, the school system was obsolete and inadequate. As part of its development program, the school district erected this modern field house and gymnasium.

The gymnasium floor is 86 by 100 feet, and the playing area, when the spectators' folding seats are in open position, is 58 by 100 feet which is adequate for a regulation basketball court. In the rear of the building are a band room, shower and clothes-drying rooms, and locker and storage rooms.

It is a fireproof building with a Spanish tile roof supported on steel trusses. It is one story in height with brick, cement, and wood finished floors over concrete slabs. It has tile wainscots.

It was completed in January 1937 at a construction cost of $114,064 and a project cost of $121,030.

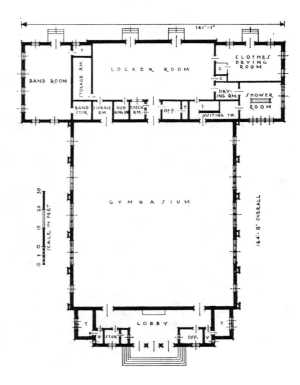

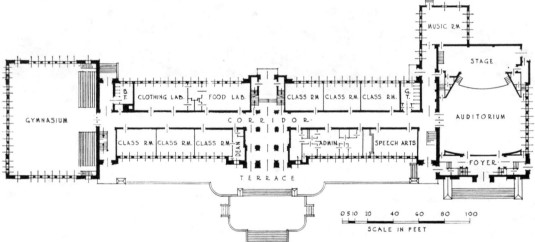

## North Side Senior High School

### *Fort Worth, Texas*

One of the units of the large school building program undertaken by Fort Worth was the North Side Senior High School which has a student body of 1,000. It is 3 and part 4 stories in height and contains 28 standard classrooms, laboratories, an art room, shops, a target range, library, cafeteria, double gymnasium, and an auditorium seating 1,200. It is fireproof except for the roof, and the exterior walls are a light, cream-colored brick trimmed with cast stone and black brick. It has a total floor area of 91,863 square feet. It was completed in February 1938 at a construction cost of $459,410 and a project cost of $477,181.

High School Stadium and Offices, *El Paso, Texas*

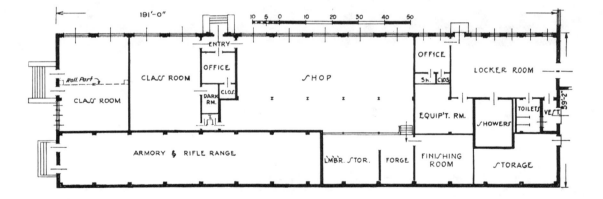

This Austin High School Stadium was constructed for the use of three high schools and one college. It provided the city with its first enclosed athletic field.

It has a seating capacity of 3,500 spectators and adjoins an auditorium at one end. It is 191 feet long by 59 feet wide. An unusual feature is the incorporation under the seats of a shop, rifle range, classrooms, and locker and shower rooms.

The stadium seats are constructed of reinforced concrete. The wall construction is steel, reinforced concrete, and brick.

It was completed in January 1936 at a construction cost of $67,641 and a project cost of $70,838.

Daniel Webster High School, *Tulsa*, *Oklahoma*

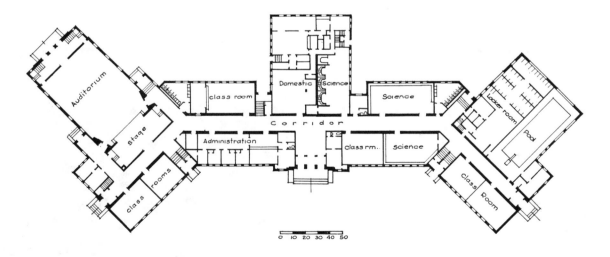

The Daniel Webster High School is a two-story and basement structure which contains 15 classrooms, a library, 2 cafeterias, a lecture room, corrective gymnasium, girls' gymnasium, auditorium seating 400, domestic-science department, 2 manual training rooms, 3 laboratories, offices, swimming pool, dressing rooms. Another adjacent building houses shops, boys' gymnasium, and lockers. Both structures are fireproof. Exterior walls are brick with stone trim. Both buildings were completed in July 1938 at a construction cost of $662,855 and a project cost of $768,257.

Port Allen High School, *Port Allen, Louisiana*

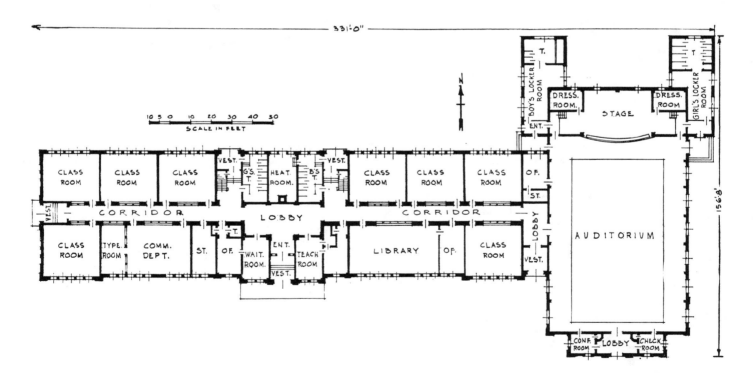

Port Allen is a town of 1,500 inhabitants, across the Mississippi from Baton Rouge. Its new high school is 1 story and part 2 stories in height and contains on the first floor 10 classrooms, administrative offices, and a first-aid room. The second floor has the science laboratories and an office. Connected with the building is the auditorium with a seating capacity of 700, a well-equipped stage and dressing rooms. The wall construction is concrete with a machine-rubbed finish on exterior. The project was completed in July 1938 at a construction cost of $158,795 and a project cost of $169,693.

## Hollywood High School, *Los Angeles, California*

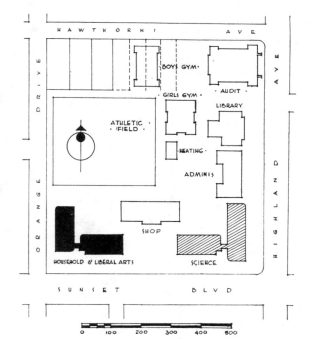

The science building, and the liberal- and household-arts building illustrated on the next page, are two units of this institution constructed with P. W. A. aid. Their plans are similar. The science building contains 11 classrooms, recitation rooms, laboratories for physics and biology, and lecture rooms. The liberal- and household-arts building contains 14 classrooms and special rooms for art and domestic science. Both structures are fireproof, of reinforced concrete, and designed to resist earthquake shocks.

The science building was completed in November 1935 at a construction cost of $186,748 and a project cost of $208,968. The liberal- and household-arts building was completed in March 1938 at a construction cost of $210,838 and a project cost of $230,425. Both structures are outstanding examples of concrete finish.

*Continued on following page*

Hollywood High School, *Los Angeles, California*

*Continued from preceding page*

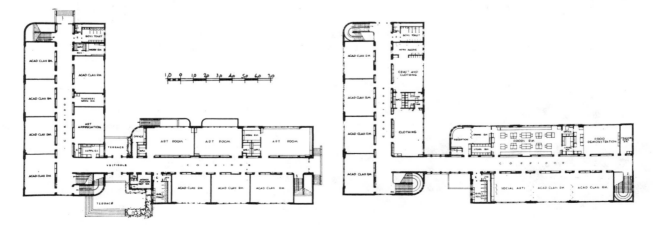

## Palm Springs High School, *Palm Springs*, *California*

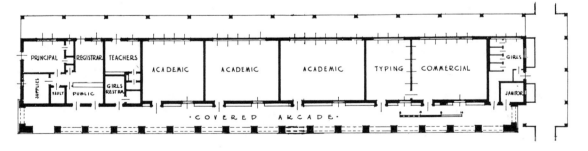

This project consisted of two buildings at Palm Springs and one building at Banning. The illustrations show the south wing at Palm Springs, the other buildings being similar in character. They are all constructed of reinforced concrete designed to resist earthquake shocks. The project was completed during 1938 at a construction cost of $303,282 for all three and a project cost of $331,550.

South Pasadena High School Auditorium, *South Pasadena, California*

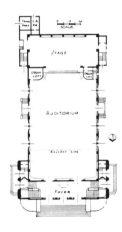

This building was rehabilitated to withstand seismic disturbances, with the construction of new concrete exterior and interior walls. It is approximately 81 by 150 feet and has a seating capacity of 1,160.

The size of the stage enables the production of major plays. Covered passageways connect the auditorium with the other buildings of the school plant. The inside is finished with acoustical plaster. An organ is installed by the stage.

The project was completed in April 1937 at a construction cost of $113,528 and a project cost of $126,378.

## Redlands High School Girls' Gymnasium

### *Redlands, California*

Redlands is approximately 60 miles directly east of the city limits of Los Angeles, near San Bernardino Mountain. In 1930 it had a population of 14,177.

The basement of the old school was formerly used as a gymnasium for the girls. It was intended to accommodate 150 girls and was being used by over 350. Physical education is a part of the required curriculum.

The new building contains 15,867 square feet of usable floor area. The gymnasium is 70 by 100 feet. It has a gallery along the wide side which will accommodate a large percentage of the student body for viewing the many types of competitive athletic sports and games.

In addition to the gymnasium, the building contains a corrective relaxation room, a large locker room, a room for individual showers, and another for open showers, a kitchen with adjoining classroom, three rooms for toilets, two offices and examination room, and a room for storage of equipment. Consideration was given in the design to reduce to a minimum the operating and maintenance cost and to provide sufficient room for future expansion.

The building is constructed entirely of reinforced concrete, except for the roof over the gymnasium itself, which is

*Continued on following page*

238

Redlands High School

Girls' Gymnasium

———

*Redlands, California*

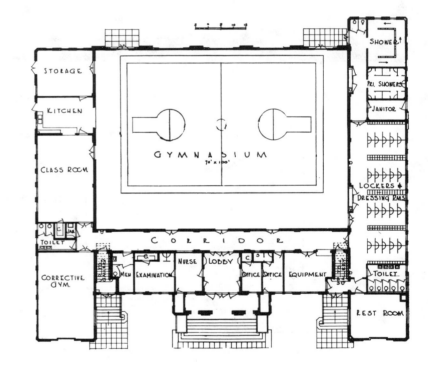

*Continued from preceding page*

spanned by lightweight steel trusses. The exterior of the concrete walls is left exposed with form marks showing.

The gymnasium provides two small basketball courts or one large standard court. The walls have a wainscot of wood. The structure was designed to withstand minor and major earthquake disturbances.

This project was completed in December 1936. The cost of construction was $105,496 and the total cost of the project was $115,493.

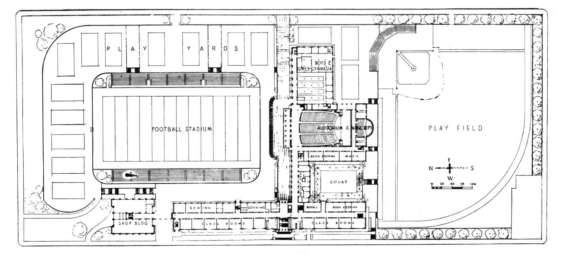

## George Washington High School

### *San Francisco, California*

This building was constructed to reduce overcrowded conditions in other senior high schools. It has 39 classrooms, boys' and girls' gymnasiums, a large auditorium with stage, a small music hall with platform and sloping floor, numerous special service rooms for sewing, cooking, bookkeeping, and other subjects.

It was completed in 1937 and is one of 12 elementary and high-school buildings under this docket. The construction cost of this building was approximately $782,302. The project cost of the 12 buildings was $2,997,302.

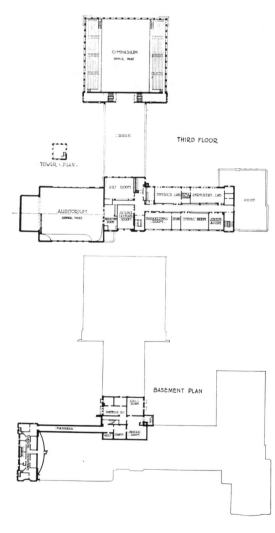

## High School, *Boulder, Colorado*

This new two, part three and part basement building replaced an obsolete structure built in 1895 for a student body of 300 whereas the student body in 1935 had increased to 800. The accommodations of the new school may be seen on the illustration of its plans and it may also be noted with what ease future additions can be made when needed. The auditorium will seat approximately 1,500. The construction is fireproof and the exterior walls are faced with a random ashlar of native stone trimmed with rubbed concrete. The project was completed in September 1937 at a construction cost of $475,005 and a project cost of $550,467.

Gymnasium and Shop Buildings, Gilbert High School, *Gilbert, Arizona*

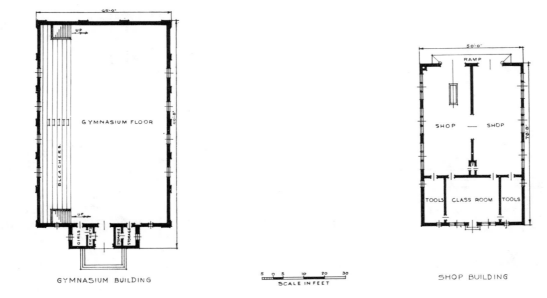

GYMNASIUM BUILDING                    SCALE IN FEET                    SHOP BUILDING

The illustration shows the new gymnasium for the Gilbert High School with the new shop building in the background. The gymnasium provides a playing floor, 45 by 90 feet, and has bleachers along one side underneath which are locker and shower rooms. The shop building provides a classroom and two shops each 25 by 54 feet and each having a storage room for tools and supplies. Construction of both buildings is concrete-block, stuccoed and wood-roof construction. They were completed in March 1938 at a construction cost of $32,554 and a project cost of $34,979.

242

## Gymnasium-Auditorium, Mohave County Union High School

### *Kingman, Arizona*

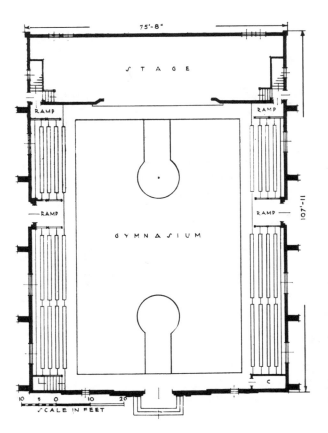

This combination gymnasium-auditorium has permanent seating at the sides and will accommodate approximately 400 spectators for athletic and dramatic events. Its construction is of interest. The foundations, first-floor slab, and buttresses are concrete, exterior walls of painted brick and the roof of Lamella type, the thrust of which is taken by the buttresses.

The project was completed in March 1936 at a construction cost of $28,237 and a project cost of $30,285.

Ogden High School

*Ogden, Utah*

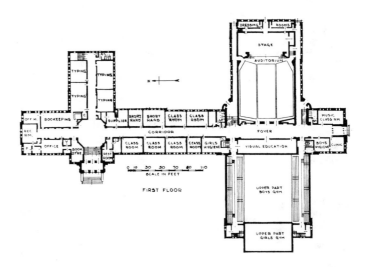

The airplane view of the Ogden High School shows the entire plant as well as most of its site which is a plot of ground 660 feet square. The figures on the illustration indicate the various parts of the building. No. 1 is the classroom section; No. 2, the auditorium; No. 3, the gymnasium; and No. 4, the shops building and R. O. T. C. headquarters.

It is one of the largest high schools in the State and will care for an enrollment of 2,000 students. The classroom section, which is 4 stories in height, contains 40 classrooms, domestic arts and science rooms, a cafeteria, 69 by 122 feet, physics, chemistry, and biology laboratories, and a library, 60 by 80 feet. The gymnasium section contains a boys' gymnasium, 2 stories in height and 70 by 100 feet, and a girls' gymnasium, 40 by 70 feet, and the necessary locker and team rooms. The auditorium wing is 168 by 105 feet and provides the auditorium with a well-equipped stage and a choral room.

The entire structure is fireproof. The construction consists of a concrete frame, reinforced concrete floor and roof slabs, and exterior walls faced with a light-colored brick trimmed with stone.

The project was completed in November 1937 at a construction cost of $1,028,916 and a project cost of $1,077,568.

## Bellingham High School, *Bellingham*, *Washington*

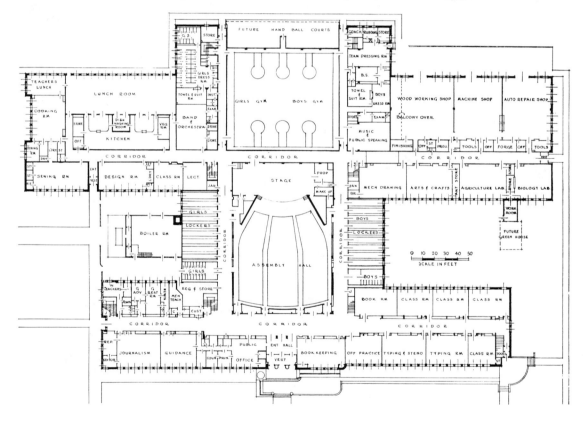

The Bellingham High School is one of the largest and finest structures of this type erected recently in northwest Washington. It is 3 stories in height with sufficient basement to take care of the heating system. It provides 20 standard classrooms; laboratories for chemistry, physics, biology, and agriculture; a woodworking shop; a machine shop; an automobile repair shop; rooms for music, arts and crafts, mechanical drawing, domestic science, office practice, typing, and stenography; a band and orchestra room; lunchrooms; a boys' gymnasium; a girls' gymnasium; an auditorium with a stage; a library; conference rooms; study rooms; and administrative offices.

The construction is entirely reinforced concrete with a stucco finish on the exterior walls. The project was completed in May 1938 at a construction cost of $757,678 and a project cost of $856,898.

## Senior High School, *Salem, Oregon*

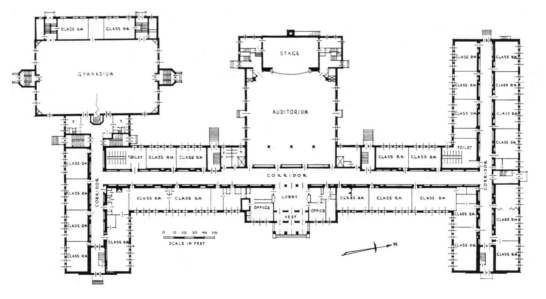

This building is somewhat removed from the center of the city but is located with reference to the school population and is situated next to the junior high school which is equipped with an athletic field.

The structure is 2 stories in height, with a basement used only for storage purposes and the heating plant. It provides 32 classrooms, a commercial department of 7 rooms, 14 laboratories, a library, an art department of 2 rooms, a music room, 4 administration offices, 5 teachers' rooms, and a clinic of 4 rooms. The auditorium is 88 by 100 feet and

seats 1,750 persons; the cafeteria, 78 by 92 feet, is below the auditorium. The gymnasium is 76½ by 122 feet and has a seating capacity of 780, and there is a shop building containing 5 classrooms, 4 shops, and an office. The plant accommodates a student body of 1,800.

Construction is steel and reinforced concrete. The exterior walls are brick backed with tile and trimmed with terra cotta, and the roof is covered with slate.

The project was completed in June 1937 at a construction cost of $670,875 and a project cost of $741,351.

## Corvallis High School, *Corvallis, Oregon*

Corvallis is in the middle eastern section of Oregon on the Willamette River. It is the Benton County seat. The population in 1930 was 17,985.

Besides classroom facilities, this senior high school contains a gymnasium and auditorium. The exterior walls are concrete, covered with stucco. The interior framing is concrete, steel, tile, and wood. Sloping roofs are covered with

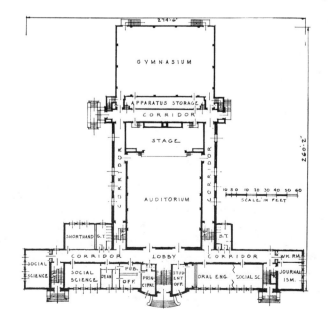

asbestos shingles. It has an adequate heating system and a modern electric school signal system.

The classroom section is approximately 40 by 275 feet and the gymnasium-auditorium is about 100 by 220 feet.

It was finished in October 1935 at a construction cost of $293,250 and a total project cost of $315,860.

247

Auditorium

Roosevelt High School

*Honolulu, T. H.*

The Roosevelt High School Auditorium is one of 10 units included in a single P. W. A. docket. It was constructed as an important element of this institution which is one of the largest high schools in Hawaii.

The building is rectangular, 72 by 150 feet, in plan. The auditorium seats 1,050, and its floor slopes down to the stage which is of sufficient height to provide space for shifting scenery and for lighting. Dressing rooms are provided for the stage and there is a motion-picture projection booth.

The construction consists of reinforced concrete columns and floor slabs, suspended ceilings hung from steel trusses, hollow-tile walls plastered on the inside and stuccoed on the outside, and clay-tile roofs.

The project was completed in July 1935 at a construction cost of $71,821 and a project cost of $77,052.

Junior High School, *Richmond, Rhode Island*

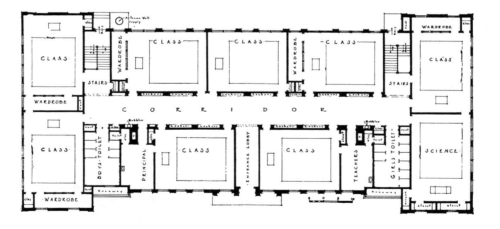

The town of Richmond had a population of 1,535 in 1930. This school building is an elementary and junior high school located on a lot approximately 8 acres in size, in the general center of the town.

The building has one story and basement. The basement contains a drawing room, woodworking shop, finishing room, cafeteria, cooking and sewing rooms, assembly room with stage, and boiler room. The first floor has nine classrooms and rooms for the principal and for the teachers.

The building is not fireproof. The exterior walls above the concrete basement are constructed with wood studs faced with brick veneer in front and rear and with clapboard wood siding elsewhere. The walls are insulated and on the interior are covered with wallboard or plaster. The doors and windows are generally wood, but are metal where required by code for exits.

The basement has a concrete floor and a plaster ceiling on metal lath. The roof construction is wood and is covered with slate.

The dimensions of the building are 159 by 69 feet. It was completed in April 1935. The total construction cost was $66,654 and the total project cost was $72,098.

The town of Cabot is located in the northeastern part of Vermont, in Washington County. Employment is afforded by wood-working plants producing novelties.

The school is in the residential section of the town and replaces an inadequate two-story condemned wooden building. There are five classrooms, a library, domestic science room, principal's office, and teachers' rooms. The walls are insulated.

It was completed in October 1938. The construction cost was $36,434 and the total project cost was $39,903.

## Cabot Village School

### *Cabot, Vermont*

## Old Saybrook Consolidated School
### *Old Saybrook, Connecticut*

This town is located near the mouth of the Connecticut River on Long Island Sound. This project replaced an old wooden elementary school and included the construction of a new elementary school building, a combination auditorium-gymnasium, and additions to and refacing the existing high school.

The building accommodates 500 pupils and has a volume of approximately 500,000 cubic feet. It contains 17 classrooms, an auditorium and gymnasium, lunchroom, three workrooms, and offices.

The walls are common red brick, the floors are concrete supported on steel-bar joists, and the doors and windows are steel.

The entire project was completed in February 1937 at a construction cost of $147,724 and a project cost of $159,896.

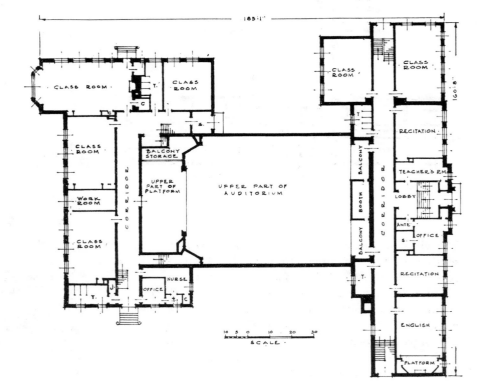

## Mahopac Central School, *Mahopac, New York*

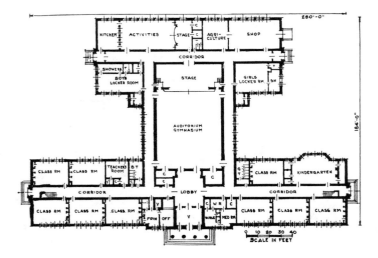

with acoustical plaster and the floors in the corridors are finished in terrazzo. The interior doors are oak. The exterior walls are pink and gray granite ashlar, with limestone copings. The sloping roofs are covered with slate. It is located on a 10-acre lot and faces west. There are 33,000 square feet on the ground floor and the volume of the building is 1,300,000 cubic feet.

It was completed in October 1937 at a construction cost of $459,320 and a project cost of $538,643.

The village of Mahopac is located on Lake Mahopac in the south-central part of Putnam County. In 1930 its permanent population was 407. It is also a summer resort.

This new school building accommodates 800 pupils from the vicinity. Besides the classrooms, it has a bus garage, bowling alleys, and a combination gymnasium-auditorium. It replaced old frame buildings which have been abandoned.

The construction is fire resistant. It is built with structural steel frame and concrete subfloors. The ceilings are covered

## Livingston Manor Central School, *Livingston Manor*, *New York*

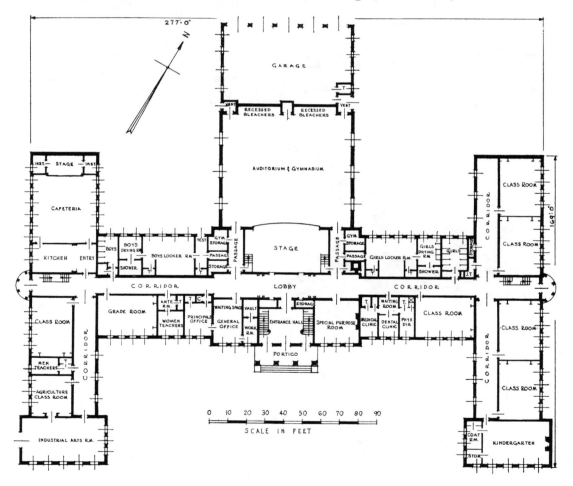

The site of this project is a peninsula, locally known as "The Island" and in addition to the school building, there are baseball and football fields, a running track, tennis courts, and a park containing beautiful old trees. The school, which is 2 stories in height, contains 28 classrooms, a combination gymnasium-auditorium, a kindergarten, cafeteria, library, rooms for domestic science, medical and dental clinics, and a garage for 5 school buses. Construction is semifireproof. The exterior walls are brick trimmed with cast stone and the roofs are covered with slate. The project was completed in April 1939 at a construction cost of $582,244 and a project cost of $642,496.

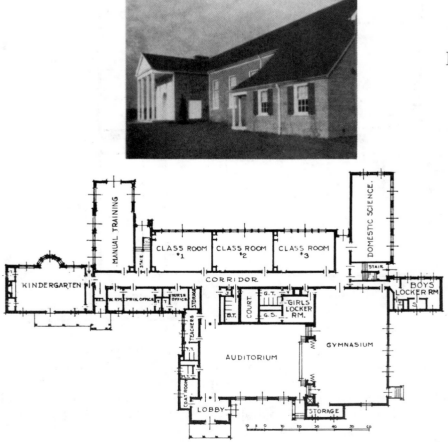

## Ho-ho-kus Public School
### *Ho-ho-kus, New Jersey*

Ho-ho-kus is a residential community composed primarily of commuters to New York City and has grown considerably in recent years. The new building replaces a structure 30 years old which had only four classrooms, necessitating combining the lower grades and sending the seventh and eighth grades to a school in Ridgewood.

The new school occupies the corner of a 7-acre lot, permitting the development of athletic and play fields. It is a combination grade and junior high school and provides an auditorium and gymnasium, as well as the necessary classrooms and special rooms. It is of semifireproof construction and was completed in April 1937 at a construction cost of $198,628 and a project cost of $219,275.

Carryville School, *Campbell County*, *Tennessee*

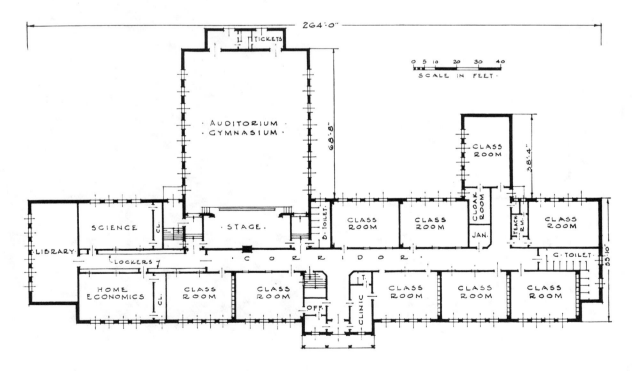

This project consisted of the erection of 9 school buildings and repairs and additions to 4 others. The Carryville School is a combination elementary and high school, one story and part basement in height, and contains 11 standard classrooms, a library, and an auditorium. It is a nonfireproof building, being of frame construction, except the exterior walls which are brick trimmed with wood. The roof is metal. This building was completed in November 1938 at a construction cost of $66,026 and a project cost of $76,930. The entire project cost was $327,875.

## R. J. Delano School, *Kansas City*, *Missouri*

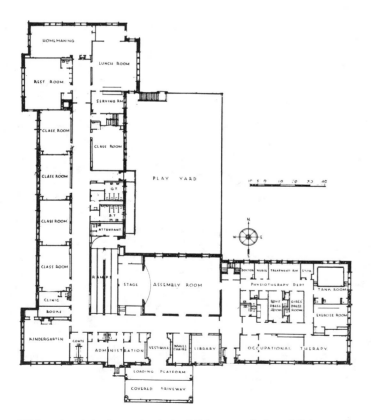

This school is for crippled children and for children who are deficient in sight or hearing or who are cardiac cases. A partial basement provides a manual training department, a playroom, and three unfinished rooms. The first floor has four divisions: (a) Administration, library, and assembly rooms; (b) five classrooms and kindergarten; (c) home eco-

nomics, restroom, and lunchroom; (d) hydrotherapy, physiotherapy, and occupational therapy.

The construction is fireproof. No stairs are used, ramps taking their place. The building will accommodate 125 children. The estimated construction cost was $324,775 and the project cost was approximately $362,396.

## Young School for Colored Children

### *Independence, Missouri*

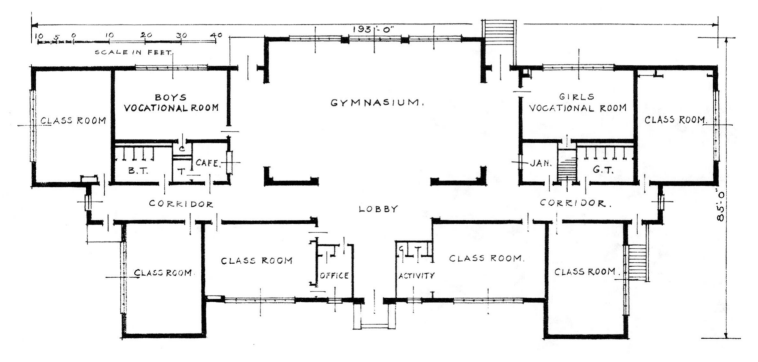

The construction program of the school district at Independence included the Young, Columbian, and Southwest Schools. The Young School, illustrated on this page, is one story in height with a small basement to contain the heating plant and locker rooms for boys and girls. The main floor contains six standard classrooms, two vocational rooms for boys and girls, a gymnasium, and an office. The ground floor slab is concrete, the exterior walls are brick trimmed with cast stone, and the roof is wood, covered with built-up roofing material. It was completed in September 1935, at a construction cost of $25,348 and a project cost of $29,244. The construction cost of all three schools was $245,689 and their project cost $278,739.

School Building, *Moose Lake, Minnesota*

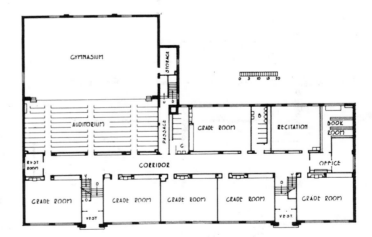

This building is a combination elementary and high school erected by the independent school district No. 3 in Carlton County.

It is 2 stories and a basement in height and provides 14 classrooms, 2 libraries; laboratories for science, agriculture, and domestic science; administrative offices, and a combination auditorium-gymnasium.

The building is fireproof with exterior brick walls trimmed with stone. It was completed in April 1936 at a construction cost of $125,047 and a project cost of $130,361.

## Oliver P. Morton School, *Hammond, Indiana*

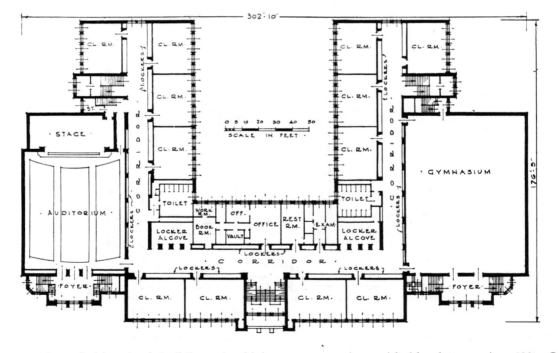

Before the construction of this school building, the high school students of Hammond were quartered in 15 inadequate, temporary, or portable buildings.

The new structure is 3 stories in height and is built around a court which is landscaped as a formal garden. On the ground floor are 12 classrooms, a band room, shop, kindergarten, 2 museums, girls' and boys' shower and locker rooms, lunchroom, and kitchen. The first floor has 12 classrooms, administration offices, an auditorium seating 800, and a gymnasium with bleachers seating 600. On the second floor are a library, 6 classrooms, and rooms for domestic science, sewing, art, physiology, and general science. The boiler room, a separate 1-story building, encloses the court on one side. Construction is fireproof and the exterior walls are faced with pressed brick and trimmed with stone and marble. The project was completed in June 1937 at a construction cost of $543,702 and a project cost of $580,083.

259

## Lander Grade School, *Lander, Wyoming*

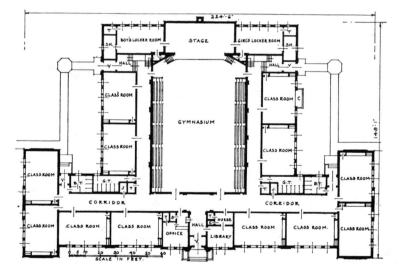

Lander is the county seat of Fremont County and has a population of approximately 12,500. This new building was erected for school district No. 1 and replaces both the old grade school and junior high school which had been condemned for defective construction.

The structure is T-shaped in plan and one story and part basement in height. It contains a combination gymnasium and auditorium with a stage, 12 classrooms, a library, administrative offices, and locker rooms on the first floor. The manual-training and domestic-science departments, music room, and boys' and girls' lunchrooms are in the basement. Bleachers are on each side of the gymnasium, and there is a projection booth opposite the stage above the first-floor corridor.

The building is semifireproof. The floor is concrete and the roof framing is wood. Steel trusses span the gymnasium. The exterior walls are brick trimmed with terra cotta.

The project was completed in February 1938 at a construction cost of $108,505 and a project cost of $119,527.

## Combined Elementary and High School
### *Orick, California*

The illustrations on this page show the old and new schools in the village of Orick and provide a good example of the type of obsolete structure used for school purposes in many places, and the type of modern building that has been made possible with the aid of the P. W. A. The new building contains two large and two small classrooms with a stage at the end of one of the larger classrooms, a typing room, a library, a general laboratory, and a principal's office. It is not fireproof and its plan leaves much to be desired from the point of view of school functional planning. However, it is adequate, sanitary, and provides well lighted and ventilated rooms. It was completed in May 1936 at a construction cost of $25,911 and a project cost of $29,194.

Murphy School Auditorium, *near Phoenix, Arizona*

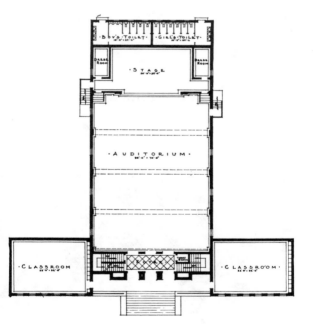

This project consisted of the erection of the Murphy Auditorium, the alteration of an existing school building to provide offices for the principal and nurse, and the equipment for two buildings.

The auditorium is a T-shaped structure approximately 120 by 120 feet in its over-all dimensions. It provides an auditorium 50 by 70 feet with a stage and dressing rooms, and two classrooms each 23 by 32 feet which are connected to the auditorium but not a part of it. These classrooms were added under another P. W. A. docket after the construction of the auditorium.

The construction is semifireproof of brick, concrete, and frame.

The project was completed in March 1939 at a construction cost for both dockets of $49,534 and a project cost also for both dockets of $55,220.

## Skagway Public School, *Skagway, Alaska*

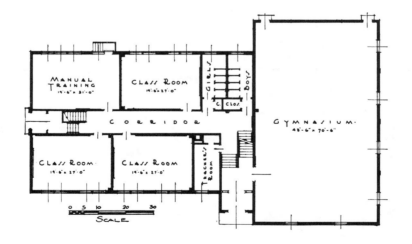

Skagway is in the northwest corner of the first judiciary division of Alaska, which is the southern strip separating the ocean from British Columbia. It is about 100 miles north of Juneau, adjacent to the Canadian line.

This building was constructed for grade and high school pupils from the neighboring community. In the basement are boys' and girls' dressing rooms, showers, and the boiler room. On the first floor are three classrooms, teachers' room, manual training room, and a gymnasium 43½ by 70½ feet without a stage. On the second floor are three classrooms, a library, physics room, and administrative quarters.

The building is fireproof. The structural framing including exterior walls are reinforced concrete. The surface of the exterior walls is covered with stucco.

The project was completed in September 1938. The cost of construction was $59,671 and the project cost was $63,274.

## State Normal School, *Bowie, Maryland*

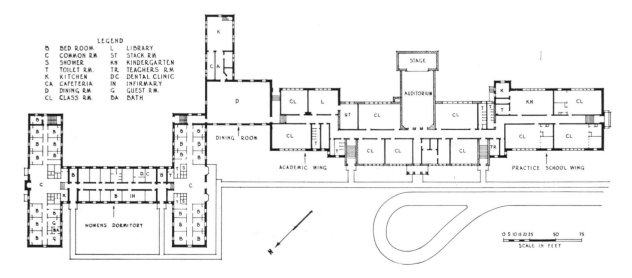

The State Normal School at Bowie is the only school of this character in Maryland. Due to a great increase in the student body the existing plant had become intolerably over-crowded and this project provided two additional wings to the girls' dormitory, each with an area of 4,300 square feet, an addition to the dining room and academic wing of 4,600 square feet, alterations to the boys' dormitory, and an addition to the practice school of 5,800 square feet. It also included the con-struction of a water tank, a system of fire protection, sewers, and walks. The construction consists of brick exterior walls, wood joists and stud partitions on the interior, and slate-covered pitched roofs and slab roofs on the decks. All stairways are concrete and enclosed in fireproof wells. The project was completed in February 1939 at a construction cost of $272,774 and a project cost of $291,994.

## Los Angeles City College, *Los Angeles, California*

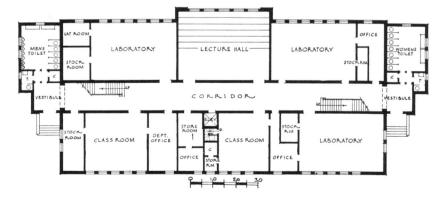

This institution covers an area of approximately nine city blocks. The life-science building, the chemistry building, and the library are included in this project. The life-science building contains on two floors two zoology, one anatomy, one biology, one botany, and one physiology laboratory; two lecture rooms, two classrooms, two workrooms, a dark room, and offices, stockrooms, and storerooms.

The construction, of concrete, is fireproof and designed to resist earthquakes. It was completed in May 1938 at an estimated construction cost of $108,667 and a project cost of $119,845.

## Field House and Auditorium

## Oklahoma Military Academy

*Claremore, Oklahoma*

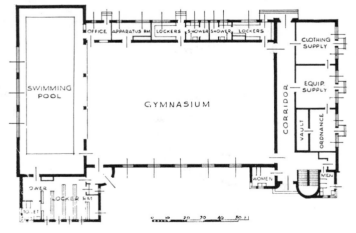

The auditorium building has a seating capacity of 600 with an additional 200 in the b alcony, which is sufficient to accommodate the student body and faculty and a reasonable number of visitors.

The entire project was completed in November 1936 at a construction cost of $257,128 and a total project cost of $277,399.

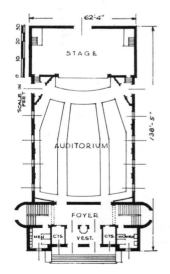

These buildings are part of the Oklahoma Military Academy, a State institution since 1919. Increased enrollment necessitated construction of more units, including the field house and auditorium buildings.

The field house contains a gymnasium with a playing area 70 by 100 feet, and a swimming pool 30 by 75 feet, with locker rooms and storage for military ordnance. Three classrooms and two offices are in the small second-floor portion at the front.

## Pasadena Junior College, *Pasadena, California*

The Pasadena Junior College has a student body of 4,300.  It occupies an area of nine city blocks and has one of the most beautiful campuses in the State.

This project consisted of the erection of three structures, one of which is the administration building, and two of which are science buildings.  The science buildings contain a total of 32 classrooms.  The administration building, in addition to administrative offices, has 64 classrooms, a rest room,

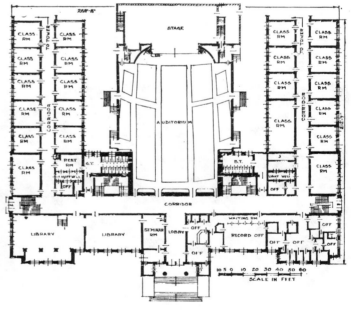

library, and an auditorium with a seating capacity of 2,500.

The construction is earthquake-resistant and consists of reinforced-concrete bearing walls, foundations, and floor slabs.  The exterior walls are finished with stucco and cast-stone trim.  The roof is composition on concrete roof slabs. The project was completed in October 1937 at a construction cost of $1,191,030 and a project cost of $1,468,046.

Commerce Building, Fullerton Junior College

*Fullerton, California*

Fullerton is 15 miles south of Los Angeles. Other buildings included in the school plant are those for administration, social science and student body, arts and crafts, and general science.

This junior college also accommodates students from 8 neighboring towns. It has an enrollment of approximately 1,000. The curriculum of the school includes studies in physical and social science, and in business education.

The new Commerce Building has 12 classrooms, 2 offices, a lecture hall, a workroom, a banking room, and 2 rest rooms. The building is 70 by 150 feet and 2 stories high. It is constructed of reinforced concrete designed to resist major seismic disturbances.

It was completed in October 1936. The construction cost was $131,503 and the project cost $144,805.

*Continued on following page*

## Commerce Building, Fullerton Junior College, *Fullerton, California*

*Continued from preceding page*

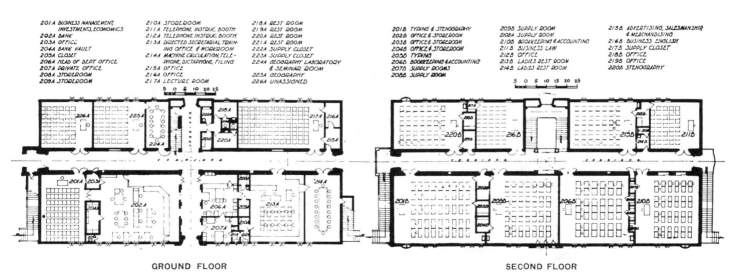

201A BUSINESS MANAGEMENT, INVESTMENTS, ECONOMICS
202A BANK
203A OFFICE
204A BANK VAULT
205A CLOSET
206A HEAD OF DEPT OFFICE
207A PRIVATE OFFICE
208A STOREROOM
209A STOREROOM

210A STOREROOM
211A TELEPHONE INSTRUC. BOOTH
212A TELEPHONE INSTRUC. BOOTH
213A DIRECTED SECRETARIAL TRAINING OFFICE & WORKROOM
214A MACHINE CALCULATION, TELEPHONE, DICTAPHONE, FILING
215A OFFICE
216A OFFICE
217A LECTURE ROOM

218A REST ROOM
219A REST ROOM
220A REST ROOM
221A REST ROOM
222A SUPPLY CLOSET
223A SUPPLY CLOSET
224A GEOGRAPHY LABORATORY & SEMINAR ROOM
225A GEOGRAPHY
226A UNASSIGNED

201B TYPING & STENOGRAPHY
202B OFFICE & STOREROOM
203B OFFICE & STOREROOM
204B OFFICE & STOREROOM
205B TYPING
206B BOOKKEEPING & ACCOUNTING
207B SUPPLY ROOMS
208B SUPPLY ROOM

209B SUPPLY ROOM
210B A SUPPLY ROOM
210B BOOKKEEPING & ACCOUNTING
211B BUSINESS LAW
212B OFFICE
213B LADIES REST ROOM
214B LADIES REST ROOM

215B ADVERTISING, SALESMANSHIP & MERCHANDISING
216B BUSINESS ENGLISH
217B SUPPLY CLOSET
218B OFFICE
219B OFFICE
220B STENOGRAPHY

GROUND FLOOR                                                  SECOND FLOOR

Long Beach Junior College, *Long Beach*, *California*

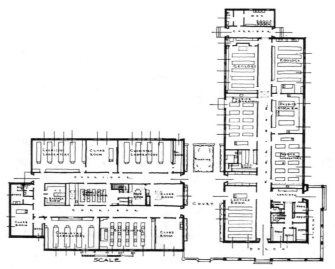

This project consists of three buildings, replacing the former school plant destroyed by earthquake in 1933. The upper illustration is of the physical-science building and the lower of the English building. The former is constructed of steel frame and studding, providing approximately 24,000 square feet of usable floor area; the latter is of wood frame and stucco, with 17,400 square feet of floor space.

The three buildings were completed in 1935. The language and social-science building is not shown. It has 20,700 square feet of floor area and is constructed of wood frame and stucco.

The buildings were erected at a construction cost of $206,477 and a project cost of $225,191.

## Carbon County Junior College

*Price, Utah*

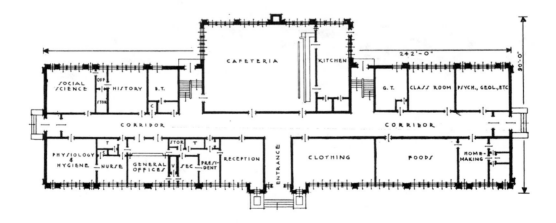

The Carbon County Junior College is the first institution of this kind erected in this section of the State, as a result of State legislation. The project consisted of the administration building, illustrated on this page, and the industrial-education building, as well as the equipment for both structures. The administration building is two stories in height with a small basement at the rear to accommodate the heating plant. It contains on the first floor administrative offices including an office for the president of the college, a cafeteria with a kitchen, a small clinic, and rooms for the teaching of social science, history, physics, geology, homemaking,

foods, and clothing. On the second floor are rooms for the teaching of bookkeeping, typing, stenography, art and chemistry, physics and biology laboratories, three English classrooms, a lecture room, a room for the language department, and a large library with a stack room adjoining.

The building is of fireproof construction with a frame of structural steel, concrete floor and roof slabs, and exterior walls of brick trimmed with stone. It was completed in June 1939 at a construction cost of $178,447. The project, including the industrial-education building, was constructed at a cost of $258,676 and the project cost was $276,019.

## Normal School Gymnasium

———

*Lewiston*

*Idaho*

The city of Lewiston is in Nez Perce County in northwestern Idaho and in 1930 had a population of 9,500. The Normal School had an old gymnasium which was inadequate in every way and this project consisted of the erection of a new building to provide for the athletic requirements of the institution. The gymnasium room is flanked on two sides by bleachers and there are additional seating spaces over the entrance lobby and locker rooms. Doors at the rear of the building open directly to the athletic field. The exterior walls are concrete with a rubbed finish and are painted with cement paint as a protection against moisture. Interior partitions are wood. Windows above the bleachers and three skylights provide ample light. The old building was remodeled for use as administrative offices for the school. The project was completed in November 1938 at a construction cost of $74,310 and a project cost of $79,381.

## Mabel Louise Southwick Memorial
## University of Vermont
### *Burlington, Vermont*

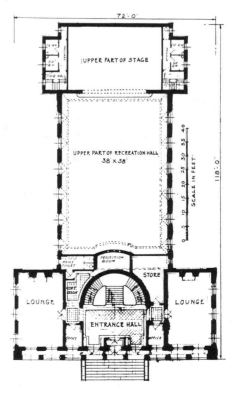

The University of Vermont and State Agricultural College was organized in 1865. Its courses include agriculture, mechanical arts, military science and training, medicine, and general college courses. Its student body increased from 515 in 1910 to 1,266 in 1930.

The Mabel Louise Southwick Building is the women's recreation building at the university. It is T-shaped in plan and is two stories and a basement in height. The basement contains a combination recreation hall and auditorium with a large stage, locker and utility rooms. Lounges and sitting rooms occupy the first floor. On the second floor are meeting rooms and a recreation hall with a small stage.

The structure is fireproof throughout, the exterior walls being red brick trimmed with marble. It has a volume of 458,000 cubic feet and was completed in November 1936 at a construction cost of $263,237 and a project cost of $281,139.

Students' Dormitory, Virginia Polytechnic Institute

*Blacksburg, Virginia*

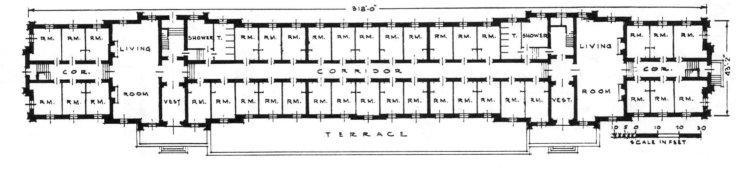

The Virginia Polytechnic Institute undertook an extensive building program with the aid of P. W. A. It included the students' dormitory, a faculty dormitory, a utilities building, and a teaching and administrative building. The four structures were let on one contract and were built at the same time.

The students' dormitory accommodates 276 students in rooms which open off a central corridor, and there are six living rooms, 22 by 44 feet, each with two fireplaces. The building is four stories in height.

The construction is fireproof throughout. The exterior walls are rock-faced native limestone trimmed with sawed limestone and the roof is slate.

The project was completed in May 1937. The construction cost for the four buildings was $1,089,987 and the project cost $1,199,507. The cost of the dormitory was $191,026.

274

### Students Activity Building

### Virginia Polytechnic Institute

### *Blacksburg, Virginia*

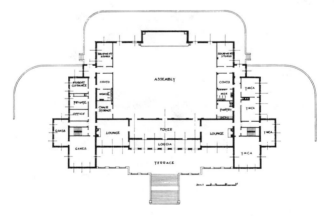

The Virginia Polytechnic Institute has an annual enrollment of 2,400 students.

A number of buildings have been added to its plant with the assistance of the P. W. A. and of these the students' activity building is perhaps the most interesting. It is three stories in height and provides a large assembly room and dance hall, bowling alleys, a room for pool and billiard tables, a refreshment stand, reading rooms, and group conference rooms.

The building is semifireproof. Foundations, frame, and floors are reinforced concrete, exterior walls are face brick trimmed with cast stone and backed with hollow tile, pitched roofs are slate and flat roofs composition. It was completed in August 1937 at a construction cost of $234,073 and a project cost of $251,717.

The Citadel, South Carolina Military School Barracks, *Charleston, South Carolina*

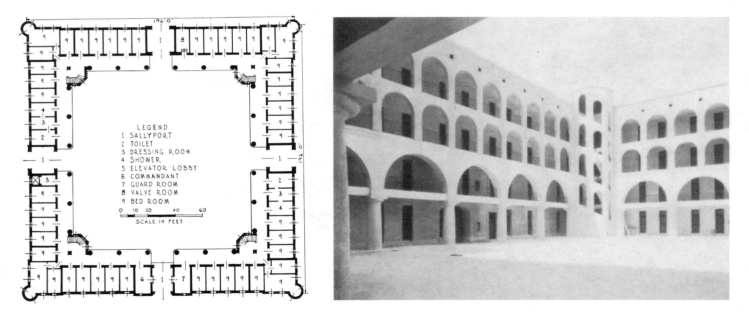

The lack of facilities in the plant made it impossible to meet the demand for an increase in the student body until funds appropriated by the State legislature and a P. W. A. grant made possible the construction of several buildings, one of which was this barracks. It is substantially the same both architecturally and as to construction as the Murray barracks which were built in 1926. It is 4 stories in height and is built around an inner courtyard surrounded with balconies. It provides 52 rooms, 2 toilet rooms, 2 dressing rooms, and 2 shower rooms on each floor.

The construction is frame except the outer walls which are brick and tile stuccoed. The project was completed in April 1939 at a construction cost of $254,306 and a project cost of $264,495 for the barracks only.

*Continued on following page*

The Citadel, South Carolina Military School Chapel, *Charleston, South Carolina*

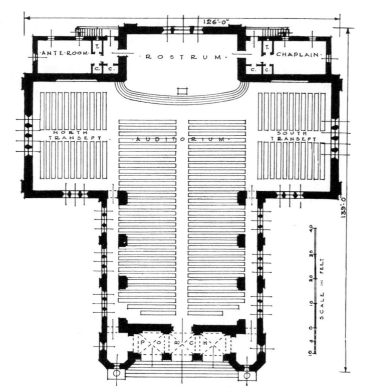

*Continued from preceding page*

Another of the new buildings at The Citadel is the chapel, a pseudo-gothic structure, which is in keeping with the traditional architecture of the school. It can seat the entire student body of 1,000. It is built with tile walls finished with stucco on the outside while the inside is plaster with a wood roof and ceiling of simple beam construction. The chapel was completed in December 1937 at a construction cost of $147,637 and a project cost of $160,596. The total project cost of all the work at The Citadel was $612,996.

## Green Hall, State College of Agriculture, *Kingston, Rhode Island*

The State College of Agriculture at Kingston is a land grant college supported by the State and Federal Governments.

Green Hall forms the focal point of the college and houses the library and administrative offices. The building is T-shaped in plan and the main section is two stories and a basement in height with the rear section three stories high. The offices of the president, vice president, dean, and other administrative offices are on the first floor. The main library, periodical, reading rooms, and offices are on the upper floors, and the rear section is occupied by the bookstacks.

The construction is fireproof. The exterior walls are faced with granite and the roof is covered with slate. Green Hall is one of 10 granite-faced buildings at the college.

The project was completed in September 1937 at a construction cost of $245,927 and a project cost of $255,641.

*Continued on following page*

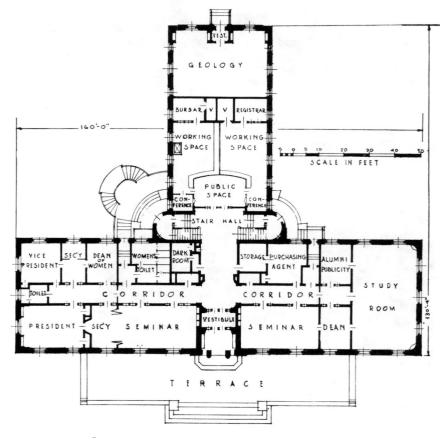

State College of Agriculture

Women's Dormitory

*Kingston, Rhode Island*

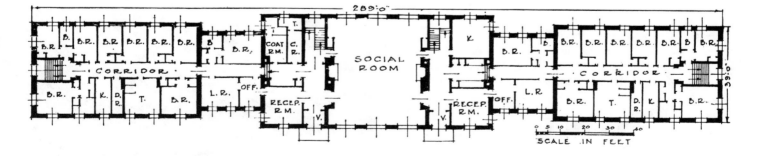

*Continued from preceding page*

This building is 4 stories and part basement in height with 2 wings, each 1 story lower. It provides quarters for 103 women students in double study-bedroom units and in 43 single rooms. It is completely fireproof and its exterior walls are brick trimmed with stone and wood. The roof is covered with slate. Before its construction there were no adequate quarters for housing the women students. The project was completed in 1937 at a construction cost of $199,408 and a project cost of $207,789.

## Brooklyn College
### *Brooklyn, New York*

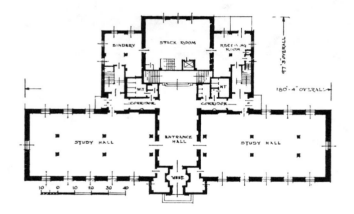

president, the board of higher education, the faculty, the deans, the departments of art and music, four lecture halls seating 800, and a cafeteria seating 1,750 students. The science building is similar in size to the academic building and houses the departments of chemistry, physics, and biology. The gymnasium building has gymnasiums for men and women, four exercise rooms, a hospital, and a swimming pool.

Construction is fireproof throughout, exterior walls being of brick and roofs of slate. The project was completed in December 1937 at a construction cost of $5,450,170 and a project cost of $5,847,776.

Brooklyn College is part of the College of the City of New York and is located on a 40-acre plot of ground in the geographical center of the Borough of Brooklyn. It consists at present of five buildings grouped in such a way that they will eventually form part of a much larger group.

The campus is oval in shape. The library with its tower is at one end of the oval flanked by the academic and science buildings and faced at the opposite end by the gymnasium. The heating plant is placed off campus but near enough to be easily connected to each building by tunnels.

The library contains about 125,000 volumes and seats 700 students in addition to rooms for general study. The academic building contains 200 classrooms, offices for the

## Gymnasium Building
## State Teachers College
### *Mansfield, Pennsylvania*

Three new buildings were constructed for the State Teachers College with P. W. A. aid, one of which is the gymnasium, the other two being the training school and the science and home-economics building.

The gymnasium building is separated into two parts, the front portion containing the gymnasium which has galleries for spectators, and the rear part housing a swimming pool.

It is a fireproof structure with exterior walls of brick trimmed with stone. The project for the three buildings was completed in May 1939 at an approximate construction cost of $497,200 and a project cost of $543,296.

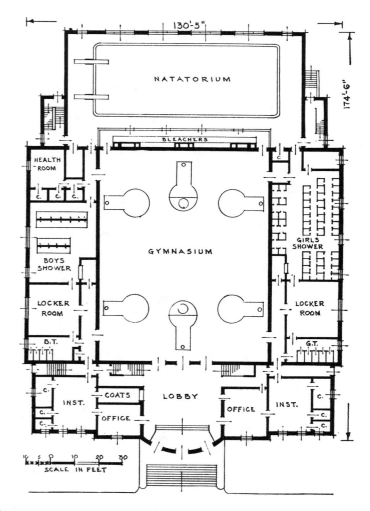

## Auditorium

## State Teachers College

### *Lock Haven, Pennsylvania*

This auditorium at Lock Haven provides a hall seating 700 people, a well-equipped stage, and dressing and work rooms. It is fireproof throughout with exterior walls of brick trimmed with limestone. It is part of a project that included a library building, a gymnasium and swimming pool building, and a central heating plant to serve the entire college. All these structures are fireproof and are finished, like the auditorium, in brick trimmed with limestone.

The four buildings contain approximately 1,973,106 cubic feet and were all completed in July 1939 at an estimated construction cost of $535,967 and a project cost of $586,698.

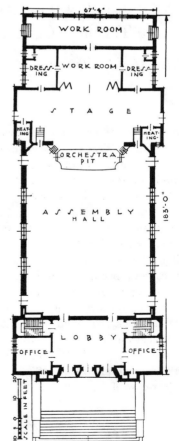

Men's Dormitory, Miami University, *Oxford, Ohio*

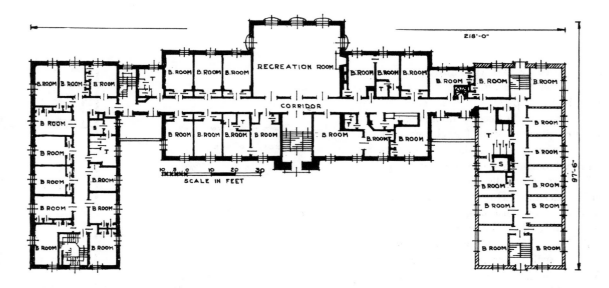

Miami University is now 130 years old. It is one of the oldest colleges in the State. It has a 268-acre campus. The students come from every Ohio county and from many neighboring States. Its enrollment at the time of the P. W. A. application was 2,700, with a faculty of 190.

This new freshman dormitory provides living, dining, and social quarters for 220 men. The north wing at the left of the photograph was built before P. W. A. The building is fireproof. Heat and light are from the college central-heating plant.

The project included some reconstruction to the north wing.

This project was completed in June 1936 at a construction cost of $243,043 and a project cost of $250,425.

## Agricultural Engineering Building, Pennsylvania State College

### *State College, Pennsylvania*

This is one of the 10 buildings constructed with the aid of P. W. A., as described on page 115. It contains classrooms on the second floor and, on the first floor, rooms for classes and demonstration with a large field-machinery laboratory and a machine shop.

The exterior walls are brick-bearing with limestone trim and hollow tile back-up. The framing is structural steel with reinforced concrete floors and roof slabs. The ceilings are covered with acoustical plaster. The ceilings in the lobbies are ornamental plaster. The lobbies have slate and marble trim with terrazzo floors.

The building was substantially completed in June 1939 at an approximate construction cost of $111,360 and a project cost of $122,490.

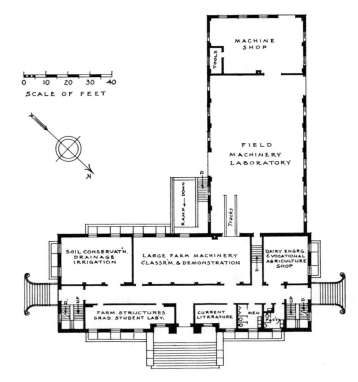

## Dental College Building
## University of Illinois
### *Chicago, Illinois*

The University of Illinois is located at Urbana and has an enrollment of about 14,300. In Chicago, the University, cooperating with the State Department of Public Health, developed a city block as the "Chicago Campus." On this campus it has its medical and dental colleges. This concentration of public health and educational facilities necessitated the tower-type building.

The building is air-conditioned. It has dental chairs to serve 400 dental students. The medical students use the four lower floors. It has a circular amphitheater on the fourth floor and is 9 stories in height and 14 including the tower. The structure is fireproof, is constructed of steel and concrete, and has over 100,000 square feet of floor area.

It was completed in September 1937. The construction cost was $1,353,570 and the project cost was $1,453,221.

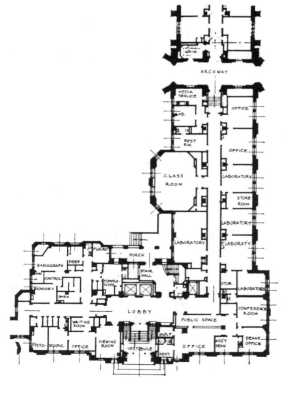

Eastern State Teachers College, Health Education Building, *Charleston, Illinois*

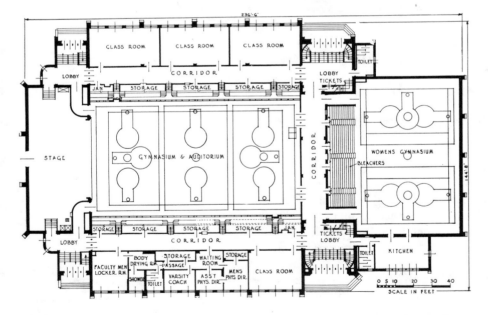

The P. W. A. project of which this health-education building is a part, included also a science building illustrated on the next page. The health-education building provides a men's gymnasium-auditorium, a women's gymnasium, a corrective gymnasium, classrooms, and the necessary shower and locker rooms.

The structure is fireproof, with a steel frame and concrete floor slabs, and the exterior walls are a light-colored brick with stone trim. The interior finished floors are wood, terrazzo, or tile according to requirements.

The total project cost of the two buildings was $812,827 and the health-education building cost $463,782.

*Continued on following page*

## Eastern State Teachers College, Science Building, *Charleston, Illinois*

*Continued from preceding page*

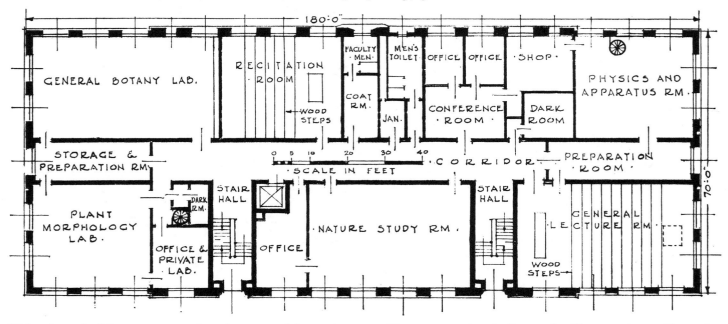

This science building represents the other part of the project of which the health-education building was the first. It is 4 stories in height and contains 10 general classrooms, 4 chemistry laboratories, 2 laboratories for zoology, 3 physics laboratories, 6 other laboratories for minor sciences, a general lecture hall, offices, conference rooms, rooms for photographic work, and stock and store rooms.

The construction is fireproof. The exterior walls to the second-story sills are faced with limestone and above this point are brick with a considerable amount of stone in bands and as trim. Sculpture in stone is used over the entrance doors and at the tops of piers. The project was completed in January 1938 at a construction cost of $327,129.

## Student Union Building
### University of Cincinnati, *Cincinnati, Ohio*

The University of Cincinnati was one of first city colleges in the United States and at the time of the construction of this project it had an enrollment of 9,000 students.

This building has a volume of 1,644,000 cubic feet. It contains the University Book Store, a light-refreshment stand, a general lounge, a faculty dining room seating 125, a main cafeteria dining hall seating 700, six private dining rooms, and the necessary accessory rooms.

The building is fireproof and is heated from the central heating plant. The main rooms have been given acoustical treatment and have special ventilation.

The project was completed in October 1937 at a construction cost of $564,005 and a project cost of $599,747.

288

## Field House and Men's Gymnasium
## Purdue University
### *West Lafayette, Indiana*

This project as developed provides a compact and complete athletic plant. The gymnasium unit is 210 by 110 feet and contains three basketball courts; arenas for boxing, wrestling, and fencing; courts for squash, racquet, and hand ball; a swimming pool 40 by 75 feet with seats for 500 spectators; and in the basement a rifle range and golf driving nets. The field house unit is 302 by 180 feet. The floor is clay and sawdust and the basketball floor is removable. Permanent steel bleachers seat 3,900 and temporary bleachers can be erected, increasing the capacity to 8,500.

The exterior is brick trimmed with stone and the field house is spanned with welded, haunched, two-hinged steel arches. The project was completed in November 1937 at a construction cost of $681,148 and a project cost of $712,164.

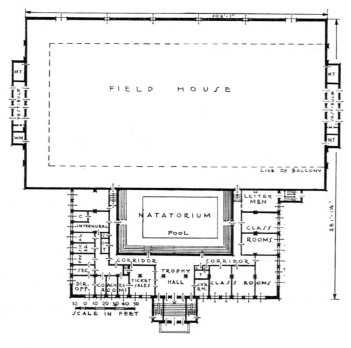

## Indiana University
## Administration Building

### *Bloomington, Indiana*

Indiana University was founded 119 years ago and occupies a spacious campus in Bloomington, Indiana. Its enrollment was 5,891 in 1930 and by 1938 it had increased to 7,113.

With P. W. A. assistance, the administration building, a laboratory building, a women's dormitory, a medical building, and a music building were added to its plant. The total cost of these five structures amounted to $2,158,277.

The administration building provides approximately 50,000 square feet of floor area and has offices for the president, the trustees, the bursar, the registrar, and the deans, together with the necessary conference and committee rooms. The top floor accommodates the photostat, accounting, and multigraph departments.

The architectural character conforms to many of the earlier buildings of the university. The construction is of reinforced concrete and the exterior walls are faced with a random range ashlar of limestone.

The volume is approximately 600,000 cubic feet and its construction cost was $377,961. The project cost was $401,628. It was entirely completed in December 1936.

*Continued on following page*

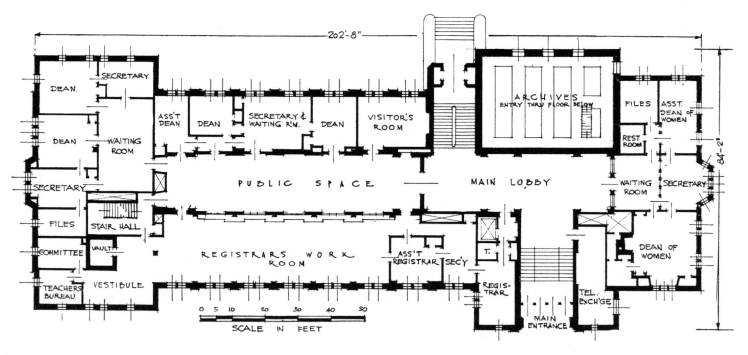

## Indiana University
## College of Music

### *Bloomington, Indiana*

*Continued from preceding page*

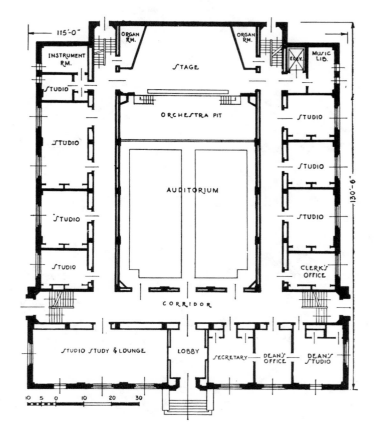

The new music building is approximately 115 by 130 feet. On the first floor is a practice auditorium, seating 320, with stage and orchestra large enough for symphony rehearsals. On this floor are also 7 practice studios, the music library, instrument rooms, a student lounge room, and the dean's offices. On the second floor are 2 library rooms, 3 classrooms, a phonograph-recording room, record-storage room, and 4 practice studios. A balcony of the auditorium, seating 80, opens off the corridor. The third floor contains 55 practice studios. An elevator is provided to handle pianos.

The building is fireproof, the exterior walls being faced with limestone. The volume is approximately 640,000 cubic feet.

The building was completed in December 1936 at a construction cost of $337,286 and a project cost of $360,471.

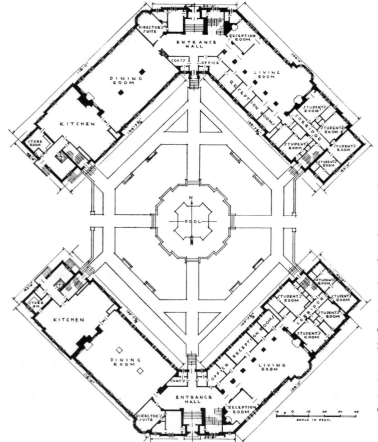

## Women's Dormitory
## Purdue University
### *West Lafayette, Indiana*

Purdue University is a "land-grant college" organized in 1865. It has a 700-acre campus. When the P. W. A. application was made it had an enrollment of about 3,700 students, approximately one-sixth of whom were women.

The building shown is one of two buildings erected in 1934 and 1937 with P. W. A. assistance. They provide for complete living quarters and social activities of the occupants. The picture shows the building constructed in 1934 which accommodates about 240 women.

The exterior walls are variegated red brick. The construction is masonry and reinforced concrete with slate roofs on gypsum slabs. Quarry tile is used in some rooms for floor finish.

This building was completed at a construction cost of $211,618 and a project cost of $223,783. The two buildings have a volume of about 1,160,000 cubic feet and the project cost of the two was $537,874.

William and Mary College Extension, *Norfolk, Virginia*

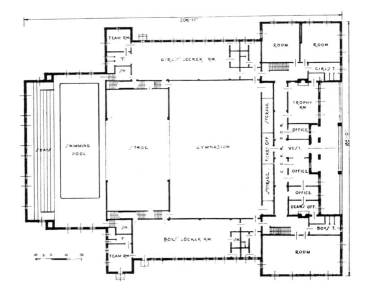

In 1930 the College of William and Mary in Williamsburg established the "Norfolk Extension" on a 5-acre tract of land which had been donated to the college by the city of Norfolk.

The structure illustrated on this page is a combination lecture hall and gymnasium and includes a swimming pool.

Its architectural character conforms to that of the main college in Williamsburg and has exterior walls of red brick trimmed with stone and wood. The floors and roof are bar joist and concrete construction except over the gymnasium where the roof is supported on steel trusses.

The project was completed in July 1936 at a construction cost of $117,826 and a project cost of $127,022.

## Laboratory Building, State Teachers College
### *Bowling Green, Kentucky*

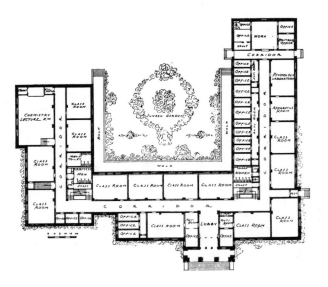

Western Kentucky State College has an enrollment of about 4,000 students, which is one of the largest student bodies of the State teachers colleges in the country.

This project replaces an old, insanitary building which was a firetrap. The P. W. A. grant enabled the board of regents to finish this project. The front portion is 243 by 57 feet. One wing is 131 by 57 feet, and the other is 77 by 68 feet. There are 12 laboratories, a book store, and post office in the basement. There are 50 classrooms and offices on the first and second floors and 16 on the third floor. The building is fireproof.

It was completed in December 1937. The P. W. A. part of the construction cost was $494,724 with a project cost of $556,266.

Laboratory Building, University of Georgia, *Athens, Georgia*

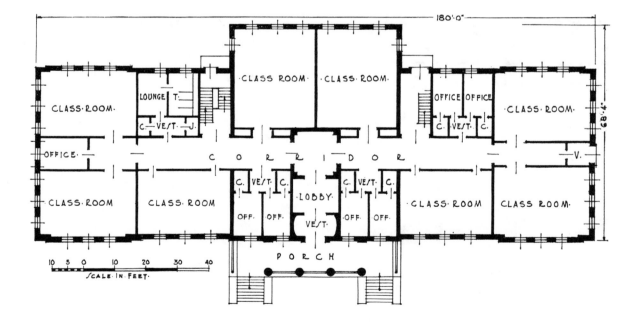

This project, known as the "Laboratory Building," is 2 stories and a basement in height. The basement contains the manual-training department, recreation rooms, an infirmary, a sewing room, kitchen, cafeteria, and the heating plant. On the first floor are 8 classrooms and the administrative offices. The second floor contains 10 classrooms and offices for instructors.

The construction is nonfireproof. The exterior walls are brick trimmed with limestone, and all the rest of the building is wood. The project was completed in January 1939 at a construction cost of $133,634 and a project cost of $137,178.

## Stadium, William and Mary College
### *Williamsburg, Virginia*

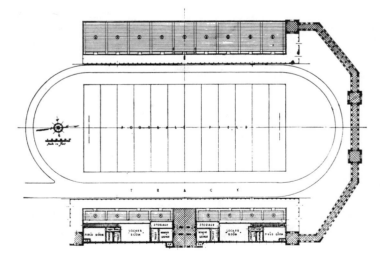

with field rooms and locker rooms underneath, flank the football field on the east and west sides and are connected on the north end by covered arcaded corridors. The bleachers seat 10,000 spectators.

The construction is reinforced concrete with all exterior walls faced with red brick of the type used throughout the college.

The project was completed in January 1936 at a construction cost of $185,585 and a project cost of $196,085.

The College of William and Mary, with the aid of the P. W. A., made several much-needed additions to its plant, among which was the stadium. The original plans called for a students' activity building as well, but investigation of the proposed site showed that this was not feasible on account of soil conditions. The site of the stadium was changed to a much better location but this meant an increase in the cost of the structure.

Two bleacher sections, each approximately 360 by 60 feet,

## Gymnasium and Swimming Pool
## University of North Carolina, *Chapel Hill*, *N. C.*

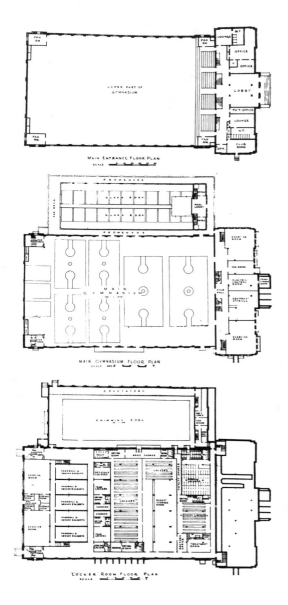

The University of North Carolina, which is more than a century old, had an enrollment of 2,706 in 1935 and 3,500 in 1938. The facilities for outdoor athletics were ample but the gymnasium was too small and inadequately equipped.

The new gymnasium building has a floor 150 by 250 feet in size, provided with removable bleachers seating 3,000. In front of the playing floor is a 2-story and basement unit providing administrative space. The swimming pool is a separate structure but is connected with the gymnasium at the locker-room level. Both buildings are fireproof.

The project was completed in March 1938 at an estimated construction cost of $508,983 and a project cost of $534,836.

## Classroom Building, University of Georgia, *Athens, Georgia*

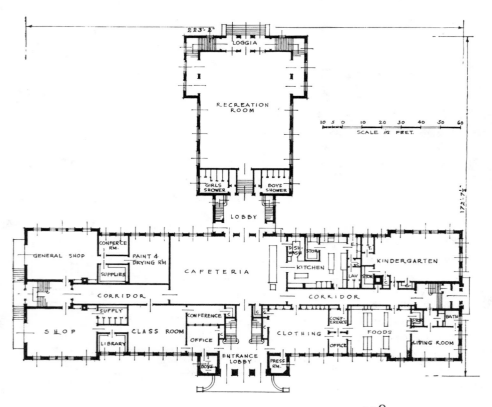

In 1933 the State legislature made it possible for the University of Georgia to secure grants from the P. W. A. with which to carry out an extensive building program to accommodate its increased student body and to replace obsolete equipment. The classroom building is 3 stories and a part basement in height and provides 15 classrooms ranging from a kindergarten through the sixth grade, shops, a model living room with bath, clothing, food and science laboratories, conference rooms, administrative offices, a library, cafeteria, recreation room, and an auditorium with stage.

The area of the building is 30,700 square feet. The construction is semi-fireproof. Exterior walls are limestone to the second floor level and brick with limestone trim above this. The cornice is wood and the columns are painted metal.

The project was completed in December 1938 at a construction cost of $203,479 and a project cost of $215,880.

## Southern Experimental Station, Bureau of Mines
## University of Alabama, *Tuscaloosa, Alabama*

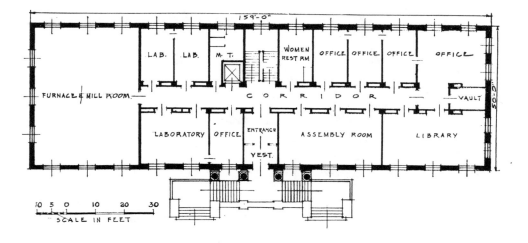

Of the 11 experimental stations of the Bureau of Mines, 9 are located at State universities where they have the advantage of educational facilities and cooperation with the State agencies. This one, at Tuscaloosa, was built on a site of 2½ acres donated by the university.

The building is three stories in height and 50 by 159 feet in plan and provides offices, conference rooms, assembly rooms, a library, a machine shop, assay rooms, and several laboratories for many different purposes. These laboratories are so arranged that they may be expanded and all are equipped with the most modern apparatus.

The exterior walls are brick trimmed with limestone. The total floor area is 20,854 square feet and the volume 356,000 cubic feet. The project was completed in March 1936 at a construction cost of $192,734 and a project cost of $200,000.

Engineering Building, University of Alabama, *Tuscaloosa, Alabama*

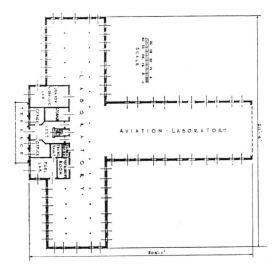

The University of Alabama has an enrollment of more than 5,000 students. The new engineering building permits it to include in its curriculum a complete course in mechanical arts which had not been possible before.

The new structure is T-shaped in plan, the front portion being 2 stories in height and the rear wing 1 story. On the first floor are hydraulic, fuel, and aviation laboratories together with instrument and storage rooms. On the

second floor are 10 classrooms, offices, and an auditorium.

The building is fireproof throughout. The exterior walls are faced with red brick and trimmed with limestone. The pitched roofs are covered with asbestos shingles and the flat roofs with composition. The project was completed in September 1936 at a construction cost of $167,010 and a project cost of $174,205.

## Student Activities Building

## University of Nebraska

### *Lincoln, Nebraska*

This structure is three stories and a basement in height and approximately 100 by 190 feet in over-all dimensions. It contains a main lounge 45 by 90 feet, a ballroom, a dining room, several private dining rooms, kitchens, a students' lunch room, a library, recreation rooms, and offices.

It is of fireproof construction throughout. The exterior walls are red face brick trimmed with limestone. The pitched roof is covered with slate and the flat roofs are composition.

It was completed in May 1938 at a construction cost of $388,964 and a project cost of $417,908.

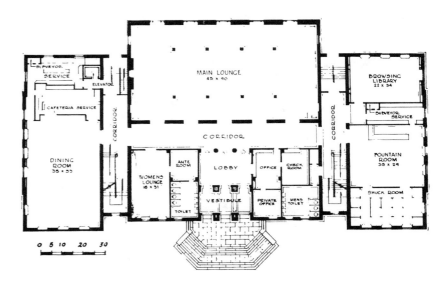

Men's Dormitory, University of Minnesota, *Minneapolis, Minnesota*

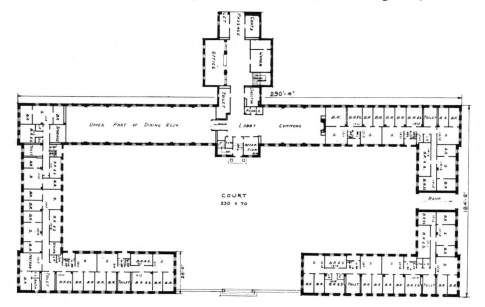

The men's dormitory, known as "Pioneer Hall," at the University of Minnesota, is four stories and a basement in height and is built around a central court or quadrangle open to the outside only for a short distance on one of its long sides.

The dining hall is in the basement and is two stories in height and is served from the kitchen in another building through a tunnel. The first floor has a lobby and a commons room as well as offices and living quarters. The upper floors are devoted to living quarters.

Construction is fireproof, the exterior brick walls being trimmed with stone. The project was completed in October 1934 at a construction cost of $314,013 and a project cost of $327,900.

## Student Cottages, *Canyon, Texas*

The West Texas Teachers College has adopted this unusual and interesting method of housing its students rather than the customary dormitory. Under conditions of high land values and building costs it would not, as a rule, be possible, but as an exception it has much interest.

Each building provides a living room, kitchen, bathroom, and three bedrooms, and accommodates six students. The rent is $30 per month, or $5 per student if the house is fully occupied.

The foundations are concrete, exterior walls are masonry with a stucco finish, and the balance of the construction is frame.

The 10 units were completed in September 1936 at a construction cost of $36,683 and a project cost of $38,983.

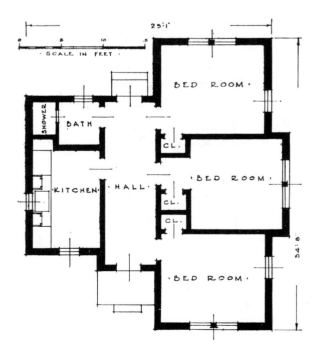

# University Theatre, State University of Iowa

## *Iowa City, Iowa*

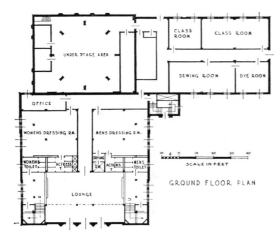

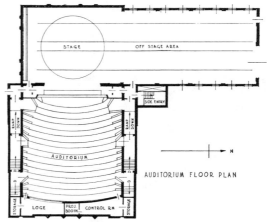

This structure is devoted to experimental work and teaching of dramatic arts. It consists of an auditorium seating 500, a large stage with a high fly loft and a grid, a revolving stage, 38 feet in diameter, and a well-equipped workshop forming a continuation of the stage. In addition there are classrooms, a sewing room, dye room, dressing rooms, and a large lounge below the entrance foyer.

The building is fireproof. The walls below grade are concrete and brick backed with hollow tile above grade. The floors are reinforced concrete slabs and the roof structural steel framing and gypsum plank.

The project was completed in July 1936 at a construction cost of $166,635 and a project cost of $166,930.

Fine Arts Building, State University of Iowa, *Iowa City, Iowa*

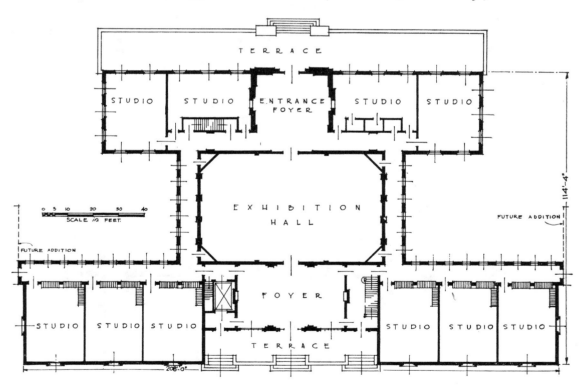

The Fine Arts Building stands on the bank of a stream not far from the University Theatre. It contains a centrally located exhibition hall, 42 by 73 feet and 20 feet high and 10 studios all oriented so that they receive north light through windows or skylights which is supplemented by adjustable reflectors for artificial light. Construction is fireproof of reinforced con-crete with exterior walls faced with brick and trimmed with stone. Indirect lighting in the ceiling, lights the exhibition hall. The project was completed in July 1936 at an esti-mated construction cost of $181,195 and a project cost of $181,489.

Veterinary Clinic Building, *Ames, Iowa*

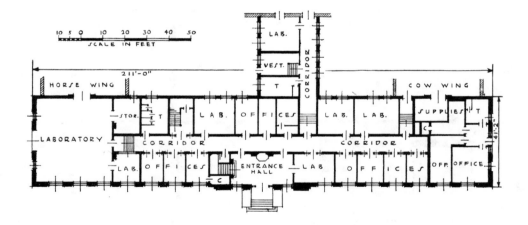

The Iowa State College of Agriculture and Mechanic Arts provides courses in veterinary medicine, surgery, and animal husbandry, and this building supplies the necessary plant and equipment for carrying on these studies.

The building is two stories in height and constitutes an addition to existing cow barns and buildings for housing animals. It contains administrative offices and an operating section as well as laboratories and rooms for special work and study.

The construction is fireproof throughout. The exterior walls are faced with brick and trimmed with stone and on the interior, floors are terrazzo, and walls of glazed terra-cotta blocks.

The project was completed in December 1937 at a construction cost of $178,101 and a project cost of $183,910.

Dormitories, University of Texas, *Austin, Texas*

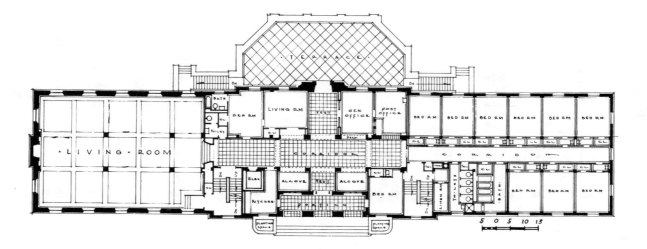

The student body of the University of Texas increased from 6,000 in 1920 to 10,000 in 1930, necessitating an extensive building program for the university. Carothers Dormitory for girls was one of the first buildings constructed.

It is three stories and a basement in height and provides 61 double bedrooms, living room, dining room, matron's suite, staff bedrooms, and the necessary kitchens and service rooms.

The building is semi-fireproof, the exterior walls being of brick trimmed with stone and stucco. It was completed in March 1937 at a construction cost of $250,572 and a project cost of $264,923.

307

Music Hall, College of Industrial Arts, *Denton, Texas*

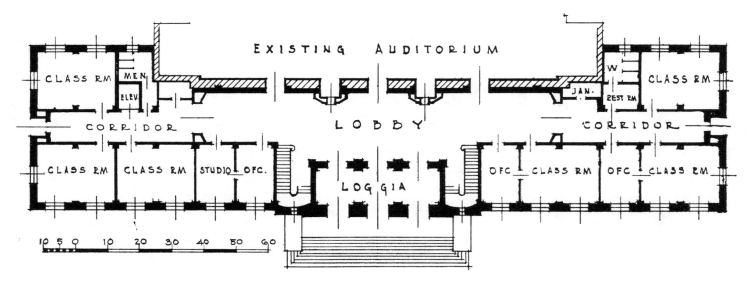

Among several new units constructed by the College of Industrial Arts is the music hall which is an addition to the front of the existing auditorium.

The structure is 3 stories in height and contains 10 standard classrooms, 22 small classrooms, 19 practice rooms, and a small auditorium for group work. A large foyer provides entrance to both the music hall and to the auditorium.

Construction is reinforced concrete, with the exterior walls faced with brick and trimmed with stone.

The project was completed in June 1937 at a construction cost of $160,289 and a project cost of $172,783, both estimated.

## Students' Union Building, University of New Mexico
### *Albuquerque, New Mexico*

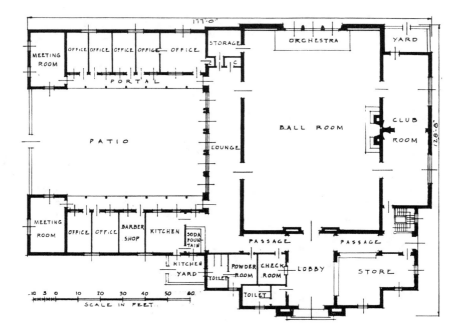

This project, in addition to the students' union building, included a central heating plant and irrigation system, a library, and a health laboratory.

The students' union building includes a large central ballroom around which are placed clubrooms, lunch and fountain-service rooms, cooperative stores, and students' offices. The ballroom is large enough to accommodate 250 couples on the floor and the clubrooms can be opened and used as an overflow.

The building is semifireproof. The exterior walls are finished in stucco and its effect together with the architectural design is to give the structure the appearance of an ancient Indian pueblo.

The project was completed in April 1938 at a construction cost of $97,809 and a project cost of $104,355. The cost of of the entire project was $694,086.

## Administration and Laboratory Building
## University of New Mexico
### *Albuquerque, New Mexico*

The new administration and laboratory building for the University of New Mexico is designed in the "Pueblo" style to conform to the other buildings on the university campus.

It consists of a 3-story central unit flanked by two 2-story wings. The first floor contains the administrative offices and the department of anthropology, the latter including a museum and rooms for laboratory and research work. On the second floor are the departments of geology and physics

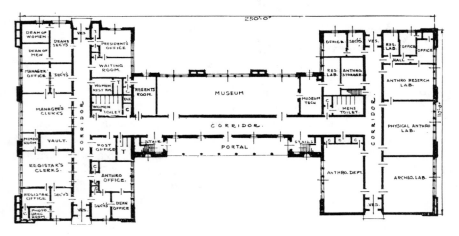

and part of the department of psychology. The third floor accommodates the remainder of the department of psychology.

The construction is semifireproof. The exterior and bearing walls are brick and other walls tile, the exterior finish being stucco and the interior plaster. Exterior trim is wood.

The project was completed in April 1936 at a construction cost of $254,609 and a project cost of $275,796.

Fine Arts Building, State Agriculture College, *Monticello, Arkansas*

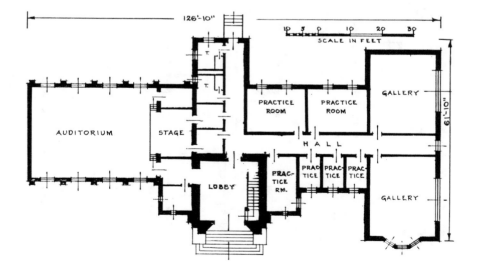

This structure houses the various fine arts departments of the college. On the first floor are the offices, recitation and class rooms, and a small auditorium seating 185. The second floor is given up entirely to recitation and practice rooms.

The building is semifireproof, the exterior walls being faced with random rock-faced stone ashlar trimmed with cut limestone. The plan permits of easy enlargement. The project was completed in May 1935. The construction cost was $94,856 and the project cost $105,897.

## School of Medicine, University of Arkansas

### *Little Rock, Arkansas*

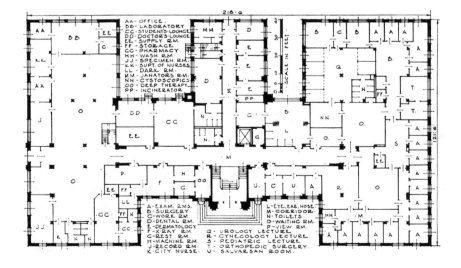

The University of Arkansas is in Fayetteville but its school of medicine is in Little Rock, and its new building has been erected on a site adjoining the city hospital, thus affording the students better opportunities for study and for contact with the hospital staff. Formerly the school occupied the old capitol building which had not been sufficiently remodeled to make it practical for school purposes.

The new building is 5 stories in height and provides a clinic, laboratories, a library, an amphitheatre, classrooms, and lecture rooms, and all necessary facilities for the instruction of 500 students. It has exterior walls of brick trimmed with stone. It was completed in February 1936 at a construction cost of $457,633 and a project cost of $506,318.

## President's House, Arkansas State Teachers College
### *Conway, Arkansas*

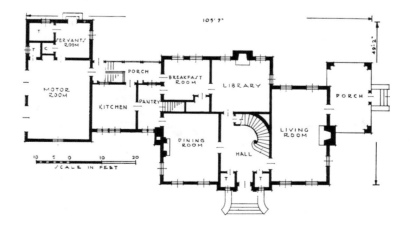

The president's house was one unit of a P. W. A. docket which included the construction and equipment of six separate units for the Arkansas State Teachers College. It is a two-story structure containing a two-car garage, living room, dining and breakfast rooms, library, and kitchen on the first floor; and three bedrooms, a sleeping porch, and baths on the second floor. The design is colonial and is carried out in red brick with wood trim and a slate roof. It was completed in June 1937 at a construction cost of $17,520 and a project cost of $21,498, both estimated.

## Men's Dormitory, University of Arkansas
### *Fayetteville, Arkansas*

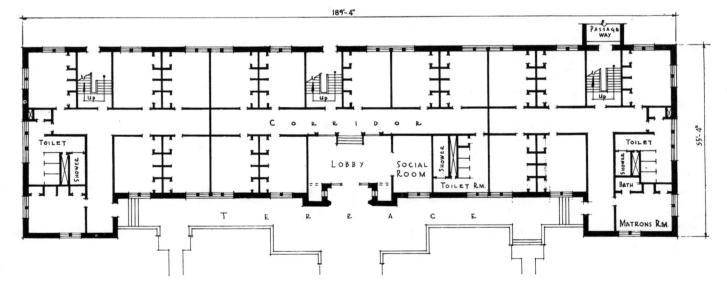

The new men's dormitory at the University of Arkansas is divided into three separate units, each having its own entrances and stairway.

The building is 55 by 189 feet in plan and 3 stories in height. On the first floor are 19 double rooms, a lobby, and a social room. The second and third floors each provide 21 double rooms, so that the entire building can accommodate 122 students.

The structure is fireproof, with reinforced concrete floor and roof slabs and exterior walls of brick trimmed with stone. It was completed in August 1937 at a construction cost of $143,549 and a project cost of $156,803

## Field House, University of Arkansas, *Fayetteville, Arkansas*

Previous to the building of this new field house, the old auditorium of this university could not seat more than 650 spectators. It was a frame building unsuited to the needs of the university.

The new building is 3 stories in height. On the ground floor are locker, storage, and utility rooms. The gymnasium and auditorium occupy the entire first floor. A small second floor, across the front of the building, contains offices. There is an additional entrance to the ground floor from the out-

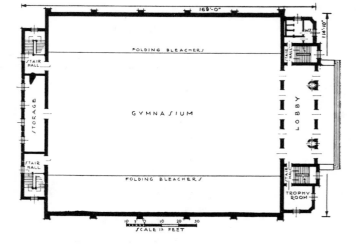

side. The building is 115 by 169 feet. The playing floor of the gymnasium is 103 by 135 feet, sufficient for 2 practice basketball courts when the bleacher seats are folded. When these seats are open the floor space provides a standard basketball court, and 2,112 spectators may be seated. When used as an assembly hall, it seats 3,250.

The building was completed in August 1937. The construction cost was $152,137 and the project cost $165,505.

Field House, University of Colorado
*Boulder, Colorado*

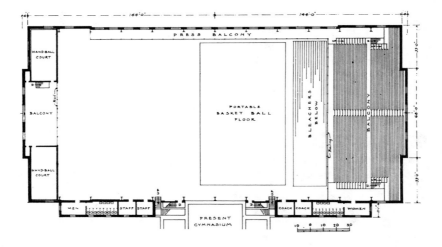

The new field house for the University of Colorado is approximately 144 by 296 feet in over-all dimensions. The large hall has an earth floor with a cinder running track 12 laps to the mile, and is provided with a removable wood basketball floor, 60 by 90 feet. Permanent bleachers seat approximately 2,000, and removable bleachers on both sides of the basketball court can seat approximately 1,900. There are 2 handball courts as well. The exterior walls are in random ashlar of native stone. The wood roof covered with tile is supported on steel girders and purlins.

The project was completed in September 1936 at a construction cost of $114,156 and a project cost of $122,295.

Women's Club Building, University of Colorado, *Boulder, Colorado*

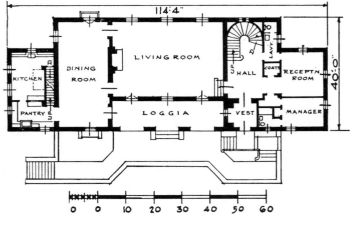

Before the construction of the new women's club, the University of Colorado had no suitable facilities for the holding of social functions by women.

The building is two stories in height and contains on the first floor a living room, approximately 40 by 25 feet, a dining room, reception room, manager's office, kitchen, and pantry. The second floor is devoted to bedrooms.

Construction is fireproof with a reinforced-concrete frame and floor slabs, exterior walls of native stone, and a roof covered with tile. The building was completed in September 1937 at a construction cost of $65,707 and a project cost of $69,236.

Auditorium and Commons Building, University of Wichita, *Wichita, Kansas*

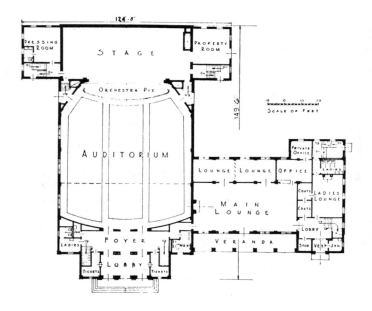

The construction of this building has provided a recreation center for the students as well as releasing space formerly used for such purposes, for classrooms. It is a 2-story structure somewhat irregular in plan and contains an auditorium, seating 1,200 on the floor and 600 in the balcony, and is provided with a well-equipped stage. Adjoining this are a lounge and small clubrooms. On the second floor are the main dining room, a private dining room, and the kitchen. The construction is semifireproof. Exterior walls are faced with brick trimmed with stone and wood. The project was completed in October 1936 at a construction cost of $182,544 and a project cost of $191,834.

Liberal Arts Building, University of Wyoming, *Laramie, Wyoming*

This building houses the entire liberal arts department of the University of Wyoming.

It is rectangular in plan with an auditorium in the center, surrounded with classrooms, and is four stories and basement in height.

The first floor contains the auditorium and its stage, the entrance lobby, offices, and classrooms. Dressing rooms for the stage are in the basement. The second floor has seven classrooms, offices, two political economy rooms, a lobby, and the balcony for the auditorium. On the third floor are seven classrooms, rooms for English, history, Latin, and offices. On the fourth floor are offices and a lecture room.

The structure is entirely fireproof and the exterior walls are faced with a rough ashlar of local stone obtained in a quarry owned by the university. The spandrels and parapet copings are dressed stone.

The project was completed in June 1936 at a construction cost of $339,311 and a project cost of $366,775.

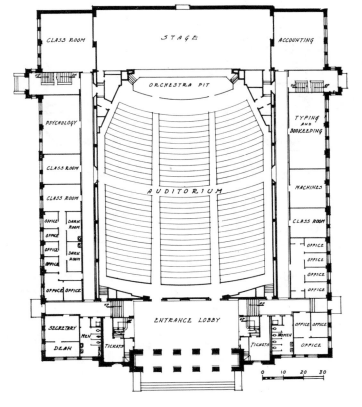

## Auditorium and Gymnasium, Georgia School of Technology, *Atlanta, Georgia*

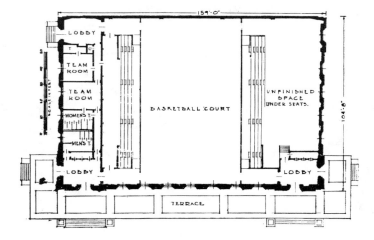

The Georgia School of Technology has an enrollment of more than 2,000 students but until the completion of this project had never had a gymnasium or an auditorium.

The building is 105 by 159 feet and provides floor space for basketball and a permanent seating capacity of 2,000. Portable seats placed on the playing floor can increase the seating capacity to 3,000.

The construction is monolithic concrete and due to soil conditions the structure rests on concrete piles. It was completed in January 1937 at a construction cost of $91,196 and a project cost of $92,911.

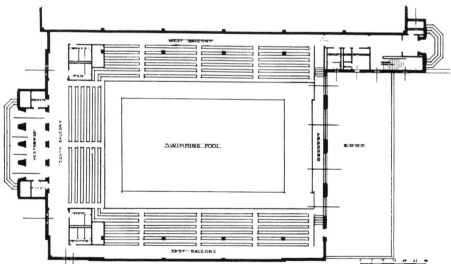

## Swimming Pool Building
## University of Washington
### *Seattle, Washington*

This structure, housing the swimming pool, was erected as an addition to the physical-education building. The swimming pool is 42 by 75 feet and galleries for spectators are provided to seat 1,000.

The construction is reinforced concrete with exterior walls faced with brick and trimmed with cast stone. The steel roof trusses support a wood roof.

The project was completed in September 1938 at a construction cost of $193,818 and a project cost of $205,887.

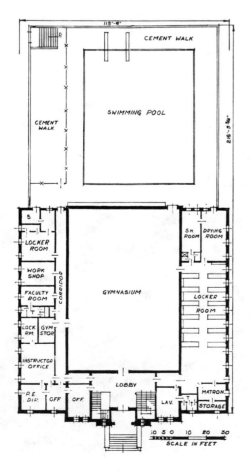

## Women's Building
## University of Arizona

*Tucson, Arizona*

The University of Arizona carried out a rather extensive building program with the aid of the P. W. A. The women's building is characteristic of the architecture that was adopted for all buildings and has a somewhat north Italian medieval flavor and blends with the surroundings.

The building is part one and part two stories in height. On the first floor is a women's gymnasium, 61 by 90 feet, with special exercise and locker rooms adjoining. There is also a swimming pool, 30 by 75 feet, furnished with underwater lighting and a modern sterilizing and filtering plant. On the second floor is a recreation hall, 86 by 114 feet, which may be used for dances. The orchestra is provided with a music shell on one side of this room.

The structure is semifireproof, exterior walls being brick trimmed with terra cotta, and the roof, tile. The project was completed in March 1937 at a construction cost of $96,309 and a project cost of $104,316.

Washington State College Stadium, *Pullman, Washington*

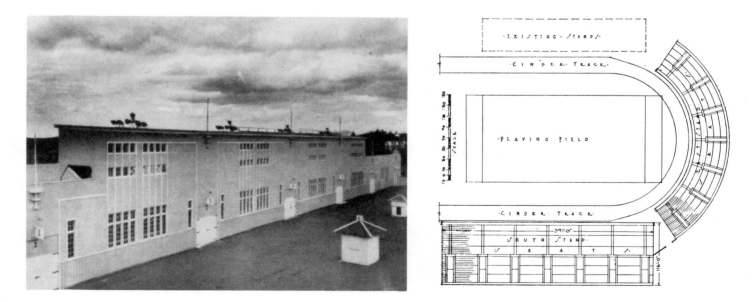

The location of the Washington State College Stadium was determined upon after considerable study by the designers of the campus plan. A site was selected where the natural contours of the ground sloped down to the athletic field and the seating was made to conform to these slopes, thus reducing the construction work and the cost.

This project consists of 2 sections, the south stand being rectangular and the east stand in the shape of an arc of a circle. The 2 together seat 21,000 people.

The construction is concrete on natural grade or fill 60 percent of the distance to the top, and frame the rest of the way up. The date of completion was September 1936. The construction cost was $104,062 and the project cost $107,617.

## Athletic Field Pavilion, *Cranston, Rhode Island*

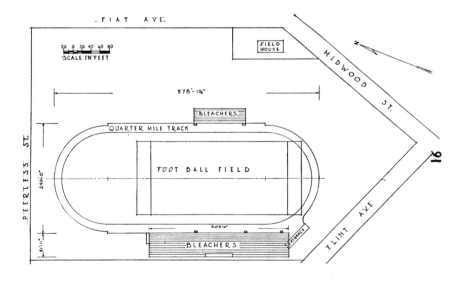

Cranston is the fourth city in size in Rhode Island. It was incorporated in 1910, and in 1930 had a population of 42,910.

This pavilion is at the recreation center and replaces portable wooden bleachers. It seats 6,000 people, and a press box enclosed for radio broadcasting surmounts the central section. Below the seat construction are ticket offices, storage for park tools, and sanitary conveniences.

The athletic field is lighted for night use and the pavilion provides seats for spectators for football and baseball games, track meets, band concerts, and pageants.

The entire construction is reinforced concrete. The project was completed in October 1936 at a construction cost of $53,955 and a project cost of $61,321.

## Field House and Stadium for the Public Schools, *Westfield*, *New Jersey*

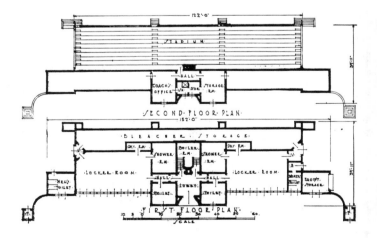

This structure supplements an athletic field which had been developed on the grounds of the Lincoln School. It consists of bleachers to seat 788 spectators with a field house underneath providing locker and shower rooms and rooms for coaches and equipment. The construction is reinforced concrete with exterior walls of stuccoed concrete block. The project was completed in September 1936 at a construction cost of $32,283 and a project cost of $35,577.

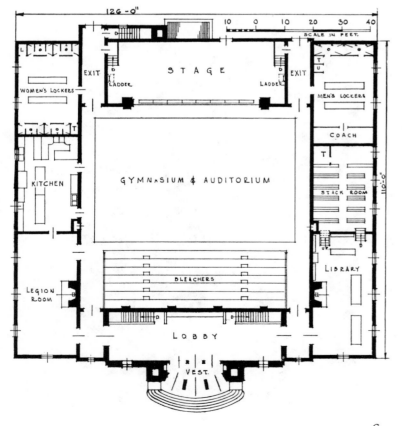

## Mills and Petrie Memorial
### *Ashton, Illinois*

This building constitutes a cultural and recreational community center. It was constructed with a donation of site and of $40,000 by a citizen of Ashton and with the aid of the P. W. A. It provides a public library, a stack room, a combination auditorium and gymnasium with a stage and men's and women's locker rooms, a kitchen, and a room for the American Legion.

It is a fireproof structure and the exterior walls are a light-colored brick trimmed with stone. The auditorium-gymnasium is used by the high school as well as by the public. It was completed in June 1936 at a construction cost of $103,701 and a project cost of $106,702.

## Outdoor Swimming Pool

### *Wheeling, West Virginia*

This swimming pool in Wheeling Park is part of a project which included, also, the houses and a small pavilion for a municipal golf course in the same park. It is 80 by 200 feet in size and is surrounded by concrete walks. Facing the deep end of the pool is the bathhouse which contains dressing and shower rooms for men and women, rooms for life guards and for concessions, and the filter room. There is a terrace for spectators on part of the roof.

The project was completed in July 1937 at a construction cost of $90,266 and a project cost of $95,728. The cost of the golf-course pavilion was approximately $8,000.

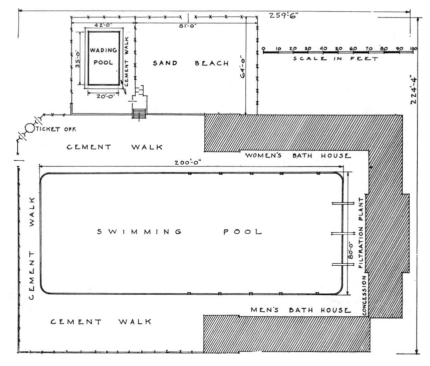

## Swimming Pool and Pavilion, *La Grange, Georgia*

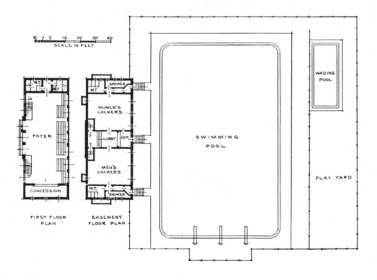

shower rooms and the office are on the first floor, and the second floor is used as an observation gallery. The construction is fireproof, and the water for the pools is properly sterilized by filteration and chlorination.

The project was completed in April 1935 at a construction cost of $37,952 and a project cost of $39,594.

La Grange is an industrial city of 20,000 population in the western part of the State. It decided to provide a recreation center for its citizens and included in this program a swimming pool which was constructed in a public park which adjoins the residential district.

The project consists of a swimming pool, 75 by 125 feet, a wading pool, and a two-story bathhouse. The locker and

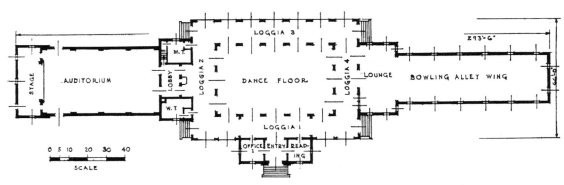

## Recreation Center

### *St. Simons Island, Georgia*

St. Simons Island is a popular resort, and this building was constructed to replace the county-owned casino and pier which were destroyed by fire in 1935. The project consisted of the casino and a swimming pool, 50 by 100 feet.

The building contains an auditorium, bowling alleys, and dance hall, while locker rooms are placed underneath the walks surrounding the swimming pool.

Construction is fireproof. Exterior walls are faced with brick and the roofs are slate. The project was completed in September 1936 at a construction cost of $71,471 and a project cost of $77,275.

Municipal Stadium, *Miami, Florida*

 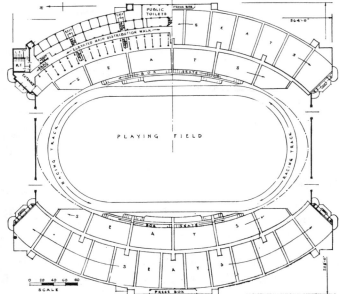

The city of Miami had no proper accommodations for spectators at its athletic field except wooden bleachers accommodating 10,000. The demand for a modern field became so great that this development was deemed necessary. The new stadium is called the "Orange Bowl" and has become nationally known in athletic circles. It has a seating capacity of 22,000. It is of steel-frame construction with wooden seats and has a concrete front on the field side and at the 2 ends. It is equipped with all conveniences for athletics and spectators, and is provided with illumination by reflectors on steel towers for athletic events held at night.

It was completed in September 1937 at a construction cost of $306,041 and a project cost of $324,627.

Swimming Pool and Bathhouse, *Des Moines, Iowa*

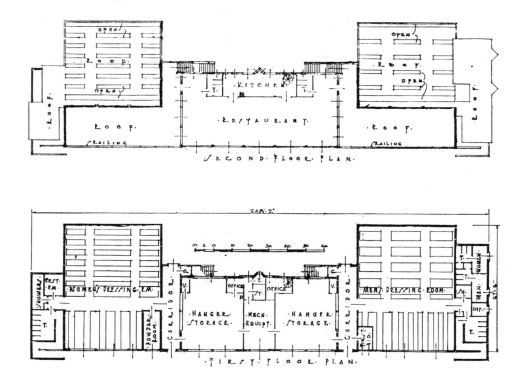

This swimming pool and bathhouse was constructed in the municipal park by the city of Des Moines.

The swimming pool is reinforced concrete, measures 57 by 164 feet, and is provided with a modern filtration, circulating, and sterilizing plant. The bathhouse is two stories in height and contains on the first floor dressing and shower rooms for men and women. On the second floor is a dining room, a kitchen, an observation deck, and a small dance floor. The bathhouse is built of structural tile painted on the outside.

The project was completed in June 1936 at a construction cost of $103,565 and a project cost of $109,992.

Sonotorium, *Kearney, Nebraska*

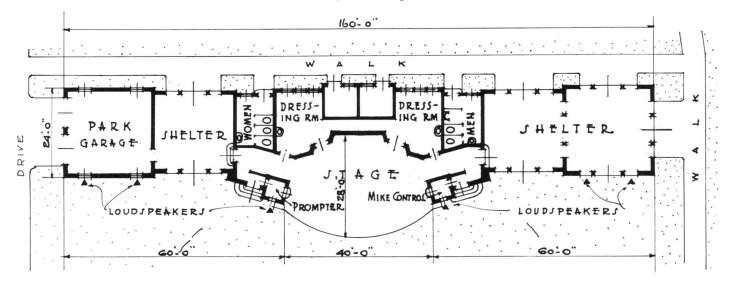

The word "Sonotorium" is a coined word used to name this open-air theater which includes, in addition to its stage and dressing rooms, park shelters, comfort stations, and a park garage. It is used for radio programs, theatrical productions, and public speaking. The stage and pylons are constructed of reinforced concrete while the shelter houses are frame covered with cement stucco. The stage is equipped with a public-address system, six loudspeakers, and a radio-program pick-up. The project was completed in June 1938 at a construction cost of $11,438 and a project cost of $12,081.

## Swimming Pool and Bathhouse

### *Marshall, Minnesota*

The illustration is a view of the new bathhouse constructed in connection with the swimming pool at Marshall. The central pavilion contains attendants' and equipment rooms with a covered bandstand on the second floor. Flanking this are the men's and women's dressing and shower rooms. Over these are open terraces for spectators, approached by stairways at each end. The swimming pool is 60 by 120 feet and is constructed of reinforced concrete and provided with modern sterilizing equipment, diving boards, and guard towers. The walls of the bathhouse are local field stone.

The project was completed in July 1938 at a construction cost of $31,506 and a project cost of $33,741.

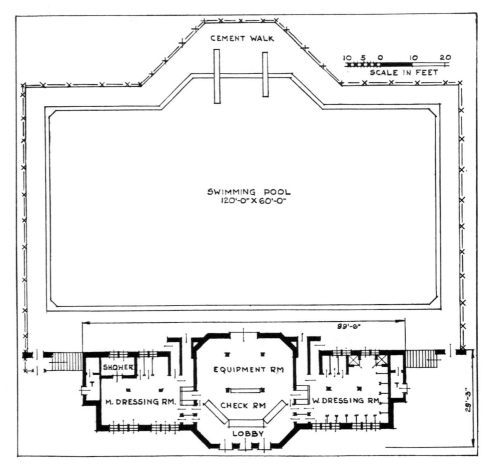

## Sylvan Lake Hotel

### *Rapid City, South Dakota*

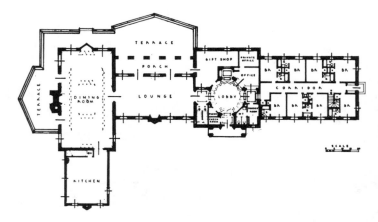

The Sylvan Lake Hotel, erected for the Custer State Park Board, is located about 37 miles southwest of Rapid City on the shore of a beautiful lake, surrounded by rugged hills and woods.

The building contains 29 guest rooms, a large lounge, dining room, and kitchen. The lounge is the equivalent of 2 stories in height with wood walls of random width knotty-pine boards, exposed wood roof trusses, a wood ceiling, and a random width oak-plank floor.

The construction is a combination of native-stone walls and wood frame.

The project was completed in September 1937 at a construction cost of $140,008 and a project cost of $151,628.

Municipal Swimming Pool and Bathhouse, *Big Spring, Texas*

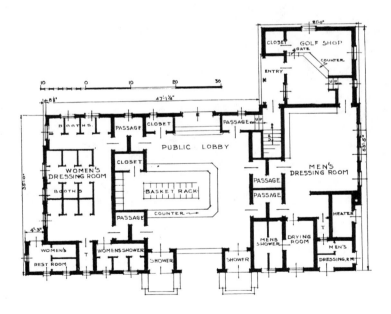

The population of this city in 1930 was 13,735, which had increased 9,462 in 10 years. It was necessary to expand all municipal accommodations accordingly.

The swimming pool is 60 by 150 feet, with depth varying from 3½ to 10 feet. The bathhouse has a lobby and locker and dressing rooms for men and women. The caretaker lives on the second floor. The swimming pool is reinforced concrete. The bathhouse is wood frame with brick exterior walls.

The project was completed in October 1935 at a construction cost of $33,023 and a project cost of $35,079.

Municipal Swimming Pool, *Santa Barbara, California*

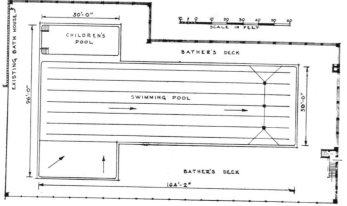

The evident thought and care exercised in the design and planning of this municipal swimming pool has resulted in a satisfactory architectural composition.

The pool is L-shaped, 50 by 165 feet on the long leg and 15 by 50 feet on the short. The smaller leg is for the use of children. The bathhouses and other necessary facilities are adequate and the most modern methods are used for sterilizing the water of the pool. This project was completed in October 1938 at a construction cost of $70,931 and a project cost of $78,845.

## Recreational Building

*Huntington Beach, California*

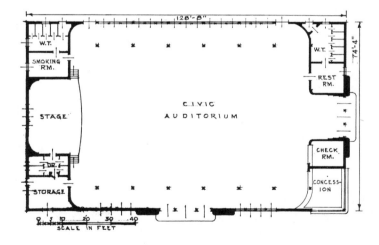

This project consisted of the erection of the recreational building and improvement of the approaches and beach front. The building is located at the shore end of the existing municipal pier. The beach south of this pier attracts a large number of people as it is especially safe and attractive for bathing.

The recreational building is two stories in height and approximately 75 by 129 feet. The lower floor is used as a lunchroom for picnic parties and on the upper floor is a dance floor, 55 by 75 feet, with a raised platform at one end which may be used for orchestras or for theatrical performances, and also concession space for beverages and refreshment.

The construction is frame and the structure is supported on creosoted wood piles. The exterior finish is stucco with wood trim.

The project was completed in May 1938 at a construction cost of $55,569 and a project cost of $59,998.

## Painted Desert Inn, *Petrified Forest National Monument, Arizona*

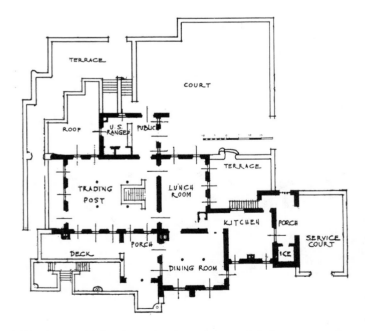

The building contains a dining room and a sandwich shop with kitchens, an Indian museum, a trading post for products of Indian make, a ranger's quarters, a naturalist's office, and eight rooms for lodging tourists. These rooms are on different levels and each has a walled and landscaped terrace.

The over-all dimensions of the structure are approximately 100 by 75 feet. Its walls are rubble masonry with a plaster finish.

The project was completed in April 1939. The P. W. A. allotment, which included the purchase of land, was $130,888.74.

This inn, which gives the impression of being an ancient construction of the Indians, is a modern hotel. It was built on the southern edge of the Painted Desert, 25 miles east of Holbrook, Arizona, by the National Park Service.

## Municipal Park Improvements
## Club House
### *Dorris-Norton Park*
### *Phoenix, Arizona*

In order to provide its citizens and its large transient population with better park facilities, the city of Phoenix undertook the rehabilitation and beautification of existing parks and the acquisition of lands for the creation of new mountain and city parks. The type of buildings erected in these parks was similar in all cases and their character and design blend with the brilliant sunshine and the native foliage. The illustration on this page is a view of the club house in the Dorris-Norton Park. It is one and part two stories in height and contains a large public dining room, a lunchroom, living quarters, and an office for the club manager and is connected to the boat house by a pergola. It was completed in June 1937 at a construction cost of $37,000 and a project cost of $45,872, not including equipment.

*Continued on following page*

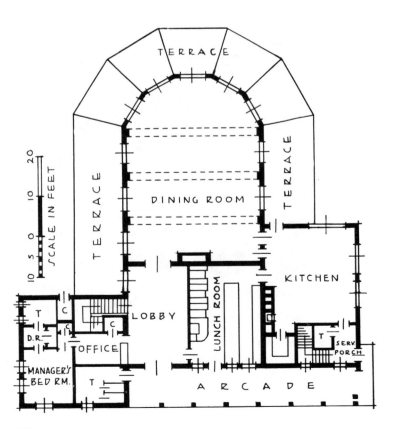

## Municipal Park Improvements, Boat House and Locker House,
### *Dorris-Norton Park, Phoenix, Arizona*
*Continued from preceding page*

The upper illustration shows the boathouse and dock in the Dorris-Norton Park. It was completed in 1937 at a construction cost of $3,400 and a project cost of $4,850. The locker house (illustrated above) contains locker and shower rooms for men and women. Its exterior walls are painted brick and the roof is covered with Spanish tile. It was completed in June 1937 at a construction cost of $10,500 and a project cost of $13,457. This does not include equipment, electrical work, sewer, or water connections.

*Continued on following page*

## Municipal Park Improvements

## Band Shell

## *Dorris-Norton Park, Phoenix, Arizona*

*Continued from preceding page*

The revival of interest in listening to music out of doors has not been overlooked by the city of Phoenix in its park improvement program, and this band shell in the Dorris-Norton Park provides a place where the bands and orchestras of the city can play. The shell is constructed entirely of wood covered with stucco and has been designed to reflect and amplify the sound over a large area of the park. It was completed in June 1937 at a construction cost of $5,400 and a project cost of $6,731 which did not include electrical connections for lighting or amplifiers.

The entire docket included improvements in 14 different parks and provided for tennis courts and other recreational areas, grandstands, paths, landscaping, water and sewer lines, and various appurtenant buildings. One unit of the park system, the archaeological development, consisted of the construction of laboratory facilities, archaeological excavation, and reconstruction of ruins for which work $15,000 was authorized. All improvements were completed in May 1937 and involved a total project cost of $923,041.

## Seattle Park Clubhouse, *Seattle, Washington*

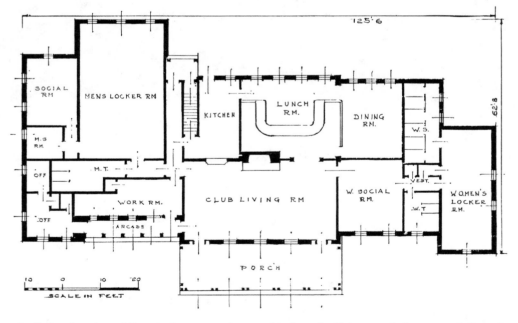

This clubhouse was built by the city of Seattle in connection with one of its public golf courses that are included in the city park and recreation areas.

The building has a small basement, a first floor, and a partial second floor. The heating plant occupies the basement; the first floor contains a spacious living room, locker rooms for men and women, a dining room, lunchroom, and kitchen facilities; and the second floor has quarters for the custodian.

The basement and first floors are concrete, but otherwise this building is frame with exterior brick veneer walls.

The project was completed in September 1936 at a construction cost of $29,225 and a project cost of $31,037.

## Bluebeard Castle Hotel

### *St. Thomas, Virgin Islands*

Among the several projects in the Virgin Islands was the Bluebeard Castle Hotel. The group of buildings was erected on the summit of a hill 200 feet above the sea. An ancient stone tower with walls 5½ feet thick, is supposed to have been the watchtower of the famous legendary pirate, Bluebeard. The building on the right in the larger illustration contains the lobby, administrative offices, dining room, bar, kitchen, and service rooms. A detail of its entrance portico is illustrated on the right side of this page. Terraces planted with palms, tropical flowers, and foliage surround all the buildings. The building in which Bluebeard's tower is incorporated is one of the guest houses and, with other guest houses and cottages, provides accommodations for 100. Much of the construction is concrete or stone, some is frame, and the roofs are mostly metal. Since no well water is available it is necessary to catch all rain water which is stored in large cisterns under the buildings. The project was completed in May 1938 at a total cost of $271,842 of which amount the P. W. A. appropriated $133,644, the Virgin Islands $20,000 for the land, and the W. P. A. $118,198.

# INDEX

Note to the Da Capo Edition: This index, reprinted from the original book, refers to the original pagination, which has been retained for the Da Capo edition in two volumes. Buildings with page references of 1-343 will be located in Volume I; those listed for pages 344-666 can be found in Volume II.

176638

## *Titles of Related Interest —*

**A MONOGRAPH OF THE WORKS OF McKIM, MEAD & WHITE 1879-1915**
New introduction by Paul Goldberger

**ITALIAN VILLAS AND THEIR GARDENS**
by Edith Wharton

**IN THE NATURE OF MATERIALS:**
**The Buildings of Frank Lloyd Wright 1887-1941**
by Henry-Russell Hitchcock

**THE STONES OF VENICE**
by John Ruskin

**THE LEAN YEARS: A History of the American Worker 1922-1933**
by Irving Bernstein

**GRAPHIC WORKS OF THE AMERICAN THIRTIES**
by the American Artists' Congress

**AGAINST THE AMERICAN GRAIN:**
**Essays on the Effects of Mass Culture**
by Dwight Macdonald

**JAZZ MASTERS OF THE THIRTIES**
by Rex Stewart

**THE 20's: The Lawless Decade**
by Paul Sann

**STRUCTURES: Or Why Things Don't Fall Down**
by J. E. Gordon

*Available at bookstores or direct from*

**DA CAPO PRESS**
**233 Spring Street**
**New York, NY 10013**
**Toll-free 800-221-9369**